Bearding The Lion That Roared

The Levinson Cornerstones
in
Organizational Consulting Psychology

Immersion & Diagnosis
Courage
Leadership

A. M. O'Roark, Ph.D. ABAP, Editor

Bearding the Lion That Roared, The Levinson Cornerstones
Copyright © 2010 Ann Marie O'Roark, PhD.
Cover and interior design by Ann Marie O'Roark. All rights reserved.
Copy Editor Nancy Quatrano

Levinson, Harry
Bearding the Lion That Roared, The Levinson Cornerstones
     220 p. ill. cm.
     ISBN 978-0-9799623-5-6   e-book 978-0-9799623-6-3
     1.   Applied Psychology
     BF636
     158
     LCCN 2010930991

Articles by Harry Levinson, PhD., Michael Diamond PhD., and Diana Gordick,
PhD., are used with the permission of the authors.

ClearView Press, Inc.
PO Box 353431
Palm Coast, FL 32135-3431
www.clearviewpressinc.com
                Printed in the United States of America

TABLE OF CONTENTS

BEARDING THE LION THAT ROARED: THE LEVINSON CORNERSTONES

A. M. O'Roark, Ph.D., ABAP, Editor

OVERVIEW

Bearding the Lion that Roared, showcases chapters published by Harry Levinson, corporate consulting pioneer and founder of psychoanalytic organizational theory and practice (Diamond, 2003). Levinson advises consulting psychologists to be grounded in psychological theory, regardless of the individual's preferred orientation or school of training. Working from a theoretical frame of reference is a unique characteristic of scientific methodology and a distinguishing hallmark of the psychologist dedicated to organizational psychology: A critical aspect of the psychological diagnostic procedure that leads to a practitioner's determination of consulting interventions.

Articles selected to be presented here illustrate Levinson's consulting work with senior executives, managers, and leaders in emotionally challenging circumstances and use his theory to interpret observations and design interventions consistent with theoretical principles in a contemporary psychoanalytic frame of reference enlarged and adjusted to workplace applications.

Articles for this volume could have been selected based on primacy of "theory" in scientific disciplines and on the historical path leading the development of consulting psychology in the mid-twentieth century. Another compelling reason to consolidate articles and chapters written by Dr. Levinson across the evolution of psychological organizational consulting practice is that Harry Levinson as an active member in the American Psychological Association (APA) and Division 13 (the Society of Consulting Psychology.) Across more than fifty years, he has inspired countless next-generation psychologists with his dedication to advancing organizational consulting psychology, whether their fundamental theoretical framework was psychoanalytic, behavioral, perceptual, or cognitive. Harry's keen observations, easy to read case studies, and insightful interaction with consultants as well as clients, led to him being recognized as a legend in his own time, in the professional community to whom this volume is dedicated. His professional innovations and contributions include seminars, workshops, mentoring, and, most recently, distance-learning/teaching-coaching of early career psychologists.

Harry and Miriam Levinson created an SCP/APA Foundation award [1992-2008] to recognize outstanding creative psychologists working as organizational consultants. Recipients of the prestigious award, carrying the largest stipend of its kind, were selected because their work shows exceptional ability to integrate a wide range of psychological theory and concepts, then to convert that integration into applications that enabled leaders and managers to create more effective, healthy, and humane organizations. In 2008, Harry and Miriam transformed the stipend into a scholarship to be administered by the American Psychological Foundation.

Harry continues to support SCP's role in the advancement of consulting psychology through *Consulting Psychology: The Second Century.* Dr. Levinson not only encouraged the development of the paperback book series, but he also contributed materials reprinted here and in an earlier volume (Freedman & Bradt, 2008), assigning royalties from this volume to SCP in the hope of defraying costs of providing SCP members with complimentary copies and of seeding further publications.

Psychological Roots

Bearding the Lion that Roared bridges psychology's first and second centuries by focusing on one of the earliest and most enduring scientific building blocks: Theory. The practice of consulting psychology proceeds from a recognized theory, testable hypotheses, and systematic research methodology to consultant interventions that include evaluation and reporting of results.

Psychology's first one hundred years as an independent discipline, as measured from the time of Wilhelm Wundt's psychological laboratory in Leipzig (1879), produced theory-grounded hypotheses and postulates about human behavior that continue to stand as valid and to be demonstrated as efficacious in multiple cultural and cross-generational settings (Tanaka-Matsumi, 2008). *Bearding the Lion that Roared* - present Levinson articles that range from a discussion of the entrepreneurial ventures of Sigmund Freud, who was semi-contemporary with Wundt, to turn of the next century corporate executives. The articles were selected for their durability, their relevance in the 21st century global community, and their ongoing practical value to the consulting psychology community.

Theory as a foundation for intervention. Michael Diamond (2003, reprinted by permission) reviews key concepts in Levinson's adaptation of basic psychoanalytic theory. Diamond provides operational-definitions of psychological terms and concepts that served as Levinson's building-blocks for developing his organizational consulting practice.

Diamond describes how Levinson, acknowledging his full agreement with Kurt Lewin about the value of a good theory, used psychoanalytic theory to inform how he shaped his approach to consulting. Harry stresses how beginning with a good theory and proceeding with scientific methodology were and remain essential to effective consulting practice as well as to the establishment of psychology as an independent scientific discipline.

Michael Diamond's chapter (2003) from *Organizational & Social Dynamics* 3(1): 1-18 is reprinted here to provide readers with theoretical / conceptual background information and a bibliography of Harry Levinson's publications from 1953 through 2002. He traces Harry's career from the wizard of Oz state, Kansas, to the wisdom center of academia, Harvard. Diamond reports Harry's stated professional objective: *to develop a more sophisticated understanding of the psychology of leadership and organizational processes; and to apply psychoanalytic theory to managerial practice and organizations.*

Living and Working In a Global Community. Next, consulting psychologist Diana Gordick reports on an interview with Harry Levinson. Gordick's description of her conversation with Harry reflects Dr. Levinson's natural ease when communicating his concepts, adapting information to that individual, and referencing current social and cultural variables. The conversation with early career consultant, Gordick, in contrast to Levinson's psychoanalytic theoretical context for his conversation with seasoned consultant Diamond, emphasizes how he and his associate gained insight, early in their careers, to an important durable fact: "what psychologists know about developing people in healthy ways [is]…unknown to management…" (Gordick, 2003, reprinted here).

Gordick's review provides evidence of Levinson's impact being without borders: Harry's wide-ranging work moved beyond Menninger Foundation and Kansas to Harvard School of Business Administration and the Sloan School of Management at MIT, New York's Pace University, to projects with the Finnish Government Institute of Occupational Health and the Institute of Public Administration in Jaipur, India. Gordick interprets the consulting concepts Levinson shared during their conversation as grounded in individual, structural, social, and cultural influences applied in real world examples.

Harry credits Dr. William C. Menninger with directing his attention to organizational consulting in 1954, when Dr. Menninger asked Harry to do something about keeping well people functioning well. Harry Levinson began with a focus on the betterment of the *client*, expanded his focus to attend to the work and preparation of the *consultant*, which culminated in his template for the *practice* of organizational consulting psychology.

Concern for the client and acknowledgment of employees need for emotional support were highlights of Harry's work on the Menninger Foundation assignment. Publication of results of this early-career investigation is considered a harbinger of today's employee assistance programs (Diamond, 2003). In addition, Levinson's "psychological contract" – drawn from principles of ego-ideals and object relations, mutual needs and expectations --- provided an alternative to the humanistic and behavioral approaches to organizational consulting.

Interest in consultants and psychologists' special training in systematic observation and listening resulted in one of Harry's major conceptual contributions: Beginning consultation by immersion in the organization. Harry compares the consultant's immersion to the ethnographic field methods of the anthropologist when learning about a new tribe, or culture.

The psychological consultant, working from the psychoanalytic theory base, refrains from discussing intervention options (team building, executive coaching, strategic planning) until after immersion, the gathering of information: factual, historical, genetic, interpretive. Levinson advises the consultant to become a participant-observer, keeping an open mind to tune-in to the story and dynamics of the work group[s]. Immersion enables the consultant to analyze what is going on at deeper and less obvious levels. He advises the consultant who chooses to practice using his model to become self-aware and to be prepared to deal with repressed, sensitive, and difficult barriers that interfere with well-people functioning well.

The practice of consulting, as envisioned by Levinson, requires caring deeply about the client, so deeply that the psychologist is willing to fully invest one's self when entering the world of the client and to maintain an open mind. That invested self that remains consciously grounded in theory and self awareness that includes the dynamics at work in self, others, and the dynamics of the interaction, such as transference and countertransference. Consulting practice, as described here, begins with humility and courage. Humility as expressed in the acknowledgement of "not knowing" is a deliberate suspension of the assumption of knowing, especially, of knowing the best method for working with a client. Diamond lists Levinson's questions from The Psychological Man (1976) to summarize how immersion enables the consultant to move deeper into diagnosis of dysfunctions and surface problems: *Who is in pain? When did it begin? What's happening to needs for aggression, affection, and dependency? What is the nature of the ego-ideal? Is the problem solvable?*

After immersion, a consultant is advised to exercise interpersonal sensitivity and consideration as well as courage when giving interpretive feedback or serving as a truth teller. Courage and humility are considered paramount when going with the client into the darkest shadows and fears of loss and grief. Levinson chose to address unconscious or latent dynamics beneath the surface as CEOs or employees strove for meaning and dignity in their workplace. A critical turning point in this model of psychological consultation is the shift into problem analysis and applying psychoanalytic template for analyzing troublesome human relations at work.

Harry acknowledges that psychological consulting using psychoanalytic theory is not for everyone as it is intense, comprehensive, and involves a long time commitment. He recommends a consultant's consultant for those who do chose to work with this approach. The Levinson chapters included in Bearding the Lion illustrate how Harry worked with theory to diagnose situations, and how theory influenced the choice of interventions. Much of his work was with chief executives and the volume is titled for the first Levinson chapter which is a case study of his consultation work with a troubled and tyrannical leader. He is widely known for introducing the case study as a training tool for developing consulting psychologists.

Immersion

Bearding the Lion that Roared: A Case Study in Organizational Consultation. Levinson, H. with Sabbath, J. & Connor, J., *Consulting Psychology Journal, 44:4*, 1-16, Fall 1992
The Practitioner as Diagnostic Instrument. In A. Howard, (ed.). *Diagnosis for Organizational Change.* New York: Guilford Publications, 2, 27-52, 1994.
A Psychologist Looks at Executive Development. *Harvard Business Review*, 40:5, Sept-Oct, 1962, 69-75.

The three chapters in the first section immerse the reader in Levinson's consulting work and methods. The first emphasizes the well-being of the *client* and is an executive case study, an in-depth look at a successful and diagnosable CEO. The case study is a hallmark Harvard Business School teaching tool, and long associated with Dr. Levinson's compelling and instructive methods for preparing next generation consultants and executives. In this narrative, with one of Harry's famously clever titles [e.g., Ready-Fire-Aim; The Great Jackass Fallacy; Why the Behemoths Fell], the reader is given a mystery-story trip through a consultation filled with theory-based diagnosis. We track how the consultant team converted their analysis into recommendations for solutions to the presenting problems in the organization [turnover] in ways that also addressed the deeper issues within the CEO. Ironically, and in keeping with the diagnostic inferences of the consulting team, the CEO managed to actualize the recommendations all the while denying that those recommendations were any more useful than "putting a condom on a stud bull."

The second chapter emphasizes the work of the *consultant* and the dedication of the consultant's whole unbiased self to be the *instrument* of diagnosis and treatment. The first consultant competence is the ability to plan and implement a systematic method for gathering, organizing, and interpreting information about organizations. Yes, Harry begins by talking about theory for interpreting the data and he elaborates on the need for special attention to leadership: "All organizations are the lengthened shadows of their leaders." The Course of Consultation is described using a case study to illustrate the ethical application of the information collected by the consultant to prepare recommended steps for change that is in keeping with the organizations culture, capabilities, and the core problem. In this case it is developing a more sophisticated approach to management.

The third chapter addresses another reason for the *consulting practice* to give special attention to the leaders in an organization: the unparalleled importance of a next generation manager [or consultant] to have someone who has more experience, skill, and power to admire, to identify with, and with whom a strong, supportive relationship can be developed. While executive coaching by consultants can be beneficial, it in no way replaces or is as powerful as the executive being competent in mentoring and inspiring, even challenging, the up and coming junior managers. Harry addresses the issues surrounding the concept that "growth of executive capacity depends in large measure on identification with a corporate executive," such as: competitive rivalry, dependency – independency and the importance of executives giving their time for this responsibility to those they supervise – a responsibility that cannot be delegated.

Courage

On Executive Suicide. *Harvard Business Review*, 50:4, 118-123. July-Aug, 1975.

A psychologist diagnoses merger failures. *Harvard Business Review*, March-April 1970, 139-147.

Beyond the selection failures. *Consulting Psychology Journal,* 46:1, 3-8,Winter, 1994

Who's to blame for maladaptive managers? *Harvard Business Review*, Nov-Dec.1965, 143-158.

Easing the pain of personal loss. *Harvard Business Review, Sept-Oct. 1972, 82-90.*

The question of "why" is prominent in this set of articles. Harry is speaking primarily to the consultant about signs of serious inner trauma and insights for advising senior executives how to recognize destructive situations. Executive suicide describes the character elements frequently noted in suicide victims: intelligence, ambition, disappointment, and high ego ideal that revolve around power. Self directed anger follows the drive for perfectionism. Times of economic distress and over-identification with one's profession are early warning indicators of depression onsets. Harry cautions against time-off as a remedy and against sudden recovery from depression as particularly vulnerable times.

In chapter 4, Harry talks about consulting with executives in the senior partner in a corporate merger.

The first question, again, is "why?" Why did the senior partner want to merge with this company? Then, why do they have a condescending attitude toward the new partner? Fear and obsolescence are introduced as underlying motivations in mergers. Loss of flexibility and identity reviewed as key issues in the discussion of where the merger pains are being felt. An important ingredient in resolving merger discomforts is for consultants and leaders is recognizing and respecting that both senior and junior partners are equal in psychological power even when not equal in economic power.

Chapter 5 explores the why of selection failures and uses an example of an international organization's candidates for heading up their American operations. The shortfalls of headhunters and assessment centers are noted and the need for psychologists to use a multi-method approach to matching characteristics of the candidate with those of the supervising executive and the corporate culture, as well as job demands. The psychologist's advantage in identifying late bloomers, negative narcissism, and abrasive personalities are valuable assets in reducing the incidence of selection failure. Unrecognized motives of fear and obsolescence *lead* to *impulsive actions which magnify the very problems partnerships should resolve*

Chapter 7 shifts the consultant's attention away from the character related problems to six common management actions that can result in troublesome behavior among subordinates. These problem-generating actions were derived from analysis of cases presented by executives attending workshops at the Levinson Institute. It turned out that the senior executive had a part in each of the problems: encouragement of power seeking; tolerating angry behavior; stimulating rivalry; not preparing the subordinate for the unpleasant realities that will come their way along the career path; pressing people to do more than they can handle; and misplacement of people in the wrong job.

The final chapter in this section addresses easing the pain of personal loss. Personal depression and career plateau are concepts that have endured across nearly four decades and have become hot topics in the 21st century. Harry's analogy of human experience being like the roots of a tree, with life substance and support coming from those attachments we develop to people, places, things, goals, wishes, aspirations, skills, knowledge, and activities. When one feels that there is a decrease of being valued as a person, it is a precipitant of the feeling of loss of love. The organization can take action to support employees through the pain of personal loss, including employee assistance counseling, job placement services, and relating to the community in its areas or times of need. Severe personal and organizational damage can ensue when individuals are cut loose from their psychological moorings

These chapters lay a foundation for consultants understanding of the "why" behind the human pain that will be encountered in the wake of worklife's traumatic and inevitable ups and downs of change. These are some of the things that psychologists know about human growth, development, and suffering that executives and managers do not know. These are some of the concepts that Harry introduced into the practice of consulting psychology that helped him reach his career objective: *to develop a more sophisticated understanding of the psychology of leadership and organizational processes; and to apply psychoanalytic theory to managerial practice and organizations (Diamond interview).*

Leadership

Fate, fads, and the fickle fingers thereof. *Consulting Psychology Bulletin*, 37, 3, 3-11, Fall 1985.

Freud as entrepreneur: Implications for contemporary psychoanalytic institutes. In L. Lapierre (ed.), *Clinical Approaches to the Study of Managerial and Organizational Dynamics.* Montreal: *Ecole des Hautes Etudes Commerciales, May 1990.*

Age of leadership. *Pegasus.* Mobil Services Company Limited, 1974. [Discontinued internal management publication.]

These three chapters emphasize the need for consulting *practice* to be grounded in the lessons learned from its proximal and distal history. The applied psychologist planning on a career in organizational consulting benefits from immersion in the discipline of psychology and administrative techniques recommended in popular management and leadership paradigms. Levinson points out short sightedness of recent management fads in chapter 9, concluding that the fickle fingers of fads can, but do not need to, determine a consulting psychologist's professional fate. Early career consultants and veterans alike will find thought provoking considerations in the succinct summaries of management fads dating back to the 1939 Hawthorne studies, through Maslow, Herzberg, McGreggor, Blake & Mouton, and Likert, and international studies in British coal mines, Ahmadabad silk mills, and Swedish autoworkers.

A trademark Levinson argument is the practicing psychologist's ever present, enduring need to understand personality and group dynamics, observing through a template that is not based on "partial theories." He eschews manipulation of carrots and sticks in favor of favor of actions that facilitate getting the work done and keeping healthy employees healthy.

The next chapter, 10, is a unique and easy to follow history of the how and why of Sigmund Freud's establishment of a practice. Freud's Wednesday Psychological Society could be considered as a first independent practice firm and continuing education center. A determined entrepreneurial drive is credited with enabling Freud to achieve his objective of perpetuating his psychoanalytic concepts. Levinson exposes Freud's own ego-ideals and oedipal rivalry with the father as pertinent to the story of Freud's evolution of the Wednesday Psychological Society into the Vienna Psychoanalytic Society. Levinson carries the evolution of Freud's practice into the development of the current Psychoanalytic Institutes. Harry's recommendation for the future of the practice includes being incorporated into the academic institutions as a classic technique and continuation of the open ended discussions and concept evolution that Freud initiated (sometimes to his regret.).

The final chapter in this selection of Levinson's articles is about leadership and the first and last responsibility of the psychologist choosing to practice in organizational consulting: the well being and well functioning leader, identification with whom serves as the glue that holds the organization together. The leadership of the consultant disciplined in psychology enables the corporate CEO and leaders to work with the problem of change, motivation, and dependency-interdependency issues. The slow process of healthy change is easily forgotten when organizations are operated for short-term, expedient purposes. When the organization is led by someone who manages for perpetuation, Harry predicts that will be good for the people and each member of the group can reach the health-inducing, inner goal of liking themselves.

January 15, 2007, Harry Levinson celebrated his 85th birthday. In an interview that day with Arthur Freedman (personal communication to co-editors), 2007 recipient of the Miriam and Harry Levinson Award, Harry described his most rewarding and most disappointing experiences in his extensive practice.

Most rewarding: "When I was consulting in a client organization, even when I think I have done well and acted on behalf of that organization's best interests and helped them solve some of their problems, sooner or later I had to leave it---it has to go it's merry way. Well, sometimes it does and sometimes it doesn't do well on its own– sometimes because of the people, and sometimes because of the nature of the business, sometimes because of the competition. At any rate, the contribution that may have been mighty important when I made it may be vitiated or become outmoded or something else.

"The most important gratification is when somebody I have helped in an organization comes back, long after the experience, and tells me how much my help meant to him or her in terms of his or her own career direction as well as the success of the business…"

Most disappointing: "My most disappointing experience did not have to do with failure. It concerned my inability to fulfill what I thought was an important aspiration. I was consulting with a company in Argentina. I was helpful with the Chief Executive in his effort to resolve some of his organization's problems. At that time I had decided to retire....I had [two associates] take over to do some follow up work....neither of them worked out very well. The CEO....called me saying, 'Please come down to Argentina to help again.'...I could no longer travel, certainly not that distance...Although I suggested it might be worth his while to come to the United States and spend time with me, that hasn't happened yet. My own disappointment is still with me.

"My second major disappointment was the suicide of a client."

"Sometimes there are experiences that may lead to exploitation. For example, I had agreed to make a presentation to a company. Before I began, I discovered that the training person intended to record what I am doing to replay it for others in the company. This was not part of the agreement and either I have to say sorry, no thanks, and stop right away or accept that I am going to be exploited."

ORGANIZATIONAL IMMERSION AND DIAGNOSIS: THE WORK OF HARRY LEVINSON

Michael A. Diamond

It was during 1968 that Harry Levinson established The Levinson Institute during his years on faculty at the Harvard Business School. The Institute emerged from 14 years of work at The Menninger Foundation of Topeka, Kansas where he was director of the Division of Industrial Mental Health. His goal with The Levinson Institute was twofold. First, he wanted to develop and apply psychoanalytic theory to managerial practice and organizations and second, he wanted to develop 'a more sophisticated understanding of the psychology of leadership and organizational processes' (personal correspondence, 1985). This understanding 'would simultaneously inform and enrich the activities of management and leadership, and by so doing also contribute to the mental health of people who worked in organizations' (ibid.). This article is a retrospective of the work of Harry Levinson and his contributions to our understanding of organizations.

In the following, I present readers with an overview of Levinson's contributions to psychoanalytic organization psychology. Then, I share excerpts from an interview conducted with Harry Levinson in August 2002 during the American Psychological Association meetings in Chicago, Illinois. Finally, I provide a listing of his books and articles, which include published works not reviewed here. My intent is to offer readers a perspective on his impact on the psychoanalytic study of organizations.

BACKGROUND

Harry Levinson, the son of a Polish, Jewish tailor from Lodz, was born in Port Jervis, New York more than 80 years ago. Considered by many as the founder of psychoanalytic organization psychology, he was awarded the prestigious American Psychological Foundation Gold Medal for Life Achievement in the Application of Psychology in 2000. Now semi-retired and living with his wife Miriam in Delray Beach, Florida, he is chairman of The Levinson Institute, and Clinical

Professor of Psychology Emeritus in the Department of Psychiatry at Harvard Medical School. He received his BSc and MSc degrees from Kansas (Emporia) State University and his PhD in psychology from The University of Kansas, where he received clinical training in psychology at the Veterans Administration and The Menninger Foundation in Topeka, Kansas.

From 1950 to 1953, he was coordinator of professional education at Topeka State Hospital and had a central role in the reorganization of the Kansas state hospital system. In 1954 he established, and for the next 14 years directed, the Division of Industrial Mental Health of The Menninger Foundation. According to Levinson, 'I had begun the task on January 1, 1954, when Dr. William C. Menninger asked me to undertake a project that would do something about keeping well people functioning well'. He wrote later:

> *Naturally, if one is to do something in a public health sense about keeping people well, that is most easily done through social systems and primarily, therefore, with those institutions in which people work, inasmuch as their work is of great psychological significance to them. (personal correspondence, 1993)*

During the academic year 1961-1962, he was Visiting Professor in the Sloan School of Management at the Massachusetts Institute of technology and in 1967 in the School of Business at the University of Kansas. From 1968 to 1972 he was Thomas Henry Carroll-Ford Foundation distinguished visiting professor in the Harvard Graduate School of Business Administration. Throughout his career, he has sought to create a systematic application of psychoanalytic theory to management. (Levinson, 1976; W. Lorsch, ed. 1987).

CONTRIBUTIONS TO THE PSYCHOANALYTIC STUDY OF ORGANIZATIONS

Levinson is known for developing insightful and practical concepts informed by a deep appreciation of the nature of the workplace. What follows is an overview of many contributions by Harry Levinson.

The Emotional First Aid Stations

In 1954 Levinson along with William C. Menninger wrote 'Industrial mental health: some observations and trends' in the *Menninger Quarterly* and in 1956 he wrote 'Employee counseling in industry' for the *Bulletin of The Menninger Clinic*. These articles were groundbreaking in their acknowledgment of the need for emotional support and care for workers and managers. These articles were precursors of today's employee assistance programs.

The Psychological Contract

In 1962 Levinson (with Charlton Price, Kenneth Munden, Harold Mandl, and Charles Solley) wrote *Men, Management, and Mental Health*, which introduced the concept of the 'psychological contract'. In the book, Levinson explained how the psychological contract shaped the expectations of employees and the organizations they work for. Levinson's notion of a psychological contract encompassed an acknowledgement of conscious and unconscious human needs and desires that employees invest in their relationship with the organization and its leadership. He argued that unless management is psychologically aware of these manifest and latent dimensions of worker motivation, it is highly unlikely that employees will feel adequately nurtured by their employers. This oversight of course can lead to demoralization and poor performance.

The psychological contract is a valuable conceptual tool for managers and consultants as they consider failures of supervision and communication between supervisors and subordinates, executives and their staff. Application of the psychological contract between employer and employee requires perpetual dialogue between the parties, acknowledging the dynamics of mutual needs and expectations, conscious and unconscious. Levinson's use of ego psychology and the management of the ego ideal shaped his earliest thinking about motivation and emotional well-being at work.

Reminiscent of the human relations and humanist movements in management theory at the time, Levinson's psychoanalytic approach was distinctive in its application of a systematic model of human personality. His stress on the individual ego ideal and one's emotional investment in the workplace provided a deeper and more comprehensive understanding of the collision between individual and organization.

Psychological Anthropology

Men, Management, and Mental Health (1962) also provided a groundbreaking multidisciplinary study of the Kansas Power and Light Company and was an example of (what Levinson calls) psychological anthropology – a notion he uses to this day to describe a process of 'immersion' central to psychoanalytic organizational diagnosis and consultation. In the spirit of Kurt Lewin's action research model for applied social science, Levinson's notion of immersion is indicative of his belief that knowledge of organizations requires experience of the organization from the inside – what some anthropologists and social scientists would call 'participant observation'. Although, in Levinson's framework, psychoanalytic theory, self and other awareness, provide researchers and consultants with the conceptual model and potential psychodynamic awareness necessary for constructive and insightful immersion as observing participants.

Over 40 years ago, Levinson and his colleagues spent time out in the field with workers, observing, participating, interviewing and eventually understanding and documenting the crucial role of work groups and their leaders in organizations. In particular, they illustrated how the paternal foreman established meaningful and familial-like emotional ties (positive transference and counter-transference) with his workers and consequently enhanced their safety and minimized accidents under typically dangerous working conditions. For Levinson, the informal and affectionate bonds between workers and their foremen (supervisors) helped to explain effective, physically safe and emotional healthy, management performance in the workplace. The study also pre-dated much of the popular enthusiasm several decades later with organizational culture.

Management by Guilt

In 1964, Levinson observed difficulties of supervision in managing subordinate performance in the workplace. In particular, he saw a problem for managers that some individuals understood intuitively, yet had no psychological basis for articulating and correcting it. Managers often found it troubling and many felt conflicted, that is guilty, about evaluating subordinate performance, especially when the evaluation required negative and critical feedback of the employee's work.

Levinson not only explained the psychodynamics of guilt, he emphasized the human compassion inherent in and necessary for providing subordinates with unambiguous, direct, and honest feedback in performance evaluation. From the notion of 'management-by-guilt' supervisors came to better appreciate their ambivalent feelings surrounding the act of subordinate evaluations. They also came to appreciate the value of sincere feedback in the development of subordinate career opportunities. Consultants learned to pay attention to these difficulties of supervision and provide help to their clients. Out of these insights surrounding the ego ideal at work, Levinson came to stress the leadership's role in mentoring and educating workers.

The Organization as Learning Institution

In 1968, Levinson published *The Exceptional Executive*, later (1981) revised and updated in the *Executive* and published by Harvard University Press, Subtitled 'The guide to responsive management', Levinson continued his investigation of managerial performance through the lens of psychoanalytic ego psychology. Progressing on themes he started to explore in earlier writings, he argued that one of management's primary failures is their unawareness of the depth and dimensions of human needs of employees. Executives and their management must become better mentors he argued, and to do so they must become more knowledgeable about what motivates their employees. Executives and their management must become better mentors, he argued, and to do so they must become more knowledgeable about what motivates their employees.

In the *Executive* (1968, 1981), Levinson asks managers to pay attention to three primary human drives: ministration, maturation, and mastery. Ministrations, according to Levinson, takes into account needs for gratification, closeness, support, protection, and guidance. Maturation needs comprise fostering creativity, originality, self-control, and reality testing. Mastery needs encompass the demands for ambitious striving, realistic achievement, rivalry with affection, and consolidation. With these human needs in mind, executives could engage in more thoughtful and reflective dialogues with their workers and might establish management systems responsive to individual potential and desire for advancement. Motivation could be understood as multidimensional and leaders could actually facilitate growth and maturation in their own careers and the careers of their employees. One cannot help but reflect on how challenging such sensitivity to human needs of workers has become in our contemporary global economy of volatility, downsizing, and re-engineering.

A Framework for Problem Analysis

In the *Executive*, Levinson (1968, 1981 revised) provided a psychoanalytic framework for problem diagnosis as well. The framework was designed to assist managers in problem solving focused on personnel conflicts and performance issues. Here he presented a template for analyzing troublesome human relations at work and a practical application of psychoanalytic theory in the workplace.

Consistent with his earlier writing, he suggested examining the individual ego ideal in the work setting and the degree to which the individual manager, executive or worker feels he or she has lived up to this ideal. Many consultants and researchers of organizations can recall the frequency with which workers feel they fall short of their personal goals or are not working at their level of competency and training.

Next, Levinson looked at how the individual deals with needs for affection and his or her desire to develop close ties with colleagues in the workplace. Certainly, Levinson's earlier experiences in the field indicated that informal attachments in work groups, such as the case with his study of the Kansas Power and Light Company, are often critical to understanding dynamics in the organization. Then, he asked how the individual copes with feelings of aggression at work. Here, the influences of drive theory and ego psychology come through in an implicit acknowledgement of the role of work as a form of sublimation and the absorption of aggressive energies. Finally, Levinson encouraged paying attention to how workers react to dependency demands (1981, p. 33). Given the hierarchic structure of most organizations, the phenomenon of dependency enabled consultants and researchers to examine more closely the nature of super- and subordinate relationships at work.

In *Psychological Man* (1976), this framework is formulated into questions. In a rather simple and unforgettable outline, Levinson asks the following: Who is in pain? When did it begin? What is happening to needs for: aggression, affection, and dependency? What is the nature of the ego ideal? Is the problem solvable? If so, how? Thus, Levinson illustrated how one could arrange and interpret data (in a psychoanalytically informed way) around problems and conflicts in the workplace that might otherwise leave managers and executives perplexed and seemingly without recourse. His (1972) book *Organizational Diagnosis* expanded this capacity for analyzing problems to the systemic level of analysis.

Organizational Diagnosis

In 1972 Levinson's book Organizational Diagnosis was published by Harvard University press. The book is a comprehensive guide to analyzing organizations and arranging the complexity of varied data (factual, historical, genetic, interpretive) into a systemic understanding of its integrative and adaptive processes. According to Levinson:

...this was an adaptation of an open system biological model, which had been applied to individuals, for the study and analysis of organizations. It emphasized the need to understand organizations and their problems before trying to intervene into them. The diagnostic emphasis was a uniquely clinical contribution because so much of what had been done in organization development was essentially ad hoc application of established techniques without adequate diagnosis. (correspondence, 1985)

Organizational diagnosis, arguably, may be Levinson's most important contribution and in 2002 the American Psychological Association published an updated and revised version in *Organizational Assessment: A Step-by-Step Guide to Consulting.*

For many organizational analysts and consultants, particularly some psychoanalytically oriented, organizational diagnosis became the central component to comprehensive processes for 'real' organizational change. The meant that prior to engaging or contracting for a particular intervention strategy, (such as strategic planning, reorganization, team-building, executive coaching, and the like), the client and consultant would agree to a comprehensive study of the organization as an open system. This meant that, regardless of the executive leadership's assumptions of 'the problem', these assumptions would need to be suspended until a comprehensive analysis of the organization was complete and not until the consultants collected historical, factual, and interpretive data through extensive interviews and observations. In other words, strategies of intervention and change, in Levinson's model of organizational diagnosis, would follow and be governed by an organizational assessment. It was also in this extensive work that Levinson articulated the nature of transference and counter-transference between the organizational consultant and clients, encouraging consultants to pay attention to how they are received and 'used' emotionally and psychologically by their clients.

Loss In Organizational Change

In his 1972 *Harvard Business Review* article 'Easing the pain of personal loss', Levinson explains the psychodynamics of organizational change from the standpoint of change as a personal experience with loss. Here and elsewhere in later publications, he described processes of grief and mourning that gave emotional legitimacy to the human defenses and reactions of denial, anger, searching for the lost object, disorganization, and reorganization. Management from this point on was encouraged to acknowledge that changes in the workplace are not effectively implemented without processes that acknowledge participants' feelings of attachment to routines and structures and the pain of relinquishing social defenses and embracing the uncertainty of the future workplace. Difficulties in mourning or inadequate attention to the emotional dynamics of loss could sabotage an otherwise systematic effort at organizational change.

The Fallacy Of Reward-Punishment Psychology

In his (1973) The Great Jackass Fallacy, Levinson explains why the carrot and the stick are ineffective management techniques. His psychoanalytic framework for understanding human motivation and the vicissitudes of the ego ideal shape his criticisms of most traditional management theories of motivation and performance. These theories often apply a 'rational economic man' model and ignore unconscious and latent dynamics beneath the surface and inside the worker. Certainly the 'carrot and stick' approach cannot address the sentient world of workers and their search for meaning and dignity through their productive lives in the workplace or as part of a profession.

Following this overview of Levinson's contributions to a psychoanalytic study of organization, I provide the reader with the text of an interview with Harry Levinson during the annual meetings of the American Psychological Association.

HARRY LEVINSON INTERVIEW (CHICAGO, IL, JUNE 2002)

MD: What are your concerns with the state of theory and practice of organizational diagnosis today?

HL: I see a pretension to knowledge without knowledge. By that I mean a pretence among consultants of paying attention to unconscious processes within and between the consultant and client. Without the concept of unconscious processes, consultants work at a manifest and superficial level of structure and strategy without understanding the psychological meaning of these perpetuated structures and strategies and thereby without a lens for interpreting irrational and dysfunctional practices.

MD: What drives the analysis of organizations deeper?

HL: The framework for organizational diagnosis was intended to provide analysts and consultants a method for studying manifest and latent organizational dynamics by combining factual, genetic and historical data with crucial interpretive [or narrative] data. More importantly, it enables consultants to root their articulation of organizational problems in a consensually validated narrative.

MD: Can you say more about this issue of 'knowing without knowing' in the practice of organizational consultation?

HL: Another dimension of 'knowing without knowing' refers to the consultant's use [or lack thereof] of self.

MD: Do you mean self as instrument of observation, interpretation and understanding?

HL: Psychoanalytic organizational consultancy, unlike most consultancy practices, requires a stance of open mindedness – an acknowledgement of 'not knowing' and thereby a suspension of the assumption of knowing. This humility is derived from self-knowledge. My concern with the theory and practice of organizational diagnosis today is that some organizational analysts and consultants, particularly those who claim to assume a psychoanalytic orientation, are not sufficiently equipped with adequate insights into their own defensive proclivities and are thereby incapable of differentiating between their private world of internal object relations and that of their clients and their client systems. In other words, unanalyzed or unacknowledged emotional immaturity and narcissism in the consultant will lead to incapacity to adequately delineate self and object, internal and external realities.

MD: Are you suggesting that organizational analysts and consultants ought to be psychoanalyzed?

HL: I think consultants who claim to work psychoanalytically ought to get psychoanalyzed. We risk pretension without confidence in a method of working with the client and the client system and without having undertaken psychoanalysis. Psychoanalysis is a theory of human needs and is a clinical practice for organizational research and consultation is best practiced and more deeply understood when the organizational researcher or consultant has had a personal analysis. Among organizational analysts and consultants today I see an 'absence of understanding the dynamics of repression'. Many consultants working without the methodology of organizational diagnosis ignore the impact and significance of historical data for present day organizational challenges and for understanding more deeply the stories and themes of interpretive data. Without the concept of repression (or suppression) the organizational analyst cannot find meaning nor locate psychic reality in the workplace because he or she is unaware of the multiple functions and dimensions of stories (much like dreams) and the degree to which they operate as defensive screens concealing fundamental issues, problems, and motivations. Without the experience and conscious awareness of how one's own repression functions, the consultant will be incapable of sensing, feeling, and observing these repressive processed within the client system.

MD: How does theory shape your work with organizations?

HL: In the Lewinian sense I believe in the value of good theory and by that I mean that theory informs practice and is simultaneously reformulated based on practice. Students need to immerse themselves inside organizations in order to learn and experience firsthand what goes on in system they wish to understand and help. We need to stress the critical importance of *immersion* in the training and education of psychoanalytic organizational consultants. Again, by immersion I mean the integration of theory and practice in the context of ongoing fieldwork and consultation experience under the supervision of a practiced mentor. In sum, humility about what you do comes from immersing yourself in the work – in the field.

MD: What additional oversights do you find in the present work of psychoanalytic organizational students and practitioners?

HL: I do not see a sufficient emphasis on understanding and applying transference and counter-transference among consultants in dealing with the client and the client system. There are multiple dimensions of transference and counter-transference that if not understood and incorporated into the work, can leave the consultant vulnerable to seduction by those in positions of power and authority and can leave one vulnerable to provocation – that is being unwittingly provoked by a client. It is compelling to get close to people in power and to over-identify with them and to get manipulated by them. We [consultants] are not power people; often to the contrary, we assist people in power. Organizational analysts and consultants are frequently deluded by their proximity to power, magnifying their own narcissism, particularly if they (as consultants) are unaware of their own narcissistic injuries and proclivities and how these [unattended fragments of self] influence their work with client systems.

MD: Can you say more about the function of narcissism in the process of the consultant?

HL: Only that professional narcissism is a problem. It shuts out learning from others and their experiences.

MD: Do you mean that it [professional narcissism] works against 'knowing what we don't know' and may delude consultants into viewing themselves as experts with some magic solution to their clients' problems?

HL: Fundamentally, it [unawareness of narcissism] limits reflective learning and thereby interferes with developing insights and observations helpful to clients and their organizations. There are no built-in protections such as ethical standards against human aggression and narcissistic injury. Like Freud, we have to teach ourselves what goes on in our guts and what goes on in our clients and their systems. Organizational analysts and consultants are vulnerable here, since there can be no policy that might guard against narcissistic hunger for aggrandizement and approval. Some might argue that policy in the form of ethical standards does not necessarily work to defend against sexual improprieties either – a subject for another time.

MD: Beyond attending to transference and counter-transference as well as professional narcissism, what additional tools, conceptual and personal, are necessary?

HL: Organizational diagnosis as a method helps to manage consultant unawareness, because it requires interviewing many people. The consultant subjectivity is to some degree tempered by the methodology of data collection and interpretation – assuming that the processes of developing the organizational story involves either a team of consultants and/or an outside consultant's consultant or analyst. Psychoanalytic organizational consultants need their own consultants or analysts to assist them in processing their own internal object relations during consultations. They need someone to turn to while they're consulting with clients – the consultant's consultant or analyst. Also, keeping a diary to understand one's reactions as well as processing with the team, is helpful. Ideally, you find help from outside the consultation project as well.

MD: What are your thoughts on the popular trend toward executive coaching?

HL: I see what passes for executive coaching today as 'consultation for many'. Consultants are easily manipulated in this era of instant gratification. The model of organizational diagnosis, or what we might call psychoanalytic organizational consultation, is not for everyone. It's too complex and time intensive. There may be gradations in which people use the model and that's to be expected. Organizational diagnosis is an ideal model. People will do as much of it as they can or they may reject it. The model is a standard of practice – an ego ideal, aspiration – within it there is a possibility of continued learning and immersion.

MD: So you are saying that the psychoanalytic approach to organizational diagnosis and practice is not for everyone due to its intensity, comprehensiveness, and long-time commitment?

HL: I am critical of the 'brief time-frame' of many consultants and clients today, which does not allow for sufficient commitment of time for diagnosis and psychoanalytically informed consultation. I admittedly have moderate expectations about the future prospects for psychoanalytic organizational consultation. Clients and consultants prefer the 'quick fix' approach to organizations. This approach assumes the consultant somehow magically knows what the client and client system require without organizational assessment and diagnosis. Moreover, it is this impatience and short sightedness that has led to the acceleration and popularity of more prescriptive approaches that promise more than they can deliver. These approaches include executive coaching as practiced by many non-psychoanalytic consultants. Furthermore, these practices tend to focus on a part of or member of the system rather than the system as a whole and that contradicts the spirit of organizational diagnosis. One can imagine how this sort of orientation would leave consultants vulnerable to counterproductive collusions with the executive client, particularly in the case of narcissistic executives with mirroring self-object needs and consultants with idealizing self-object demands.

MD: Do you have other reservations on some forms of psychoanalytic consultations popular today?

HL: I am critical of those consultations that move people off-site and out of context: the work must take place in the 'natural workplace setting' rather than off-site somewhere that takes the consultancy work and a potential understanding of the systemic psychodynamics out of context. Consultants cannot understand the subjective and psychological reality of organizations without exposing themselves to the experiences of an organizational culture. This exposing or immersion, then, requires the psychoanalytic consultant to engage him – or herself in what I call psychological anthropology [psychoanalytic fieldwork and participant observation]. We need to understand that the psychoanalytic organizational consultation requires an understanding of and engagement with psychological anthropology.

CONCLUSION

Harry Levinson's contributions to the theory and practice of organizational consultancy are extensive and relentless. His commitment to psychoanalytic theory and the integrity of organizational consultation shaped by psychoanalysis are legendary. His conceptualization of organizational diagnosis has established a framework and benchmark for genuine systemic analysis and change – that is a measure of consultants and clients commitment to real change. For many individuals in the field he has been a mentor and for others he has been an outspoken yet constructive critic. In the early years of the International Society for the Psychoanalytic Study of Organizations, during my presidency of the Society and beyond, he fulfilled a learned role at the end of each symposium where he would summarize what we may have learned and where we might go next in the advancement of the application of psychoanalytic theory to organizations. Always the mentor, educator and responsive leader, Harry Levinson's impact on the field and the people he has worked closely with over the years is infinite.

Bibliography – Levinson, Harry

(1953) 'State hospitals are different now', *Menninger Quarterly*, 7: 7-12.

(1954) 'When is it sick to be sad?', *Menninger Quarterly*, 8: 16-20.

(1954) 'Industrial mental health: some observations and trends' (with William C. Menninger), *Menninger Quarterly*, VIII(4): 1-31, Fall.

(1955) 'Consultation clinic for alcoholism', *Menninger Quarterly*, 9: 14 – 20.

(1955) 'What can a psychiatrist do in industry?", *Menninger Quarterly*, 9(2): 22-30.

(1956) 'Employee counseling in industry', *Bulletin of The Menninger Clinic*, XX (2), 76-84, March.

(1956) 'Seminars for executives and industrial physicians', *The American Journal of Psychiatry*, CXIII(5): 451-454, November.

(1957) 'The illogical logic of accident prevention', *Menninger Quarterly*, 11(1): 19-25.

(1957) 'Emotional first aid on the job', *Menninger Quarterly*, 11(3): 6-15.

(1957) 'Social action for mental health', *Mental Hygiene*, XXXXI(3), 353-360, July.

(1957) 'Alcoholism in industry', *Menninger Quarterly*, XI(4), Supplement.

(1959) 'The psychologist in industry', *Harvard Business Review*, 37: 93-99, September-October.

(1960) 'Dilemmas of the occupational physician in mental health programming: Part II', *Journal of Occupational Medicine*, 2:205-208, May.

(1960) *Industrial Mental Health: Progress and Prospects*, Bureau of Industrial Relations, University of Michigan, October.

(1962) 'Seminars for executives and occupational physicians', *Bulletin of The Menninger Clinic*, XXVI(1): 18-29, January.

(1962) 'A psychologist looks at executive development', Harvard Business Review, 40(5), 69-75, September-October.

(1962) *Men, Management and Mental Health* (with Charlton R. Price, Kenneth J. Munden, Harold J. Mandl, Charles M. Solley). Cambridge: Harvard University Press.

(1963) 'What killed Bob Lyons', *Harvard Business Review*, 41(1): 127-144, January-February [reprinted as a *Harvard Business Review* 'Classic', 59(2): 144-162, March-April, 1981].

(1963) 'Work and mental health', *Encyclopedia of Mental Health*. New York: Franklin Watts.

(1964) 'What work means to a man', *Menninger Quarterly*, 18(2/3): 1-11.

(1964) 'Anger, guilt and executive action', *Think*, 30(2): 10-14, March-April.

(1964) 'Work and mental health', (with Charlton R. Price), Arthur B. Shostak and William Gomberg (eds), *Blue Collar World: Studies of the American Worker*. Englewood Cliffs: Prentice-Hall, pp. 397-405.

(1964) *Emotional Health in the World of Work.* New York: Harper & Row [revised edition: Cambridge: The Levinson Institute, 1980]

(1965) 'Reciprocation: the relationship between man and organization', *Administrative Science Quarterly*, 9: 370-390, March.

(1965) 'Who is to blame for maladaptive managers?' *Harvard Business Review*, 43:6, 143-158, November-December.

(1966) *Are You Nobody?* (with Paul Tournier, Victor E. Frankl, Helmut Thielicke, Paul Lehmann, and Samuel H. Miller). Richmond: John Knox Press.

(1968) 'Psychiatric consultation in industry', in Mendel and Solomon (eds), *The Psychiatric Consultation*. New York: Grune & Stratton, Inc., pp. 159-180.

(1968) *The Exceptional Executive.* Cambridge: Harvard University Press [revised as: *Executive*. Cambridge: Harvard University Press, 1981.]

(1969) 'On being a middle-aged manager', *Harvard Business Review*, 47:4, 51-60, July-August.

(1969) 'Emotional toxicology of the work environment', *Archives of Environmental Health*, 19:2, 239-243, August.

(1969) 'Seminars for executives and occupational physicians', in Ralph T. Collins (ed.), *Occupational Psychiatry, International Psychiatry Clinics*, 6:4. Bosotn: Little, Brown & Co.

(1970) 'A psychiatrist diagnoses merger failures', *Harvard Business Review*, 44:2, 139-147, March-April.

(1970) 'Management by whose objectives?' *Harvard Business Review*, 44:4, 125-134, July-August.

(1970) *Executive Stress*. New York: Harper and Row.

(1970) 'The impact of organization on mental health', (with Louis SWeinbaum), Alan A. McLean (ed.), *Mental Health and Work Organizations*. New York: Rand McNally.

(1971) 'Conflicts that plague family businesses', *Harvard Business Review*, 45:2, 90-98, March-April.

(1972) 'Management-by-objectives – a critique', *Training and Development Journal*, 26(4):3, April.

(1972) 'The clinical psychologist as organizational diagnostician', *Professional Psychology*, 3:1, 34-40, Winter.

(1972) *Organizational Diagnosis* (with Andrew G. Spohn and Janice Molinari). Cambridge: Harvard University Press.

(1972) 'Problems that worry executives', in Alfred Marrow (ed.), *The Failure of Success*. New York: American Management Association.

(1972) 'Easing the pain of personal loss', *Harvard Business Review*, 50:5, 80-88, September-October.

(1973) *The Great Jackass Fallacy*. Cambridge: Harvard University Press for the Division of Research, Graduate School of Business Administration.

(1973) 'Asinine attitudes toward motivation', *Harvard Business Review*, 51:1, January-February.

(1973) 'A psychoanalytical view of occupational stress', *Occupational Mental Health*, 3:2, Summer.

(1974) 'Don't choose your own successor', *Harvard Business Review*, 52:6, 53-62, November-December.

(1975) 'On executive suicide', *Harvard Business Review*, 53:4, 118-122, July-August.

(1976) *Psychological Man*. Cambridge: The Levinson Institute.

(1976) 'Appraisal of what performance?' *Harvard Business Review*, 54:4, 30-46, July-August.

(1977) 'How adult growth stages affect management development', *Training*, 14(5): 42, May.

(1978) 'The abrasive personality at the office', *Psychology Today*, 11(12): 78, May.

(1978) 'The abrasive personality', *Harvard Business Review*, 56(3): 86-94, May-June.

(1978) 'Is HRD a hoax or a necessity: answers from an organizational psychologist and a no-nonsense chief executive – how to tell if HRD is paying off in your organization', *Training*, 15(10): 52, October.

(1978) 'Organizational diagnosis in mental health consultation', in Thomas E. Backer and Edward M. Glaser (eds), *Proceedings of the Advanced Workshop on Program Consultation in Mental Health Services*. Los Angeles: Human Interaction Institute, pp 23 -50.

(1979) 'At their own hands', *Executive*, 5(2): 30, March.

(1980) 'An overview of stress and satisfaction: the contract with self', in Lynne A. Bond and James C. Rosen (eds), *Competence and Coping During Adulthood*. Vermont Conference on the Primary Prevention of Psychopathology. Hanover, New Hampshire, and London, England: University Press of New England, pp. 224-239.

(1980) 'Power, leadership, and the management of stress', *Professional Psychology*, 11(3): 497-508, June.

(1980) 'Criteria for choosing chief executives', *Harvard Business Review*, 58(4): 113-120, July-August.

(1981) 'When executives burn out', *Harvard Business Review*, 59(3): 73-81, May-June.

(1981) 'Seminar on organizational diagnosis', *Consultation*, 1(1): 45-47, Fall.

(1982) 'Professionalizing consultation', *Consultation,* 1(2): 38-41, Spring.

(1982) 'Diagnosis and intervention in organizational settings', in Herbert C. Schulberg and Marie Killilea (eds), *The Modern Practice of Community Mental Health*. San Francisco: Jossey-Bass, Chapter 11, pp. 289-311.

(1983) 'Clinical psychology in organizational practice', in James S. J. Mancuso (ed.), *Occupational Clinical Psychology*. New York: Praeger Publishers, Chapter 1, pp. 7-13.

(1983) 'Intuition vs. rationality in organizational diagnosis', *Consultation*, 2(2): 27-31, Spring.

(1983) 'A second career, the possible dream', *Harvard Business Review*, 61(3): 122-129, May-June.

(1983) 'Getting along with the boss', *Across the Board*, 20(6): 47-53, June.

(1983) 'Consulting with family businesses: what to look for, what to look out for', *Organizational Dynamics,* 71-80, Summer.

(1984) 'Organizational diagnosis', in Raymond J. Corsini (ed.), *Encyclopedia of Psychology*. New York: John Wiley & Sons, Inc., p. 460.

(1984) *CEO: Corporate Leadership in Action* (with Stuart Rosenthal). New York: Basic Books, Inc.

(1985) 'Fate, fads, and the fickle fingers thereof', *Consulting Psychology Bulletin*, 37(3): 3-11, Fall.

(1986) 'Always swamped? If it's your problem, you can solve it' (with John Elder), *Working Woman*, 11(9): 27-29, September.

(1986) 'Swamped again? Even if it's your company's fault, it's still your problem' (with John Elder), *Working Woman*, 11(11): 46-48, November.

(1986) *Ready, Fire, Aim: Avoiding Management by Impulse*. Cambridge: The Levinson Institute.

(1987) 'How they rate the boss', *Across the Board*, 24(6): 53-58, June.

(1987) 'Psychoanalytic theory in organizational behavior', in Jay W. Lorsch (ed.), *Handbook of Organizational Behavior.* Englewood Cliffs: Prentice-Hall, Chapter II, p.51.

(1988) 'To thine own self be true: coping with the dilemmas of integrity', in Suresh Srivastva and Associates (eds), *Executive Integrity: The Search for High Human Values in Organizational Life* (1st edn, March). San Francisco: Jossey-Bass, Inc.'

(1989) *Designing and Managing Your Career*. Editor, Boston: Harvard Business School Press.

(1990) '*Harvard Business Review* case study: the case of the perplexing promotion' (with Nan Stone), *Harvard Business Review*, 68(1): 11, January-February.

(1990) 'Freud as an entrepreneur: implications for contemporary psychoanalytic institutes', in Laurent Lapierre (ed.), *Clinical Approaches to the Study of Managerial and Organizational Dynamics. Proceedings of the Fourth Annual Symposium of the International Society for the Psychoanalytic Study of Organizations.* Montreal: Ecole des Hautes Etudes Commerciales, May.

(1991) 'Counseling with top management', *Consulting Psychology Bulletin,* 43(1): 10-15, Winter/Spring.

(1991) 'Diagnosing organizations systematically', in Manfred Kets de Vries (ed.), *Organizations on the Couch.* San Francisco: Jossey-Bass.

(1992) 'Fads, fantasies, and psychological management', presented to Division 13, American Psychological Association, San Francisco, August 18, 1991; in *Consulting Psychology Journal,* 44(1): 1-12, Winter.

(1992) 'How organizational consultation differs from counseling', in 'What is consultation? That's a good question', *Consulting Psychology Journal,* 44(1): 21-22, Summer.

(1992) 'Bearding the lion that roared: a case study in organizational consultation; with Joseph Sabbath and Jeffrey Connor, *Consulting Psychology Journal*, 44(4): 2-16, Fall.

(1992) *Career Mastery.* San Francisco: Berrett-Koehler.

(1993) 'Looking ahead: Caplan's ideas and the future of organizational consultation', in William P. Erchul (ed.), *Consultation in Community, School, and Organizational Practice.* Washington, DC: Taylor & Francis, pp. 193-204.

(1993) 'Between CEO and COO', *Academy of Management Executive,* 7(2).

(1993) 'Teacher as leader', in Arthur G. Bedeian (ed.), *Management Laureates: A Collection of Autobiographical Essays,* Vol. 2, Greenwich, CT: JAI Press, pp. 177-214.

(1994) 'Beyond the selection failures', *Consulting Psychology Journal,* 46(1): 3-8, Winter.

(1994) 'The changing psychoanalytic organization and its influence on the ego ideal of psychoanalysis', *Psychoanalytic Psychology,* 11(2): 233-249, Spring.

(1994) 'The practitioner as diagnostic instrument', in Ann Howard and Associates (eds), *Diagnosis for Organizational Change: Methods and Models.* New York: Guilford Press, pp. 27-52.

(1994) 'Why the behemoths fell: psychological roots of corporate failure', *American Psychologist,* 428-436, May.

(1995) 'Choosing to lead' (with K. e. Clark and M. B. Clark), *Contemporary Psychology,* 40(9): 867-868, September.

(1996) 'The leader as an analyst', *Harvard Business Review,* 74(1): 158-158, January-February.

(1996) 'Giving psychological meaning to consultation: consultant as storyteller', *Consulting Psychology Journal,* 48(2): 3-11, Winter.

(1996) 'Executive coaching', *Consulting Psychology Journal,* 48(2): 115-123, Spring.

(1996) 'A new age of self-reliance', *Harvard Business Review,* 74: 162-163, July-August.

(1996) 'Introduction' to Sperry, Len, *Corporate Therapy and Consulting.* New York: Brunner Mazel.

(1997) 'Some cautionary notes on 360-degree feedback', *Psychologist-Manager Journal, 1(1): 18-20.*

(1997) 'Organizational character', *Consulting Psychology journal: Practice & Research,* 49(4): 246-255, Fall.

(1999) 'A Recipe to change', *Consulting Psychology Journal: Practice & Research,* 49(4): 246-255, Fall.

(1999) 'A clinical approach to executive selection', in Richard Jennerett and Robert Silzer (eds), *Individual Psychological Assessment.* San Francisco: Jossey-Bass.

(1999) 'Diagnosis before investment', in Lawrence E. Lifson and Richard A. Geist (eds), *The Psychology of Investing.* New York: Wiley.

(2000) 'Approaching retirement as the flexibility phase' (with Jerry Wofford), *Academy of Management Executive,* 14(2): 84-95.

(2002) *Organizational Assessment: A Step-by-Step Guide to Effective Consulting.* Washington, D.C.: American Psychological Association.

(in press) 'On becoming an entrepreneur', *Psychologist-Manager Journal.* (in press) 'Understanding the personality of the executive' (with Leslie Pratch), in Robert F. Silzer (ed.), *The Effective Executive.*

A CONVERSATION WITH HARRY LEVINSON

Diana Gordick, Ph.D.

Retrieved 07/22/06 from:
http://www.apa.org/divisions/div13/Update/2003Fall/Spotlight2Fall2003.htm

Harry Levinson has a long and distinguished career which includes helping organizations create healthier workplaces, researching psychological concepts in the workplace, and educating others. He was a Thomas Henry Carroll-Ford Foundation distinguished visiting professor at Harvard Graduate School of Business Administration and taught at the Sloan School of Management at Massachusetts Institute of Technology, Kansas State University, Boston University School of Business Administration, Pace University Graduate School and Texas A & M. In addition, Dr. Levinson has taught internationally at the Finnish Government Institute of Occupational Health and the H. C. Mathur Institute of Public Administration in Jaipur, India. He has written 15 books and several articles which continue to be republished through Harvard Business Review as articles or book compilations. Dr. Levinson is the recipient of several awards, including: the Perry L. Rohrer Consulting Psychology Practice Award for Outstanding Achievement; the Massachusetts Psychological Association's Career Award; the Society of Psychologists in Management Award; the Organization Development Professional Practice Award for Excellence form the American Society for Training and Development; the I. Arthur Marshall Distinguished Alumnus Award of the Menninger Alumni Association, and co-recipient of the American Psychological Association Award for Distinguished Professional Contributions to Knowledge. His book creations have won awards from the McKinsey Foundation, Academy of Management, and the James A. Hamilton College of Hospital Administrators (twice!!) He has created The Levinson Institute to bring psychological concepts into the workplace by delivering training on Executive Education, Organizational Consultation and Executive Consultation. He is most known for distilling psychoanalytic concepts into workable theories and applying them in organizational settings.

Dr. Levinson participated in an interview with Diana Gordick, Ph.D. on September 23, 2003. The conversation which discusses several of his contributions to the field of organization development is presented below:

DIANA: Harry, so far your career has spanned several decades. You've published several books and articles and are widely read. You've brought psychological concepts to a diverse array of organizations and influenced the lives of thousands of people. What activities are you most proud of?

DR. LEVINSON: Among my professional activities, I'm most proud of integrating a whole range of material in a comprehensive manner that makes sense to the executive realm. I've translated psychoanalytic theory into something that can be used by executives. One of the things that pleases me the most is that I've written a number of articles for Harvard Business Review that continue to be published in the magazines. They also continue to be published in books of articles addressing several topics. Although much of my material dates back to the early 1970's, it continues to be useful and valid. The topics and their application are enduring, and I've translated the information in a way that makes it easy for others to hear and accept.

DIANA: That was one of the things that stood out to me as I read your books and articles. You present concepts in the context of individual, structural, social and cultural influences and then relate them to real world examples. Your writing and communication style if very accessible.

HARRY: (laugh) Well, it's pretty much been self-taught. When I started out I was clinically trained, but didn't know anything about business. I realized that I needed to develop myself in that area and also needed to find a way to communicate psychological concepts to business executives who had no basis of training in psychology. In turn, I had to learn about their world. The upside of that self-training is you are not limited by what went before. One way I went about my training was in my work at Topeka State Hospital. I was approached by the director with the question of "how do we keep well people well?" This is a question from a public health sense applicable to an already established organization. A colleague and I spent 18 months interviewing psychiatrists, psychologists, physicians, and other staff about how to develop people in healthy ways. We realized then that what we knew as psychologists about how to develop people in a healthy manner was unknown by the management at the time. We took what we know about making people tick and translated what we knew to organizations. I started getting involved in organizations, obtained immediate examples, and developed seminars on psychoanalytic theory and change. We had an infusion of examples to teach with.

DIANA: As you worked with people within the organization, what kinds of barrier did you find?

HARRY: Well, I've worked with the Kansas State Hospital system, AT&T, and several major corporations. I typically become immersed in management. For example, we did a two year study of Kansas Power & Light to get a sense of how work influences health. That's when we identified the psychological contract, the unconscious agreement between organizations [and their employees]. When this contract is fulfilled, everything goes well. When it's violated, performance starts going downhill. This also gave us an indication of what behaviors were healthy and characteristic of good mental health. For example, if people are active and productive, if they treat others as individuals, not devices to be exploited, but rather treat them with sensitivity and understanding. Also, if they are flexible under stress. For example, if you lose one or two sources of gratification, you have others to turn to for psychological support whether they are your church, family members, or your community. Sources of loss could be caused by the loss of a job, death of a friend, etc. You could be more patient in finding a new job if your family is supportive. When you are rooted psychologically in your environment – a tree with deep roots can weather a storm better than a tree with a single root, you have a psychological clasp that helps you function.

Although Dr. Levinson's decades of contribution cannot be easily summed into a few simple ideas, the section below provides a very brief overview.

Psychological Man: *Each person is a complex, unfolding, and maturing organism who openly engages in an interactive process with his or her environment. He or she evolved toward an idealized version of his or her hopes for himself with a complex set of drives and defenses. This idealized self is a primary motivator and a principle source of esteem.*

People typically attempt to meet the needs of their idealized self through work; as such work and the work environment have a significant effect on emotional health and motivation.

Psychological Contract: *In general, a psychological contract is an agreement between two people or among groups of people. Related to organizations, it refers to the often unspoken agreement between an individual and the organization he or she works for. Implicit in the contract is the expectation that the individual will do good work for the organization and the organization will provide work and sustenance for the employee.*

Noxious Feelings: *Uncomfortable feelings that employees experience at work as a result of change, job loss, geographical or work-group changes can have a negative impact on organizational health if not dealt with efficiently. We all seek to meet needs for love and affiliation, transforming feelings of aggression, managing dependency, and supporting self-esteem. When an individual's source of support is removed, each of these driving needs is threatened. Although people react in a variety of ways, common outcomes include depression, grief, loss and flight.*

Poor Health: *Pain and disruption stem from a breech of the psychological contract, an inability to address the four feelings above, or an inability to engage at work at the level of complexity where we function best.*

DIANA: Much of what you describe as affecting people stems from coping with changes in the current state of work, whether it's job loss, transfer, etc. There is a loss of community and day to day work friendships. How do you help people deal with these changes in their work environments?

HARRY: Well, executives really need to communicate about upcoming changes and the reasons for them. Often they are not prepared for resistance and you have to set their expectations. One has to confront people repeatedly with change and the logic behind it, and then help them mourn the loss of their precious ways of doing things. The CEO has to be chief mourner, by explaining he doesn't like the changes either, but that they are necessary. It may be terminating old friends, or finding new ways of doing things. You have to enable them to express their anger, depression and worry. You have to keep them organized so they are mutually supportive and maintain the integrity of their work group. You may have to do retraining. There is usually anxiety about learning to use new machines. They worry if they are smart enough, quick enough. Organizations ought to allow the mourning of the loss of what they already do well. It's also important to help people who have to leave the organization to find new jobs, identify skills, make initial contact and get started. Maybe provide training resources in local vocational schools. People like to know that management gives a damn and is trying to help them. When people who leave come back in a reunion, where leadership is mutually supportive with expressions of anger and disappointment, it can be helpful.

It was difficult to get some executives to believe they had to help others. I've found the lack of knowledge and information to be the biggest barrier. People go from one organization to another more readily. Today there are a lot of people without jobs due to the tech decline or have jobs unrelated to their training. They are turned loose with no regard. The Menninger Foundation just left 1000 people without jobs when they moved from Kansas to Texas. I don't know any program that could have met their needs fully. Even clinically trained people don't always know how to manage the change process. The rapid pace of change is an issue. I don't know of any program that helps managers deal with the speed at which things happen.

DIANA: In contrast, what have been the biggest success stories you've seen from investing in human capital?

HARRY: Companies in which people have worked for a long time are invested. They cost more to manage, but their reputation is more attractive to prospective employees. They can avoid possible lawsuits from terminating people and attract better talent. It is costly to do something psychologically wise and it is also costly to do something impulsively and without thought. You have to communicate a humane perspective to the people who remain. When they see the sensitivity they can be more comfortable and it dissipates bitterness and guilt. I think most people understand things have to change and people want to engage in change with management. This builds continuity and morale.

DIANA: How do firms create and sustain a psychological contract without becoming paternalistic?

HARRY: You have to have open communication about what things will happen, what the change process will look like and allow people as much control as possible.

DIANA: So you need to provide the information, and allow employee independence and some control while being involved?

HARRY: Yes, you reconstruct work groups, thrash out leadership issues, look at the hierarchy of the organization, and the alternatives to making changes. If you are engaged with people and carrying on a discussion about these things the fact of the interchange treats them as mature adults. You can't have an effective psychological contract without communication about what's going on and what's expected of each party. You describe the current reality and allow people to react with anger or mourning. You retrain them and help them deal with the fact that some people are going to lose power. A person loses prestige and the feelings of competence that went along with having that power. We have to have a way for people to cope with that. One of the major New York newspapers went to computer when my cousin was a linotype operator. He went into a shell. Management has to recognize that some people will do this. Psychological management is an issue. People need to manage psychologically as well as they manage economically. When change occurs there is a loss of role, status, and often friends.

DIANA: What kind of change do you see affecting our work environments over the next 20 years?

HARRY: The first is to recognize that people will no longer stick with a company if they are not adequately challenged and have room for upward mobility. More people are ready to move where there is greater challenge, opportunity, and compensation. A lot more attention has to be given to psychological growth. Some others will be fast movers and get rapidly promoted. Others will move more slowly. There is not much attention given to that or the implications for selection. It is important to realize people will reach a level of conceptual capacity and then taper off. We must learn more about conceptual development. The work of Elliott Jacques is a good start, and we need to meet employee needs more actively than we are currently. Second, we are having a lowering of the levels of hierarchy. There are fewer levels and greater flexibility for leaders at those levels. It's a kind of decentralization. It's good because more people will be able to rise more quickly if they have the capacity. Third, people will develop more competence. They will use training night schools as their skills rapidly become obsolete. It's a competitive swim and they will have to keep up with it. At GE, they have lower level people coming into the organization teaching existing people skills so they can keep up with the rate of change. You will also see a greater effort at keeping people together for a specific task or function. High tech people that want to follow their own noses and innovate will split off and start their own company. If there is financial support and opportunity for continuous learning available, people are more likely to stay. There is greater transiency when people have shot their wad and are no longer challenged at work. Keeping these people involved requires more attention to training and re-training. It would involve learning more cultures and languages and developing activities in other countries. Kansas State University developed a Japanese Language program – in Kansas. However, it's a hit. People are becoming increasingly sophisticated about other cultures and economics. Work requires us to move so frequently that we can no longer be isolated and ignorant of others. This parallels the growth of psychological man. There is a movement from small towns to big cities. People want to be where the action is, where jobs are, and where they can continue to be stimulated. Unfortunately, there is a loss of support and loss of previous ways of doing things when people transition. I was just reading something about a small town in Mississippi that is practically empty and I know where I grew up, people are leaving for larger towns.

DIANA: We've seen similar movements here in Georgia. One of my first consultation projects was with two elementary schools that were merging due to "urban flight."

HARRY: One of the things I really notice that helps or hinders people from adjusting well to change is the capacity for complexity. People have different capacities for managing complexity. If you look at the work of Elliot Jacques, he identifies eight levels of conceptual capacity based on how far ahead people have to look. There are different levels of complexity for different roles. So, a brick layer has to look ahead 8 to 10 months, and a CEO has to look ahead 50 years. This is even part of the reason for our divorce rate. Partners may start out at the same conceptual level, but one may develop more rapidly than the other. This psychological gap continues to grow as they mature to the point where they can hardly talk to one another. This is not addressed in our culture, these differences in conceptual capacity and growth.

DIANA: How does this play out at work?

HARRY: In order to rise up in a flatter organization you need greater opportunity and skill in doing a wider variety of things. You are not limited by hierarchy, so if you are not being stimulated it makes for greater mobility across work groups or projects. In some organizations there used to be twenty levels. If you reduce these to five levels, people soon realize whether they have the capacity for the increased demand for complexity. You will easily notice which people have the greater innovative capacity. For example, in a chain of grocery stores that is limited to five levels, you can easily see which managers have bigger imaginations, or who responds to change more quickly. There is more visibility and more opportunity for mobility. In flatter organizations people can self-evolve, and if the organization won't support it, they leave. You can see this across several companies; I just read an article about this happening at Proctor & Gamble.

DIANA: Yes, similar movement is occurring across business sectors and those who leave often start their own firms. I'm teaching a graduate level class this semester and one of the basic concepts the students are getting a grasp of is the difference between collaboration and consultation and when to use each. When you work with companies on these issues, do you typically work from a collaborative or consultative perspective?

HARRY: It depends on the company and the problem. For example, I started consulting with the CEO of a technology firm. Their in-house psychologist suggested he give me a call. The CEO was in a depressive rage. He did not want to change. I did a three-day seminar on change processes for the executive group, and continued to consult over the years. I worked with the HR department to help them carry on the steps of change by doing a series of workshops. I continued to meet with top management people until they downsized to the point where I was no longer involved. It's important to develop internal competence at companies. These concepts are teachable and understandable and can be carried out. There are several components of psychological management that you can teach on an ad hoc or ongoing basis. I've worked with IBM and GE in this manner.

What I've found with students, is it is helpful for them to get a sense of how much the client has to rigidly control what is going on. They need to work at finding ways to come at the person tangentially so you don't threaten their sense of control frontally. I try to teach them to have some judgment of the state of mind of the client. Sometimes the client is depressed. Sometimes they are dealing with a difficult problem and have thrown in the sponge. You have to look at what you need to do to bolster the client without helping them to feel more helpless. In teaching consultation, it is also important to address counter transference. I had one student who was giving feedback and completely excoriated an executive. When we worked with that we found she was responding to counter transference. Students may not be aware of that kind of problem. You also have to help them confront resistance. We had one CEO who managed to always be away when the students were on site. Finally we had the students show up when they were not expected. Sometimes people get wrapped up in avoiding and evading real and important issues.

DIANA: Well Harry, you've had a wealth of good ideas and experience. What's on the horizon for you?

HARRY: I keep one major client that I see as a member of an advisory board. It keeps me alert and on the ball. I'm also organizing some of my Harvard Business Review articles into a new book.

DIANA: I really appreciate the opportunity to speak with you informally. You have made such a valuable contribution to the fields of psychology, organizational behavior, and consultation. I want to thank you for making the time to present your thoughts for our readers and for keeping us abreast of your new work.

Diana Gordick, Ph. D.

A recent graduate, Diana has formed Gordick and Associates, and is in the process of building a service portfolio and developing client relationships. As an individual practitioner, she manages all aspects of client care and service delivery, focusing on individual assessment and development, team development, and organizational assessment.

WHITHER CONSULTING PSYCHOLOGY?
Harry Levinson's Valediction
Del Ray Beach, Florida 2009

In this, the final psychological article of my career, I should like to call the attention of my colleagues to three specific problems in consulting psychology:

1) The failure to be firmly grounded in psychology
2) The haphazard coping with practice in the field
3) The failure of consulting psychologists to tackle organization psychological problems in depth rather than management by odds and ends of group process techniques.

Firm Grounding

The Society of Consulting Psychology (SCP), Division 13 of the American Psychological association (APA) [Our division] membership is a disparate lot. Some are thoroughly trained psychologists, others are much more casual. Some are involved in intensive consultation in organizations; others offer a single technique or problem-solving activity. If consulting psychology is to be respected as a discipline, it must be more than a patchwork - a conglomeration of odds and ends of techniques and competences.

Our contemporary problem is becoming increasingly acute. APA CEO Dr. Norman Anderson reported to the Council of Representatives at the meeting in San Francisco in August 2007, that the APA will likely face a decline in membership as members age. The mean age of APA member psychologists now is 55 and only 18 percent of APA members are younger than 40. He said that the APA faces difficulty in attracting and retaining early career professionals. That has serious implications for consulting psychology. It also constitutes a major threat to psychological scientific creativity. The implication is that we must become actively involved in recruiting younger, imaginative people into our profession. However, unlike most psychologists, consulting psychologists must be able to relate to organizations and their executives, a skill that is not widely shared by other psychologists. We must seek out those, like ourselves, that are comfortable in that role.

A few years ago, the then-president of Harvard University rejected the nomination of two prospective appointees as professors whose age was 46. In effect, he was saying they were too old for innovation. Innovation is a young person's game. That action and the logic behind it suggest a number of issues that we as psychologists need to be concerned about. A likely issue is the increasing pressure for publications and for choosing people for faculties who can be productive. That, in itself, has another obscure variable. The greatest productivity occurs in young people before they become middle-aged. Once, having acquired tenure, there is less pressure to be productive. It is easier for psychologists who already have tenure to coast along for the rest of their careers at the cost of potential productivity. As Dr. Anderson points out, we are not attracting sufficient numbers of career psychologists to expand those numbers. Furthermore, with the increasing average age of the APA members there is unlikely to be a corollary increase in the number of productive psychologists and, as a consequence, a significant decline in innovative research and consulting technique. In short, we are becoming older, fewer in number, and less professionally productive. Although consulting psychologists are not noted for their research contributions, nevertheless unless they continue to be innovative and in keeping with the problems of the times, they risk becoming obsolete.

The chairman of a psychology department sent me a copy of a journal issue that he had just edited. Obviously he expected me to respond enthusiastically to its content. I was dismayed to see that two of the major articles were reporting on a survey technique that was old when I was a graduate student. A third article was a part of an old psychological technique and a fourth showed no awareness of the literature that had been published long before. My colleague was distraught when I pointed out these issues, as he indeed should have been. The implication is that there is considerable rehashing of old variables in our psychological journals and innovation is hard to come by.

Perusing another psychological journal, I was astonished to see that a number of the articles had new labels for topics that were established practices when I was a graduate student. In still another journal, a prominent highly regarded psychologist described not only contemporary developments in psychology, all of which were long since familiar to established colleagues, but offered no ideas for where psychology could or should be going. The implication is that much that is in the psychological literature is no longer novel and new knowledge, particularly innovative ideas, is hard to come by.

A young instructor in a major academic psychology department conveyed to me her fear of the prospect of having to write a professional article in order to sustain her position. Her problem, along with that of many other psychologists in similar positions, becomes increasingly acute as university faculties, seeking to restrain the numbers of tenured professors on the payroll, employ larger numbers of untenured instructors and are slower to grant tenure to those who remain. Unfortunately, in many cases, such instructors get little support from their seniors who might help them organize their thoughts or focus on a problem and follow it through. Such instructors are isolated and have to fend for themselves in a context that is heavily organized around seniors who have been there much longer. When those seniors who should be helpful may not be, as in this case, the individual instructor is left to flounder.

In another context, a competent professor who was being put under pressure by his dean to increase the number of students in his graduate organizational behavior class was at his wit's end. Although he was an experienced and respected professor, he was hardly likely to stand on a street corner to extol prospective students to attend his course. After much hassle, he finally resigned.

These examples, declining numbers of psychologists, potential loss of innovation, a tendency for psychologists to rehash old concepts with new labels, the decline of innovative conceptions, loss of direction and integration of younger and newer faculty members, and resulting loss of their productivity, finally coupled with increasing demands on faculty members for publications, all point to the tribulations of our profession. If consulting psychology is not to become merely a bag of old tricks, odds and ends of techniques and slogans, then there are a number of actions which we must now begin to take.

The workshops at annual and semi-annual division meetings are an important step in the right direction. They offer us also a model for how we might strengthen our professional activities. Psychologists can now choose from a wide range of short courses to keep their licenses active. That, however, is not enough. I am suggesting that we evolve a structure of formal refresher courses that cumulatively would comprise a program of professional advancement, even with formal titles or labels. In effect, these refresher courses, more systematically organized and labeled, and progressive in nature, would lead to a formal credential that would testify to the increased competence of the holder. As consulting psychologists engaged in continuing practice, we cannot afford to rest on our academic laurels. Those people who, having attained tenure and now sit on their psychological haunches, burden our profession. By involving systematic continuous training, we can communicate to fellow psychologists, clients and to ourselves that we are staying abreast of contemporary problems and techniques and that we are confronting the realities of the consulting profession. In short, we should create an internal psychological accountable experience.

A derivative of that conception would be to create local chapters of consulting psychologists that would meet regularly to support and inform each other, and train younger beginning consultants. The senior consultants would therefore be the mentors for the junior consultants and provide some internal consistency for the usefulness of local chapters. Such a program would enhance the competence of practitioners and endorse their success in the field.

Biologists who are interested in studying animals immerse themselves in the wilds of Africa. Psychologists who are interested in understanding clinical problems of human beings immerse themselves in treatment processes in hospitals, in clinics and in continued refresher activities. Organizational consultants who would keep themselves informed need to be immersed. That immersion must be formally created in the form of internships and classroom activities that give both faculty and students the opportunity to study what is going on in organizations that they will need to continue to work with. Faculty who teach organization consultation should be required to have a continuing relationship with an organization even if it is not compensated. Graduate students who are learning about organizational consultation should be assigned to a company on the first day of their graduate work and be in touch with that company throughout their graduate studies. They may merely observe, visit, or confer. Whatever the case, they too, need to have some sense of being immersed in a company, to see its problems first hand. One can teach people to understand history, literature, and languages out of books. But one cannot teach people to understand human behavior out of books alone.

Haphazard Practices

A couple of other experiences in contemporary consulting psychology give me pause.

The first occurred several years ago when one of my respected colleagues sadly said to me after reading one of my articles that he had not had a chance to learn what I was writing about. He wanted me to say something that would ease his conscience. I said simply that I did not own the material, that it was available in journals and books to everyone with all kinds of questions and that he could continue to improve his competence by following any one of several directions. He did not do any of it. His name is no longer prominent among contemporary psychologists. It is imperative that psychologists keep learning.

That is secondary to another kind of problem: the limitation of what is being taught in consulting psychology. For the past two years I have been conducting a course for beginning consulting psychologists. We meet once a month by conference call, each young psychologist presenting a case. After each presentation, there is a discussion of the case by the other participants. I follow with comments and suggestions. Thus the new consultants have an opportunity for mutual support, critical exchange, and the occasion to evaluate what they are doing in the context of what their peers are doing. Such case conferences could readily be part of local professional meetings.

The second major area which needs supervision and help is that of the trainee consultants. The repetitive problems that appear must be corrected. Some instructors who traditionally should be in contact with students' work seem to have few significant relationships with the senior executives with whom presumably they are dealing. Students have been turned loose in a company, after the instructor has been given permission for them to do a survey or other consulting activity. I am concerned that the instructor apparently has little further relationship with the corporate hierarchy. The students then must fend for themselves. They have little experience dealing with corporate power, organizational structures, and the conflicting difficult forces that they will encounter in organizations. Students may think they have really learned about a particular problem that they have studied, but sadly often have little opportunity to feed back what they have learned to elements of the power structure in the organization that really govern what goes on. The instructor, having little continuing contact with that power structure, has few ways of helping the students understand the context in which the organizational problems occur. The students now deemed the "consultants" must work on their own. This is much like medical students having to learn about patients' surgery without supervision.

Another kind of frustration is that the psychological consultants may be engaged by a variety of employers and have little contact with the core figures in the organizations where they are employed. For example, a consultant was engaged by an outside non-psychological consultant to do some psychological testing in a company. The consultant had no relationship with the significant executives in that company to whom reports would have to be given. The consultant did not have any sense of the political structure of the company or whatever else within that company that would be germane to the consultant's work. In a couple of instances like that, the consultant, after trying to work in such projects resigned.

A number of important conclusions arise from these admittedly disparate examples. Learning technical science is b a young person's game. Students should be started early in their graduate careers in organizations, beginning in one or another aspect of each organization and trying to understand its complexity and context.

At the beginning of their teaching careers, instructors in organizational psychology, organizational behavior and management leadership should arrange to become immersed in a business organization even without being paid as consultants in that organization. If they did so they then would have firsthand experience in the management of an organization by observing, taking part in and attending meetings and conferences. One really cannot teach about organizations if he or she is not so immersed. To try to teach organizational behavior without such immersion is like a medical student working without experience at cadavers. Too many psychologists teaching about organization processes have little or no experience in organizations. They are limited in what they understand and even more so in what they can teach. When such professors get tenure, they then risk becoming obsolete in role and have little to add for their students that would be up to date and vital. Little wonder that the then president of Harvard turned down the post-46-year-olds for tenure. Given the prospective APA membership figures, the likelihood is that fewer people will be granted tenure in the future unless they are more productive. Those who choose to specialize and work in organizations cannot be more productive without getting immersed in organizations.

Some years ago, disappointed with the limited research as reported in the literature, I undertook a study in the Kansas Power and Light Company with two colleagues that involved interviewing 753 employees over two-thirds of the state, getting immersed in the company, in the work, and among these employees. Instead of a simple report or some kind of test for X or Y number of people or a survey on a single topic, my colleagues and I lived with those employees on the job. We learned much about organizations that was not in the books and some that is not in the books even today. Our college professors who had not been immersed in organizations could tell us little about them. Like anthropologists who go to distant tribes to write about them, psychologists who teach about organizations should become immersed in them.

The young woman professor who was worried because she did not know what to write about would not have had that problem had she been one of my students. I would have immersed her in an organization. She would have experienced the organization rather than having learned it from books. One cannot learn enough about organizations by reading books, even mine.

However, just being immersed in an organization does not make one knowledgeable. Millions of people work in organizations and do not know very much about them. Millions more manage them and often do not know very much about them either, as reflected in their repetitive errors, failures, and major mistakes. In the process of observing, investigating and learning, one therefore must develop a frame of reference about motivation; about what makes people tick and what makes organizations function. My own orientation, which has served me in very good stead, is psychoanalysis, but perhaps other theories would be even more helpful for other consultants. Using an integrated theory of motivation helps one organize what one is observing and learning It enables the psychologist to provide a logic for his or her conclusions. Without such a theory, all one can do is paste together bits and pieces of learning without having them systematically tied together. My apologetic colleague, to whom I referred earlier, complained enviously that he did not have my training. I replied that I did not own the training. In effect, he was saying, he really ought to learn more but was not doing it.

There are many ways of learning more. One is immersion in organizations. Another is developing an understanding of what goes on in organizations by reading informative books. In one of the examples above, the graduate student undertook a study that she then reported back to the same department of the company that she had studied. One of the recommendations to that unit was highly unlikely to be applied because that unit was necessarily a component of the larger organization. She had not the least understanding of what the political problems above that unit were. Therefore she could not make recommendations which would take those realities into account. Her instructor, apparently not having sufficient experience, did not call that to her attention, nor did he help her get in touch with higher level management who could tell her about the organizational context she was studying. In effect, what she had done was an exercise in futility.

I made it a policy with all of my students to have them, as they went into organizations, talk with the dominant figures. If they were studying a part of the organization, I had them also talk with whoever headed that unit and, in turn, who is in touch with managers in authority above them.

In short, I am suggesting that students who are interested in consultation should have the opportunity to immerse themselves in organizations in the course of their training under instructors who are also immersed.

Years ago, when I was teaching organizational consultation, I assigned teams of five students each to a given organization for an academic year. They had to talk with the CEO and then present themselves all the way down in the organization as people who wanted to learn about organizations and this one in particular. Then they had to arrange an interview schedule, get data on the organization from its various reports, advertising and public communications. They had to decide where to interview samples of employees and then they discussed in class what they were learning and how to feed back to the organization. That was an intensive program. Not all faculty members and certainly not all graduate students can undertake that amount of time and effort. But basically the general idea is the same; that is if one is to understand organizations, he or she must have some way of getting immersed in them over a long enough period of time to evolve a sense of what goes on and why. There really is no other way.

When one becomes immersed in an organization, it is easy to see the limitations of the literature. The reason simply is that not many people who write have immersion experience. They only translate each other's writings but have little to speak from their own experience. Without that experience, they are also without the ability to question what is in the literature.

In the examples I offered above, the first referring to the graduate student "consultant" and the second, inadequate definition of the consulting relationship, the consultants had little or no relationship with higher management in the companies in which they were working. They simply did not have sufficient time, nor sufficient authority, nor sufficient clarity with higher level management. The consultant must communicate with whomever is accountable for the unit. He or she needs to know the expectations of higher level management. If a consultant does not insist on that kind of authoritative relationship, then much of his or her work winds up being a vain exercise.

Taking Charge

Another aspect of organizational consultation which, except for what I have written, is untouched in the literature. That is the need for the consultant, from time to time, to have to take charge of a situation. That may happen when the consultee is a weak person who needs various kinds of support to regain his or her position in the organization, or at least to be able to rise to the responsibility he or she has. That may happen if the consultee turns out to be too weak to manage a situation or is unable to take charge of the organization because of internal opposition or reluctance to be a boss or not being smart enough to carry on that particular role. Whatever the case, a consultant in such a situation finds himself or herself in the position of either withdrawing or having to take charge. If he or she withdraws, then the cause is lost and the organization is likely to go down. If, instead, he or she helps to take charge, it may be possible to strengthen either the incumbent chief or to help the incumbent choose somebody else who can take his or her place or to consider with the incumbent whether he or she should even be in that particular kind of role. From time to time every consultant will run into this kind of problem. It is an extremely difficult position to be in and a more difficult position about which to make decisions. Nevertheless, as a consultant, from time to time one must take charge. Too many consultants are much too prone to turn to group process or some other method to manage such a consultation. That sometimes may be necessary but in all organizations somebody must be in charge, whether officially, unofficially or only in a make believe fashion. Somebody necessarily is accountable. Somebody has to make final decisions. A major part of any consultant's task is to help the person in the chief executive position take appropriate action in keeping with that role. To believe that one can deal with such executive situations by some kind of group process is, in effect, to be managerially ridiculous. Wise executives know that they cannot always turn to their subordinates for advice, guidance and participation in decision making. There are always power struggles in organizations. There are always rivals for the boss's role or his or her power and position. There are always people who think everything the boss does or is trying to do and the decisions that the boss is trying to get them to make are necessarily wrong.

Some years ago the new chief executive of a major oil company was trying to get the respective vice-presidents to agree on necessary organizational changes. Despite his year- long effort, they would not budge from their fixed positions. They thought the way to run an oil company was to do as they were doing. They were not about to change. It became necessary for the CEO to take a much more active charge of what was going on. A number of the rigidly resistant vice-presidents had to leave in order for the organization to survive. I had to consult with him about the necessary steps to survive and how to cope with the resistances of vice-presidents who did not choose to yield to the new chief executive.

There are times when one as a consultant has to deal with problems of entrenched policy and help the CEO with them. It may be that a wise CEO has his own personal consultant, a fellow CEO, a friend, a neighbor, an attorney, or an accountant to whom he or she can turn. The consultant may indeed also be such a person but he or she may have to take into account the effect of the boss's other advisors on decisions that are made in the organization. Such decisions may contradict whatever is the wise psychological course that the organization should take. No psychologist working in such a situation can deal with such problems unless he or she is comfortable working with authority. Many psychologists are not. If one is not, then he or she certainly cannot work with higher management. Instead the psychologist must deal with the problems higher management causes by dealing with some of the consequences at lower levels or perhaps by forgetting about the problem altogether.

One of the touchier problems a consultant may have to deal with is a change in top management; as for example, when one organization buys another and wants to make some drastic changes. In one instance, the organization had a group of employees of very limited education who had been with it for many years. The new owners wanted to discharge them with simple severance bonuses and start the organization anew a hundred miles away, with an altogether new staff. My recommendation was that part of the terminal pay of those people who were going to lose their jobs was the requirement that they get training for new jobs. Training would be available at the local vocational schools. They could then be responsible for their own lives and their opportunity for new roles. I felt that the decision of the owners would cause terrible damage to those uneducated, untrained dependent people who with their limited training and education never before had had to look for a job. They had no experience other than in a paternalistic company they worked for all their organizational lives. The net of it was that when the new personnel director insisted that she was going to proceed in her own way, I resigned from the case.

There are times when one has to take a principled position in the interests of people who have no other way of protecting themselves. The ethics of the consultant must then come to the fore. Sometimes it is costly, as it was in this case, in the sense that I no longer had that client. Not only did the employees leave, but I left as well.

Harry Levinson, Spring 2008, Delray Beach, Florida.

CHAPTER 1

SECTION ONE

IMMERSION AND DIAGNOSIS

IMMERSION 1

Bearding the Lion that Roared
A Case Study in Organizational Consultation

Consulting Psychology Journal, 44:4,1-16, Fall
With Joseph Sabbath, M.D. and Jeffrey Connor, PhD.

Introduction

The director of human resources of a high tech company in a Chicago suburb called me, the senior author, to ask for consultation on behalf of her chief executive. She said that he was concerned because their recent turnover of upper middle management and officers was 35% higher than their norm. The president of the company had been a participant in an executive seminar conducted by the senior author some years before, and had recommended to the CEO that he call for consultation. The call was precipitated by the unexpected loss of another senior officer.

Dr. Sabbath, a senior consulting colleague, and Dr. Connor, then a junior colleague, accompanied me to the meeting in the office of the chief executive, who I shall call Mr. G. The office was in a three-building corporate complex, to which admission was controlled by security agents, because some of the company's work had to do with national defense. Mr. G welcomed us to his second floor office. He was a tall, athletically built, casually dressed 55-year-old man. His large office was decorated with a variety of paintings, sculpture, prints, and plants, as well as samples of the company's products. A large emblem of his military service decorated the wall behind him across a 1941 photo of Earth. He sat behind an outsized desk. We three sat in front of the desk: I in the center, Dr. Sabbath on thel eft, and Dr. Connor on the right. Mr. G put his stockinged feet up on the desk and proceeded to address us rapidly, including liberal quotations and metaphors, frequently in military language with such terms as "triage," "troops," and "trenches." From time to time, he would offer a homily, for example, "If you want to eat raisins, you have to spit out the seeds." He repetitively offered coffee from what seemed to be an inexhaustible pot.

He launched into a self-description: "I am an aggressive and abrasive person. I am an entrepreneur. I have been diagnosed as manic-depressive and, up till a few years ago, took lithium. I have been seeing a psychiatrist, and am not taking any medication now. You can call him if you want to. I've changed; I have learned a lot. My family made money illegally. I got into trouble as a kid. In those days, I didn't know what the truth was, but later on found people along the way that I admired and changed my mind. Two years ago, I separated from my wife. Now I want to know the truth about what's going on in my company. Whatever it is, I want to know, and want the people here to know it. You can interview whoever you want, as many as you want, including any other consultants."

He indicated in his discourse that his father had been arrested many times and that he had been reared in a difficult environment. He did not specify what his own brushes with the law had been, except to say that he had once been arrested as a suspect in a murder he did not commit and was released. He had overcome the handicaps of his upbringing to achieve a graduate degree. He had seen not one, but two psychiatrists, and a clinically trained management consultant.

I told him that Dr. Sabbath and Dr. Connor would conduct a series of one-to-two-hour interviews with people who would represent a cross section of the staff from the president on down, including a few of the officers who had left the company, and some members of the board of directors. The purpose of the study, namely to try to understand the reasons for the high turnover, would be explained to each of the executives, managers, and employees before each interview. They would be told that the interviews were voluntary and confidential, and that a summary would subsequently be prepared for Mr. G. Mr. G agreed.

Diagnostic Hypotheses

We were concerned in our post-meeting discussion with how we should deal with Mr. G. We were impressed in our first meeting with the hypo-manic, paranoid, and narcissistic features in his self-description, his denigrating view of others, and the clues to omnipotent strivings that we inferred between the lines of his comments. The risk was high that he might abort our efforts, or impulsively intrude into our work, or reject us altogether. If he were indeed in a manic phase and no longer taking lithium, there might well be no holding him down, and there was the risk that the ultimate feedback would precipitate the depressive aspects of his cycle. If the paranoid features were strong enough, then he might experience our feedback report as an attack and perceive us as enemies who were out to destroy him. The narcissistic features indicated that we must be unusually careful to support his self-image.

Clearly, he was not psychotic. Though he could be harsh to people, as he himself told us, and he had an adolescent record as an antisocial person (primarily stealing), he was not a classically antisocial personality. In fact, he had built this successful organization over 15 years, which was now doing $25 million in sales. He seemed to have considerable ego strength, despite his limited anxiety tolerance and impulse control. Although the elements of omnipotent striving and devaluation of others are prominent features of the borderline personality (Kernberg, 1977), he seemed, in the first interview at least, to be able to be warm and concerned and able also to relate to some people on a long-term basis. He seemed closer to the narcissistic personality.

Ours was not to be a therapeutic intervention. We were not here to treat Mr. G. Yet, clinical insights would be important both to understand what was happening in the organization, particularly, as was now apparent, as a product of Mr. G's personality, and what could be done about it. Even with clinically sensitive management of our relations with him, minor miscalculations could easily destroy the helping process. And then there was the whole question of what he could do about the findings. That might well take continued consultation. In the light of the previous limited therapeutic achievement, the risk was high and the prognosis guarded.

Expressive psychotherapy was clearly out of the question, nor could we resolve his managerial problems by recommending that he take his lithium again, although that might well be indicated. Given the nature of his behavior, we would have to maintain a firm, consistent reality boundary, and maximize the positive transference by demonstrating that we had our own strength and were not frightened of him. As Kernberg (1982) suggests, our supportive effort would require helping him recognize the boundaries of reality and understanding the effects of his behavior without judging him or moralizing about them. Kernberg points out that the therapist must "tactfully, yet consistently, confront the patient with how he contributes to his difficulties." Obviously, one must also work with the negative transference.

The Process Joined

The negative transference was not long in coming. When Mr. G himself was scheduled for an individual interview with Dr. Sabbath, he sent a message through his secretary that he was tied up and did not know when he would be available. Dr. Sabbath, he said, should interview some of the other people. His secretary mentioned in an aside that he had remarked that he did not like the idea of spending two hours in an interview. By this time, he himself had already abruptly called several of his top officers out of their interviews with Dr. Sabbath and Dr. Connor without explanation. Dr. Sabbath decided to go to Mr. G's office anyway.

Dr. Sabbath asked Mr. G's secretary to call him at his meeting. Mr. G was incensed that Dr. Sabbath had called and said, "Listen, my friend, I have the right to change the time when I want to. I am speaking to someone about an acquisition, and I'll be tied up for an hour or so."

Dr. Sabbath asked what other time could be arranged. Mr. G replied, "Well, maybe I'll see you tomorrow or next week." Dr. Sabbath confronted him with his prior remark about being finished in an hour and said that he would be waiting for him in his office. After a long pause, Mr. G said, "Okay, around 11:00 a.m."

Mr. G arrived exactly at 11:00 a.m. with eyes blazing. His first remark was, "You've got one hell of a nerve interrupting me. I was arranging to acquire this company in the South."

Dr. Sabbath responded that we had an appointment and had work to do.

Mr. G replied, "Don't give me that bullshit – all right now, come into the office. Don't worry, you'll get paid for your time. I resent intensely being interrupted. Sit down, and I'm taking five."

After returning from his private bathroom, he took out a tube of cold cream and began putting the cold cream on his hands, saying, "Okay, what's going on?"

Dr. Sabbath thanked him for the arrangements he had made and for the excellent cooperation on the part of the employees, executives, and managers. Dr. Sabbath reported that they had been very helpful in the consultations so far. Mr. G settled down quickly, saying, "Okay." He then started to ramble about these problems:

1) Because of the growth of the company, he cannot now know and communicate with everyone. "It is no longer like a family."

2) Some of his people are afraid of him. He does not know why. Some cower and whimper. He does not like that; he feels they must misunderstand or not hear correctly, some of his officers do not hear. He added, "I know I fire people on the spot, but I call things as I see them. Some people are serfs – they should only be emptying wastebaskets."

3) He did not want his company to grow bigger as long as people were troubled and problems were unresolved. "I've been through a lot myself, but now have never felt stronger or better."

4) "I want a fit between myself and the staff and the organization."

5) "I want to choose people who are loyal. How can we do that? Genetic engineering, maybe. There are 48 chromosomes; maybe we can splice a few good ones." He referred to one of the vice presidents

who had left as "a consummate paranoid."

During the interview there was a telephone interruption, after which he said, "I chewed that guy's ass out so hard he won't be able to sit down for a week." The interview ended with his stating that he hoped the consultants would not just be scribes, and that he would be told something that would be of use.

This interview confirmed our diagnostic hypothesis that we should maintain ego boundaries in a supportive context and see the paranoid features as typical of those more likely to be found in a narcissistic character disorder. Despite the evidence for sadistic control and for the projection of rage, there was evidence of some soft, sentimental, and tender feelings, as reflected in his yearning for a family. His insistence on high standards of production, on orderliness, precision, clarity, and control are consistent with the product and the need to maintain exacting production and clean work areas. That these obsessive-compulsive features reflect severe unresolved sadism and controlling, vengeful behavior that drives people away seemed to be secondary to the basic narcissism.

History

The subsequent interviews rounded out our initial hypothesis about Mr. G's behavior. They added perspectives on his personal life, his career, they history and current structure and functioning of the organization, and the thoughts and feelings of the executives, managers, and employees. None of those who were asked for interviews refused, but some were more cautious than others.

He had let everyone in the company know about his background, that he had grown up in a deprived environment. His parents separated early, his father was a gambler, and his mother was uninterested in him. He was reared by relatives, and in his high school years got into trouble with the law for stealing from supermarkets. He entered military service by lying about his age and then worked his way through college. During the summers of his college years, he became a research assistant to a professor with whom he is still close. He then became a salesman for a chemical company from which he was fired because he "didn't do well in a structured environment." He and two others then formed the present company in 1962. By 1972, there were 70 employees and the company was striving for $3 million to $4 million in sales.

One informant reported that the management group would come in on a Sunday. Mr. G became the leader as the other two pulled back and was made president in 1968. He is reported to have a good deal of concern about the families of the others. He himself married in 1965. (Subsequently he and his wife had four children.) Through 1978 the company was run by consensus. Eight people decided everything.

The research department evolved a new device that had a wide range of potential uses. It became an instant success and a new plant had to be found for production. The company began to expand at the rate of 70% a year and was cited in a magazine as one of the 100 fastest growing companies in America. It attracted a wide variety of young, ambitious engineers.

About this time (1981), Mr. G's mood swings became a concern for his family and colleagues. He agreed to see a psychiatrist and was put on lithium.

Serious business problems then began to develop. The new plant, which was several hundred miles away from the present headquarters, had production and labor problems, and could not keep up with the demand. It had to be sold to a conglomerate. Unfortunately, a number of key personnel, who had been involved in that project, went with the division. Apparently, that was a significant psychological loss for Mr. G. He was also in the process of separating from his wife.

The rate of growth fell from 70% to 20%. The generous price paid by the acquiring corporation was insufficient to support the number of ambitious plans that Mr. G had initiated impulsively. He embarked on rapid expansion by recruiting engineers and manufacturing personnel, and by acquiring competitors. When people left his organization and tried to compete with him, he sued them for patent infringement, so that neither they nor smaller competitors dared try to compete. He built two new buildings, bought a company airplane, and became involved in a variety of real estate deals. For three years, he would not leave his office building at night, sleeping during the day and working at night during the period of extended growth.

He saw another psychiatrist who stopped his lithium. He continued to dress informally in Pendleton shirts and Levis. His mood swings moderated. His goals were to grow 20% to 30% a year and to reach $100 million in sales with a pretax profit of 20%. He met another woman and then began to take better care of himself. He remarried in 1984.

He agreed to his board's request that he hire a chief operating officer. Nevertheless, the strain on the company increased to the point where employees left in large numbers and morale was poor. The board and the stockholders felt that they had bet on a wild man and were willing to ride with him until, in 1984, for the first time, the company failed to show a profit. Mr. G had said that his goals were to make his company a fun place and to make money. Neither was happening. Several top officers left and it was at this time that he was asked to consider consultation.

Findings

One of his longtime subordinates said, "The whole organization is set up like a garage. It hasn't left that mentality. In this organization, the focus is on people, rather than managerial processes. If a given person that you depend on is not there, everything goes to hell. As a manager, you end up doing a lot of jobs yourself because you can't trust others to get them done. Here, the service from another department is a favor and everything becomes a personal issue. A suggestion is taken as a criticism."

This is an aggressive, salesman type of organization, say the interviewees. Mr. G is not willing to accept the fact that he is not a manager. He is task-oriented, not goal-oriented. He wants immediate solutions. If someone does a snow job on him, he will change his mind. That means there is a constantly moving set of priorities. He is impulsive, a one-man company, a gunfighter. He goes off at the least sign of a challenge. He has a conflict understanding the difference between profitability and bigness. He thinks so fast, planning strategy, he does not finish before he reaches for something else. He dips into every level of operations in the company. He fires people, even groups of people, arbitrarily, for example, the quality control team. The organizational charts change every month. He has too many people reporting to him. Something is wrong in his ability to trust. He is unable to delegate. He has a group of star performers. Through superhuman effort they perform on demand, but organizationally they are disasters. When he deals with organizations or people who cannot move a tenth of his speed, he gets frustrated. When his officers are away, he finds things are wrong, and then justifies his intervention. He undercuts his officers' authorities, therefore, and puts them in a bad light with their subordinates. The top management group is seen as performing on demand and loyal to him, but some think that they have no experience running anything. Despite working 50 to 60 hours a week, the responsibilities of managers are not dear and that contributes to the high turnover.

The climate is abrasive and the casualties are high. Said one, "When he gets upset, he takes no prisoners." At a meeting, he can go from being the kindest person to being the cruelest. He can call people names and fire them on the spot. One former employee said, "Mr. G was nice to me when I was ill, then later he fired me without an explanation." The informant added, "He is preoccupied with keeping the place clean and insistent that it be kept so. He told employees when he grew up, his home was a mess and he was not going to have his plant be a mess. An officer would not go by without picking up a piece of paper on the ground. He has his 'pig of the week' to designate those whose offices or work areas are not clean. He has a shit list; he chews people out in front of others. He makes you feel guilty if you take a vacation. He will call you at any hour of the night and has nighttime and early morning meetings. It is better to admit a mistake. He thinks people are stupid and says so. If you walk slowly, it indicates to him that you think slowly. Everything is blame; no one wants to be held responsible for not achieving, not pleasing Mr. G. You never know when you are doing good, only when you're not doing good. Even when you are told you are doing well, you get only a token raise."

Few people can go toe to toe with him. For many it is not worth the fight, so issues are not dealt with. He categorizes people into tigers and turkeys. His attitude is, "What did you do for me this week?" Alternatively, "If you don't like it here, leave. You're lucky to have a job."

Other informants complain: when they talk with him, they will always come away feeling they are wrong. He decides without facts that the other person is wrong. He publicly excoriated a consultant who had been called in to speak to the group on better communications. He looks for signs of weakness in people, signs of uncertainty and fear. He believes black and white about people: they are good or no good. People are accused of "masturbating in the corner" or "playing with themselves". He is demoralizing and degrading. If you make the least mistake, he shakes you like a tiger -- turns you into a wet rag. Once a person's name is paged over the intercom, there is a fear of what he is going to be subjected to. Some people see his car in the lot and feel intimidated.

Some believe he wants to be Number One because it is good for him, not for the company. They report he buys out competitors, trying to secure 100% of market share, even though after having 80%, it is too expensive to try to get more. They say, he has a need for something successful. The company is his own baby. He wants to do so much, so it will allow him time to do things for society. It is something he does not share.

They see him as fierce and fearless in turning on the opposition and getting to the heart of a matter. Regardless of how painful it is, he exposes people. They say he will relentlessly track you down if you are disloyal. He spent hundreds of thousands of dollars trying to sue someone who left the company for another similar type of organization. In his fights with other people and customers, he goes through things from the sewer to the heavens. He is concerned about failure. He wants odds less than zero. For him, failure is not an option.

They admire his brilliant, tremendous intuition. They say he would make a good consultant. He is a superior salesman, a closer on deals. But, they note, if anyone wants a discount or a rebate, he yells, screams, and alienates some customers. His selling winds up in arguments with the customers.

They gave him credit for his persuasive presentation of the opportunities that his company offers. He took over from an advertising group, wrote the ad himself, saying that sales and profits would double in a few years.

But, they add, he has no tolerance for training people, for building from within, or developing a management organization. Women are viewed as dumb broads who have no place in management.

They complain that he does not keep written promises and salary agreements. Austerity measures affect the employees rather than the officers. Everything seems to be geared for management stock options, yet there is a good deal of loyalty on the part of lower level people and on the part of many of the technical people. The latter feel that technically it is a good environment because Mr. G does not hesitate to invest in new equipment. They feel that the corporate officers do not understand technical production and, therefore, that they have greater freedom to do their own thing. Lower level employees feel that there are too many chiefs, but that the company hires good people, provides good food, in a good building, and most of them stay, even though they feel that their friends and neighbors laugh at the style of management that they report to those people. This is an organization where one does not need much polish, nor is there a need to control one's feelings. They describe themselves as an outspoken group of individuals who have high regard for each other. The technical people see this as an exciting place to be, hectic, demanding, stressful, challenging, creative. Said one, "It's an opportunity of a lifetime to make a fortune." Some think their good performance is quickly rewarded. Mr. G has even named buildings for a couple of people and those he likes get cars, large advances, loans.

What are the consequences? Costs are out of control. There is no organized market research, for Mr. G has no tolerance for numbers and details. It is a good place for confident, competent, iconoclastic people. "You do things here to please. You modify a forecast or try to read through Mr. G's bluster. You talk about things here that are safe: topics like baseball. In order to stay, you become invaluable or adoring. Everyone is busy covering himself or herself instead of using energy to brainstorm for the common good. Headhunters refuse to send people here anymore. You need a thick skin to survive. We do a lot of things three or four times over."

The interviewees use these words to describe Mr. G: "He's wacko." "He's like a time bomb." "Certifiably crazy." "This place is run by a wild man." "He is a wild-assed entrepreneur." "He lacks control." "He's sensitive to any allusions to his integrity because of his background."

Confirmation

These responses seem to confirm our original diagnostic hypothesis, or at least to come as close to it as diagnostic formulations can. Certainly we see the self-centeredness, the grandiosity, and over-evaluation of self, together with feelings of inadequacy and both depreciation and exploitation of others. Mr. G is unable to evaluate himself and others in depth. He is not often able to empathize with, let alone sympathize with, those who seem unable to meet his demands. Paranoid trends then arise with the severe frustration or failure. Like so many who rise to leadership roles, he is highly intelligent, hardworking, and obviously capable enough to build this organization. But, certainly, he is also capable of destroying it.

However, it is striking that in the early days of his organization he was able to work cooperatively and as a team member with his colleagues. Apparently his behavior changed radically when he had to sell off what had promised to become a prized jewel and his instrument for becoming a $100 million company. The loss of support of his primary colleagues left him with few people he could trust and inadequate external controls. He had been fired earlier because apparently he could not work in a structured situation. However, with the support of that early peer group in his own organization, given common purpose and their joint effort to build an organization, he was able to accept that controlling interaction. His work efforts intensified during the period of separation from his wife, and when the loss of significant colleagues and his crown jewel occurred.

Now he is trying to beat his managers and subordinates into achieving his goals for him. He is irately frustrated because they cannot seem to rise to his level of competence or aspiration. He is unable both to lead them and to manage them. He cannot tolerate the normal frustration or the individual achievement of people if they differ with him. When they cannot tolerate his over control, he fires them impulsively or they leave abruptly. He has an easy propensity for splitting. In object relations terms, he is able only to achieve a part object rather than total object relations. Although he has the propensity for being charismatic, and is viewed by many of his subordinates as indeed giving that kind of leadership, ultimately his narcissism results in undermining the organization. He loses enthusiasm for what is no longer new and exciting, and flees into opportunistic involvements with short-term returns. He cannot meet the realistic dependency needs of his employees, nor fulfill other basic emotional needs that employees have a right to expect from their leaders (Levinson, 1981). There is, as a result, a submissive, dependent "in group" and a depressed and angry "out group."

According to Kohut (1972), narcissistic rage arises when the self or object fails to live up to the absolutarian expectations by the narcissistically fixated adult whose archaic narcissistic structures have remained unmodified. Although everybody tends to react to narcissistic injuries with embarrassment and anger, the most intense experiences of shame and the most violent forms of narcissistic rage arise in those individuals for whom a sense of absolute control over an archaic internal environment is indispensable to maintaining self esteem. The desire to turn a passive experience into an active one, the mechanism of identification with the aggressor, the sadistic tensions retained in individuals who, as children, have been treated sadistically by their parents ---all these factors help explain the readiness of the shame-prone individual to respond to a potentially shame-provoking situation by the employment of a simple remedy -- the active, often anticipatory inflicting on others of those narcissistic injuries which he is most afraid of suffering himself. In the narcissist's primitive either/or logic, one is a helpless victim or a sadistic tyrant. The first is avoided only if one plays out the second (Avery, 1977).

Action

Having reaffirmed the diagnosis and understanding both the behavior and its effects more clearly, the task was now to provide feedback to him that ideally would enable him to take positive actions. These would necessarily be of two kinds. The first would have to do with evolving accountability, task definition, criteria for performance, boundary controls, and an administrative structure. The second must facilitate separating himself from the organization to avoid his continuing intrusion that seems to be beyond his control. That second task could indeed be helpful in another sense if the consultants could help him restore the environment in which he was previously successful. In the context of a team of colleagues that could be supportive and controlling, he might be able to capitalize on his imaginative drive, while simultaneously basking in their adulation. He could also enjoy the applause that might come from others outside his organization for who he is and what he has achieved. In essence, the recommendations would need to provide for an increase in the gratification of his narcissistic needs and simultaneously enable him to step away from his organization. All this must be done by honoring his charge to present him with the truth.

The report of the consultation comprised eight single-spaced pages that represented the findings without pulling punches. The summary was as follows:

Throughout the course of the interviews, there was a spirit of interest in and concern for the company, a willingness on the part of the entire staff to do what they could to make your company succeed. They felt it was significant that you would ask outside consultants for their views and opinions. That you did so increased their hope and faith in the company.

The growth of your company from a $3 million to a $25 million company reflects your obvious talents and skills in finding a relatively unrecognized and unique product that has captured the major share of the market. You were described as a hard-driving chief executive officer who is continuing to attempt to bring the company into another period of growth and expansion. Your wish to move the organization ahead with all possible speed creates impatience and frustration not only for you, but also for those you attempt to inspire and direct. Your high-level capacity to abstract and conceptualize, the speed with which you assess and act on issues, and your ability to get quickly to the core of problems outdistances most of those with whom you come into contact. As a result, you are seen at times as intolerant, overly judgmental and critical, arbitrary, and going in several directions at once. Your standards appear impossibly high to many. This creates a conflict in the minds of staff and employees about whether you are aggrandizing yourself and satisfying your own ego, or whether you behave as you do only for the good of the company.

You are so far ahead of them that your people cannot keep up with you. They try to race to do what you want, but they can only inevitably feel disappointed, and you, in turn, can only become angrier, flail at them, and put them down. Your unrealistic expectations, therefore, are destructive to the company. Your multi varied and changing demands and hypercritical attitudes demoralize your people. They lead to an uptight organization that is losing momentum. Furthermore, by your angrily impulsive and intrusive manner, you present an image of a shop foreman and a street fighter rather than that of a corporate chief executive officer. You are not behaving in ways consistent with who you are and what your role is.

It is within this atmosphere that the high turnover rate, three times the usual level, may be understood. People feel intimidated by your attitude, afraid to communicate freely and to speak directly. There is a feeling that you do not want to listen carefully to your people, and, therefore, they feel they have no input into decisions and policies of the company. As a result, there is a conflict between what you say you want the atmosphere to be in the company and the climate that results from what you do.

They are not clear about what is expected of them. Their vague job descriptions preclude that. Further, they are not sure who reports to whom. Intrusion from higher levels undermines legitimate authority.

Rapid changes in priorities and directions further confuse them. Many, especially women, do not believe they have the opportunity for advancement, and some feel they were not given the positions or compensation they were promised. There have been layoffs without adequate explanation. Many of these conditions are known to people outside of your organization; they contaminate its primary reputation for excellence products and service.

Personal Recommendations

Having grown up with the business, you fail to recognize what you really bring to it, what business you are in, and what kinds of behavior are required of you. You must capitalize on your talents; concentrate on your bold, imaginative, and forward-looking focus; and leave the day-to-day running of the company to your officers. You need to husband your time and energy to devote yourself to product innovation and development, and to acquiring companies with complementary lines. You cannot afford to waste time and energy in being a fighting shop foreman. To carry out your role, you should move your headquarters to [the downtown area of Chicago] where you would be in continuous contact with the finance and business world.

You should select a small group of people who understand your aspirations and who can think strategically to be your headquarters staff. In this way, you could give your company the kind of corporate leadership the organization and your stature demand. By making such a move, you can better show how much you care for the company and the people in it. People will recognize the active leadership devoted to building a bigger and better organization, in contrast to their current pessimism and anger over having a harsh taskmaster with impossible standards who is too often disappointed in them. The offices in the several buildings, other than those you move to, could be brought under one roof that would help to facilitate interdepartmental communication and a greater feeling of family. The rest of the buildings could be leased, and the income could support the new headquarters.

Managerial Recommendations

1. Greater support for professional management, especially at the middle levels and among women.

2. A clear statement of organizational purpose, goals, and objectives, and preparation of better job descriptions to fit with the corporate charter.

3. An employee handbook with policies and procedures that would include hiring and firing guidelines, and a grievance and appeals process

4. Employee meetings with greater encouragement and freedom to discuss matters of importance without fear of reprisal.

5. Supervisory and managerial training and a broader range of in-house seminars. Some of these recommendations are in the process of being accomplished. We feel, however, that they should be moved forward with greater urgency.

In presenting the report to Mr. G, it was necessary to keep in mind Kemberg's (1982) observation that "patients with intense rage reactions linked to frustration of narcissistic needs, particularly if these rage reactions evolve into paranoid micropsychotic episodes, require avoiding the patient's tendency to experience any effort to clarify the immediate realities judgmental or sadistically accusatory.... It is essential for the therapist to clarify again and again that he is not blaming the patient, that, to the contrary, he is trying to help the patient understand the relation between his perception and his emotional reaction, regardless of whether these perceptions were realistic."

The three consultants met with him in his office. I read the report aloud as Mr. G followed along from his copy. When the reading was over, he said, "That's a good statement of the problem. How many people feel that way?"

I said, "The entire group."

He then said, "You're telling me that by my moving that you are going to isolate the pathogenicity, is that it?"

I said that that was not the issue, that the report was not talking about pathology; rather, the report was stressing the difference between his level of intelligence and the people he interacted with. Using gestures, I said, "You are way up there, and they are way down there. They can't keep up with you."

Again, I stressed that he should be with financial and business people in the downtown area whose respect and regard he wanted and was entitled to as a result of his own achievement. Mr. G asked how he would be able to talk with those people. I replied that he would listen. He would get their input and be aware of all the things that were going on in the financial community, as well as those that related to his business. Mr. G wanted to know if there would be enough to keep him busy. I reassured him that he would be involved with innovation, new products, new markets, key sales, and new customers. I added that this was not the only instance of a CEO moving himself and corporate headquarters some distance from operations, and offered examples from major corporations. Mr. G then wanted to know who he would take with him. I said he could take whomever he wanted to work with.

Finally Mr. G said. "I guess it's astounding what you said. It would never have occurred to me about my level of thinking. I responded once again that he wasted his time getting stuck in the mire; that, being tied down by many interfering details. he was like Gulliver. It was also as if he were trying to drive a car with the windshield covered with mud; he did not see where he was going. I reiterated that he should leave the everyday details of running the business to his officers. They could handle the details and the concrete, everyday activities. He had other things to do: to lead and to innovate. He could return to the manufacturing operation from time to time, show interest in and acknowledge the people there. That would be better than behaving in a harsh manner after being disappointed in their day-to-day inability to attain the impossible goals that he set for them.

Mr. G replied that he would try to get more people involved, but he would want ones who could stand up to him and not be afraid of him. I told him that that expectation was a two-edged sword. He wanted people with a tough skin, but not everyone who has a tough skin is competent. Tough skin usually is accompanied by insensitivity. The risk was that those people that he would like would not allow their subordinates to complain, let alone attend to the reasons from which the complaints arose. I told him that he had to let the chief operating officer be free to handle those details.

His response was. "But I felt I was a good delegator." I said that he could not be because his standards were so high that when anyone achieved anything less than perfection, he criticized him. Mr. G grudgingly acknowledged the accuracy of this statement. I then told him that the issue of leadership versus management is a continuous one for many managers; that was why so much is written about it (Zaleznik, 1977). In his case, the additional factor was his level of abstraction and the speed of his thinking, but he could work out that problem once he recognized it and made an effort to deal with it. I then said that he had to admit that he was hurting. When asked what he meant Mr. G said, "I've been an ogre, I've brought discomfort to those I wanted to help. I'm astounded by what you said about my thinking though."

Following the initial report and subsequent discussion with Mr.

G, he called me and asked that the consultants meet with members of the board. The consultants met in the corporate boardroom with three of the corporate officers, two members of the board, and a friend of Mr. G, who was also a significant investor. Mr. G was not present. The board members challenged the report and asked if any options or modifications were possible. I insisted that all options and modifications had been considered and that this report was the final result. It required no modification, and it would not be changed. A board member argued that to separate Mr. G from the rest of the organization would result in the demise of the organization. I pointed out that if that were the case, if Mr. G were to have a coronary or to become severely ill or to be hit by a bus, the company would indeed be on terribly shaky ground. I reiterated the point that Mr. G needed to be free to be his creative self and the organization needed to be free from his inappropriate intrusion. The meeting grew quite tense as the board member and I sparred. When it became unequivocally clear that the report was not going to be changed, the adamant board member capitulated and apologized for his intransigence. I had insisted on this rigidity because once the boundaries were breached, the holding pattern would be lost along with the mirroring that the recognition of his intelligence, ability, and creativity had produced. There then followed both delays and subsequent action on Mr. G's part.

Several months later, Mr. G called me and asked him to meet with him so that he could report what had happened since the consultation. When the consultants arrived, his first words were, "Well, I didn't do what you told me. It was like putting a condom on a stud bull. While your interviews were going on, the president and I did some interviewing, too. The results were absolutely the same. I decided to call everyone together, except the daily employees, because after an hour, they'd probably just be playing with themselves. I read the report to the staff, asked them for their input, and their stories of what they heard about me. I then asked if they ever tried to use intimidation to get a point across. They said they had, and I then said I used it as a bargaining chip, but never willfully with the intent to hurt. I make that distinction. I discussed the two cultures: the one that I grew up in with the people that understood and knew me and those who didn't, who didn't know the views where I was coming from. I began to realize that there was this difference."

"...People that I fired on the spot, like the quality control team, I realized that was impulsive. If they messed on the floor, I realized I should not have fired them, but should have fired their boss. Recently I restrained myself when someone came in unprepared. 1 would formerly have called him a mumbling mother fucker; instead, I told him what he had to do. If Picasso would have criticized me, I wouldn't be upset; I know I'm not a Picasso. I got upset with these people because they couldn't conform to my standards, yet, I understand. I'm now able to pass on work to the president. He's changed; he's doing wonderfully. I am now getting a top official from another company to head the research and development. We're looking ahead. I had another seminar lasting five hours to get everything out that they'd ever heard about me, every gripe, what they'd heard I've done, past misinformation, everything. Then there was a third session to make sure that there was nothing left."

"I then called the headhunters. I showed them the report and asked them what else I could do. Since that time, they have already been referring people to us."

I told Mr. G that it seemed as though now he was letting other people handle the daily details, letting others put their fingers in the dike. I said that he showed a lot of courage, a lot of guts. He expressed his thanks. When Dr. Sabbath told him that the metaphor of putting a condom on a stud bull represented some sort of a threat to him, he said, "Yeah, it was like putting a sack over my head."

Dr. Sabbath said, "Yes, a displacement from below to above."

I then suggested that Mr. G now had to continue to find stimulation in those things that he started in motion that are apart from the day-to-day management of people, that he should continue with research and new products.

He said, "Yeah, now things are going better. I confront them with the facts instead of knocking their heads off."

I suggested further that he should keep a record of what he had done, and then write it up in the form of a paper or a book because there are many entrepreneurs who find themselves in a similar situation. He again expressed his thanks to us and asked the consultants to see the director of human resources and the president.

Dr. Sabbath and Dr. Connor met with them. They reported that right after the report was presented to Mr. G, people began leaving because the report was not read to them. Five or six people a week were leaving, up to thirty in six weeks. The president went through a three-week process of trying to reason why Mr. G did not publish the report to the employees, then left for a two-week vacation. (The original contract did not call for feedback to the employees, although usually that is the arrangement.) At that point, the director of research left because he could not stand the atmosphere. Tensions seemed to have built up to an explosive level; the pain was acute.

At that point, Mr. G assumed responsibility in more than a verbal way. He asked the director of human resources to draw up a list of short and long term needs in accordance with the consultation report. He called three employee meetings. He stood up before everyone and said, "Here I am." He said he was there to talk the whole thing out with them. He read almost the whole report, except the recommendations.

Apparently, the credibility of the report was enhanced by the interviews that Mr. G and the president had conducted. As the crises and confrontations increased, he could not ignore them and the credibility of the report. He realized that he had to confront the problems and change. It was either do that or leave, which to him would have been symbolic castration. There was role reversal – he put himself at the mercy of the big collective. In going to his people and then letting them speak up, Mr. G utilized his street-smart survival instincts, much like a dog that puts himself in a submissive position, exposing his jugular, as a result of which another attacking dog would only bark but not bite. He defused the atmosphere. There was a catharsis. He then put the rest of the report suggestions into action.

Several months after the last meetings with Mr. G and with the director of human resources and the president, the director of human resources reported these changes:

1) A salary review for direct labor was made two months ahead of schedule.

2) A job posting system was formalized. Twenty employees were promoted from within.

3) There was a commitment to firm salary review dates for exempt employees.

4) Rules and regulations and disciplinary action policies were formalized and posted.

5) Grievance procedures were formalized and posted.

6) The personnel handbook was completed.

7) The human resources department now reports to the president.

8) The organizational chart was posted.

9) The employees now find G more approachable.

10) Mr. G met with recruiters and was helped to get better candidates.

11) A supervisory training program was initiated.

12) Postings of new hires and employee transfers and promotions were now a practice.

13) Three employee meetings (as reported above) were held to discuss the results of the consultation report, and employees were able to air feelings and give feedback.

14) Review committee meetings were better structured with more encouragement of the people present.

Some six months after the last contact, Mr. G called me to his office again. He told me that he was going to treat me like an insider and then reported that he decided to sell the company. He repeated once again that the consultants' recommendations had missed the mark on many issues, but others were right on. After selling the company, he would start another company with a group of people who were closest to him. He expected to be able to net $4 million to $5 million out of the sale, and perhaps to buy back one of the smaller parts of the company. He could then be both a gentleman farmer and develop his new company into a successful business. He said if he started with $5 million, the chances were that he could turn it into a $50 million business in ten years.

I pointed out that he was planning to do exactly what had been recommended, namely to get out of the annoying problems of manufacturing and to limit himself to a small group of colleagues who could be mutually stimulating and creative.

Mr. G reported that he had seen his father for the first time in 25 years. He discovered that, although he thought his father was warm, his father was more exhibitionistic and could be a buddy in a bar. He was not necessarily a warm person, according to his wife's observation. He was sorry to discover that about his father. He did not say why he had gone to see his father in a distant state. He also said that his mother was much more warm and sensitive, and that the brains of the family came from his mother. He described others in his family who were brilliant and said that his mother encouraged them. He described his present wife as warm and affectionate and said that she was able to relax in a hammock while he worked in his garden. He described how he enjoyed the opportunity to touch her and be with her. Obviously, he felt that kind of warmth to be important. We then talked about his need for stimulation. At first he thought this was a matter of his own pressure to achieve, but I pointed out that his capacity for abstraction was at a high level and that demanded continuing stimulation. This seemed to relieve some of the self-critical pressure. I pointed to the need to have continuing stimulation into late life and approved of his action because it seemed to fit with what he needed and avoided what he did not need. He seemed to be quite pleased with this and said he appreciated what the consultation had done for him. He expressed his need for continuing contact. He said he would stay in touch and would let me know how things came out. He was hoping that whoever would buy the company would carry on what had already been done and would be able to manage it more effectively. He seemed to be quite pleased with our meeting and with the conversation, and to genuinely reach out for help and support.

About four months afterward, a public announcement reported the sale of the company from which he achieved the sum he had expected. Some six months after that meeting, two years after the first contact, Mr. G. sent me a videotape of the ceremonies that marked his departure and the firm's final day as an independent company. In his letter of transmittal, he said, "If you can conceive in your wildest imagination how I may have felt and then multiply that feeling tenfold, you will then begin to realize how grateful I am for the acknowledgement given me on (the final day). If I were to be elected president of the United States, I could feel no greater joy. In the future, whenever I get a little depressed about something, I will break out this tape and remember these happy moments. To me it clearly illustrates a vital aspect of the company's culture, and because of your special relationship, I thought you would like to view it." In a handwritten postscript, he said, "You deserve to see how it all worked out! Incidentally, I am planning to start another company. G."

In the videotape of his farewell remarks, Mr. G projects his conscious good image of omnipotence, perfection, and honesty onto his followers. Those who are loyal reflect this back in superlatives. He uses human metaphors along with analogies likening business to war. The contrast between his metaphors and his wish that business should be run like a family reflects his ambivalence toward his company. He holds forth the promise, projects the image of a mentor, a generous charismatic father figure who wants to help people fulfill their dreams. But he also frustrates them, exterminates them by demeaning, cutting criticisms. He extols honesty and directness -- virtues to be sure -- but he exploits these qualities to rationalize his destructive remarks. His humor is biting. While seemingly complimenting people, his underlying sarcasm comes through. He is still fighting the unresolved issues of his own family, struggling for recognition but devastating those family people, i.e., his colleagues who he sees getting in his way or challenging him. He quotes from classical literature and simultaneously uses street language. The eulogies and his response continue to reflect his low self-image and the striving for recognition and omnipotence. He speaks of the business as being a machine that will not produce any more babies if it stops, which it may if the new owners interfere. If business is like a war and there are machines that can stop producing "babies" and business should be run like a family, then his ambivalence toward his company becomes more understandable.

Discussion

There are no details in this discussion of Mr. G's early family life, only those fragments of it that he reported in passing and communicated to the world at large. The focus of the consultation, namely enhancing the effectiveness of the organization, precluded careful investigation of his own early personal history. However, one can infer from the little biographical information he gave and the nature of his behavior that he had had a chaotic home life with inconsistent mothering and identification with part-objects. He must have been a very bright child to have achieved what he did, but he could hardly have had that kind of mirroring that would contribute to a sense of wholeness and worthiness.

One can infer from his history that he was determined to escape the poverty and chaos of his past home life. He had come to appreciate, through his subsequent identifications with the respected professor and the interaction with people at higher socioeconomic levels, that, to be like them, he had both to get money and achieve social status.

One could speculate that his preoccupation with the business as a "family" recapitulated unresolved issues from his own past life. His ambivalence was shown in his destructive acts of demeaning behavior and poor leadership, in contrast to periods of warm considerateness and discussion of his own family. There seemed to be an unconscious compulsion to repeat the parent/child relationships of his own family in his attitudes toward his subordinates. One could also speculate that in an effort to overcome a repressed bad internal object, the domineering father of whom he consciously disapproved, he was compelled to behave toward others in ways that were like that hated father. This led to a repetition of rejected or fearful parental behavior, together with the interjection of learned behavior patterns and his consequent resistance to change. Speculatively, he wanted to beat down others in order to disown his own vulnerable self.

His petty criminal father was also a poor identification figure, but nevertheless an oedipal rival. We can infer from his entrepreneurial behavior (Levinson. 1973) that that rivalry was never resolved making it impossible for him to operate in any organizational structure except at the top.   As indicated earlier. Kohut (1972) says that the narcissistically vulnerable individual responds to narcissistic injuries with shame and then fight or flight. In the logic of narcissism., a person must be either a tyrant or a victim. In manifest behavior, he was the former, in his unconscious, the latter.

That he was fortunately able to identify with his professor-friend and apparently several significant others who befriended him,. indicates a capacity for identification and attachment. That he profited from that attachment and was able to mobilize himself toward academic achievement and business success is no mean feat, a reflection of powerful ego strength.

That he recapitulated in his business the nature of his own family is no surprise. His need for absolute control of the "wimp" inside him and his intense pursuit of an impossible ego ideal led him to depreciate others, envy them, and be intolerant of their rivalry. That same narcissism made it impossible for him to evaluate himself and others accurately, and required that he surround himself with people who applauded him.

He easily split people into the black hats and white hats and let the applauders exploit his narcissism – the exploiter being exploited. His rapid shift from one thing to another in the context of his omnipotent fantasy provided him with the excitement of something new to get "on top of." His fantasy stimulated others, but its deflation, together with his underlying contempt of others, led to low morale.

Despite the diffusion of identification figures, the fact that he was able to identify with positive others who strengthened him, suggested that he might profit from the consultation, and, therefore, that the consultative effort was worth the risk. Kernberg (1977) notes that, "To the extent that chronically traumatizing or frustrating circumstances of early development, and therefore the patient's former relations with the real parents, are an important aspect of the genetic and historical background of borderline patients, the real relation with the therapist may perform parental functions the patient has never experienced before." In Kernberg's terms, the therapist is "an absorber, organizer, and transformer of the patient's chaotic intra-psychi experience... The therapist does provide auxiliary cognitive ego functions...in addition to the implicit reassurance given by his ability to withstand and not to be destroyed by the patient's aggression, by his not retaliating, by his maintaining a general attitude of concern for and emotional availability to the patient."

In this consultation, the turning point of Dr. Sabbath's refusal to be intimidated by Mr. G and the clincher was the report that helped him recognize the manifest reasons why he was having such deflating problems and how he could make use of his self-evident capacities while recreating a supportive structure for himself. His capacity to respond to the consultants and their recommendations, together with his ability to reconstruct his own life based on those relationships and that information, speaks powerfully to his adaptive strength and the usefulness of psychoanalytic thinking in management consultation.

Conclusion

The chief executive of a high-tech company sought consultation because of high turnover in managerial ranks and low morale. Interviews with a sample of employees and managers disclosed that his imaginative technical innovations were coupled with an intrusive, impulsive, demeaning, and chaotic leadership style. An important differential diagnostic problem was to determine whether he was truly in the manic phase of a manic-depressive cycle, or a narcissistic personality with borderline features. Determining the latter to be the case, the consultants took a firm stand, refusing to be intimidated by him, and recommended a course of action that supported his cognitive recognition of the rational reasons for his behavior and an alternative that would sustain his innovative capacity and his narcissistic gratification.

CHAPTER 2

SECTION ONE

IMMERSION AND DIAGNOSIS

IMMERSION 2

The Practitioner as Diagnostic Instrument

In: A. Howard (ed.), *Diagnosis for Organizational Change.* New York: Guilford Publications, 2, 27-52, 1994

Organizational diagnosis is a systematic method for gathering, organizing, and interpreting information about organizations for the purpose of helping them anticipate or ameliorate their adaptive problems. It is carried out by individuals, whether as single practitioners or in a team. The individual practitioner is his or her most important instrument or device for gathering data, making inferences, interpreting those data and inferences, and evolving modes of acting on his or her conclusions.

The independent practitioner or human resources specialist within an organization who is undertaking diagnosis may use a wide variety of methods to gather information. Inasmuch as many of the data are subjective (feelings, opinions, perceptions), the diagnostician must require confirming sources of information to accept data as valid. When there is agreement about the data from various perspectives and different sources, the practitioner is likely to have greater confidence in them. Once sufficient data are gathered, the next task is to give them meaning.

The Use of Theory

Giving meaning to diagnostic data involves two steps that must be clearly differentiated. The first is making inferences from the data. The second is interpreting the data and the inferences. The latter task requires that the practitioner have a guiding theory because of the necessarily subjective nature of interpretation and the fact that the same data may have different meaning according to the scientific or professional discipline within which the practitioner operates.

For example, assume that you, an organization consultant, are passing an automobile assembly line with the plant manager. While he is explaining aspects of the work to you, a blob of grease suddenly comes flying through the air toward you. You manage to step out of the way and avoid being smeared by it. You don't understand why this has happened, but the fact that it has makes you uneasy. Your host is embarrassed. He may offer an excuse, such as a sudden increase in pressure in the compressed air gun held by the operator, an increase that forced out a blob of grease. Without checking, he is making an inference about the cause of the event. One could make other inferences. Perhaps the gun is heavy and therefore difficult for an operator to handle. Or its mechanism may be worn and thus difficult to control. Perhaps the operator ejected the grease deliberately out of anger with the management. Conceivably, he wanted to symbolize tension and disagreement in the plant. Any of these inferences could be valid.

When the plant manager checks these varied inferences, he discovers that the gun is not too heavy. It is not unduly worn, and there was no sudden surge of air pressure. You, the observer, then develop the hypothesis that there is hostility toward the manager, if not management in general. Assuming that the blob of grease did in fact turn out to be an act of hostility toward the management, you will pursue that issue further before you can answer the question of why the hostility exists.

If you are a Marxist economist, you will likely assert that the hostile act is a product of the class struggle between the owners and the workers. If you are a sociologist, your discipline might lead you to the conclusion that social class differences are endemic in such large plants and that management and employees are treated differently by the corporation, to the envious anger of the latter. If you are a social psychologist, you might attribute the act to tensions that arise between groups, particularly when one group is given a disproportionate share of scarce resources. If you are an industrial/organizational psychologist, you might conclude that the employee is bored and angry because higher management denigrates his competence and keeps him in a passive, over controlled role. If you are a clinical psychologist, you might theorize about the worker's attitude toward those in power because of his chronic hostility to his father. In short, the meaning you attribute to the act, and the interventions you might make to cope with the problem that you think lies behind the act, would be determined by your theoretical frame of reference.

It is imperative, therefore, that practitioners be aware of the theory that guides them and that they differentiate fact from inference from interpretation. They must recognize that others might understand an incident -- or a whole set of data -- differently. Such recognition might enable practitioners to maintain a certain humility about what they believe to be the focal problem and what they propose to do about it.

In trying to understand matters psychological the practitioner will proceed backward from behavior to thoughts to feelings. In the preceding example, the worker shot the grease in your direction. That was the behavior. We don't know why it occurred. To approach an answer to that question, we must ask, "What was he thinking?" Had we asked him that question, he might have replied, "I think the manager of this plant is an SOB." However, if we are to understand why he thinks that, we must know what his feelings are and what gave rise to them. In some cases, individuals can explain the sources of their feelings. In other cases, the explanations offered mask some other motivation of which the individuals themselves are unaware, like unconscious rivalry with the person to whom they report. Ideally, our theory helps us understand the feelings and thoughts that lead to behaviors whose rationale at first appears obscure.

An important implication of the subjective nature of consultation is that all diagnosis is hypothesis. Like any scientific finding, an organizational diagnosis is a best guess. That's why the practitioner's conclusions must be refined and tested continuously and are subject to change on the basis of additional information.

A View of Organizations

Organizational diagnosis assumes that an organization is a

living organism because it comprises people. If it has a long history, that history is a product of successive cadres of people. One may therefore think of an organization in terms of biological analogies: an organization necessarily has energy, a structure, a history, and a developmental or evolutionary pattern (Greiner, 1972). Embedded in a society and composed of a collective of people, an organization also has a character, or consistent modes of acting on the basis of a set of values, and its own culture (Schein,1985; Trice & Beyer, 1984), which includes a unique language, symbols, practices, rites, and myths.

The feelings, thoughts, and behavior in an organization give it its life and are the bases of the human interactions within it. Despite efforts to make organizational decisions rational and to attenuate individual differences by structure, policies, procedures, and technical proficiency, in the last analysis organization direction, function, and activity are based on human judgment. Feelings, therefore, are its fundamental currency.

An organization, like any biological organism, is an open system. That means, among other things, that it receives information from outside itself, as well as from within itself, and processes and acts on that information. It is composed of interrelated components that affect each other and, in turn, affect the whole. It will respond to its external world on the basis of its internal processes, abilities, and capacities and those same internal processes lead it to act on the world outside itself in certain ways. It is therefore continuously engaged in maintaining an internal equilibrium among its components and an equilibrium in relationship to its external environment.

An organization necessarily requires the integrated effort of people. The devotion of people to a common effort fosters their attachment to the organization and vice versa. Cohesion is the psychological glue of integration. That sense, however, fosters organizational narcissism (Schwartz, 1991). It also leads to regression into narrower functions (Miller, 1991) and to decline of the adaptive capacity that is a product of diversity. Such major American corporations as IBM, AT&T, and General Motors, that is, corporations that narcissistically continued to do what they had always done while the world changed around them, are cases in point.

Yet an organization and the people in it are constantly undergoing change. Change inevitably occurs partly as a product of evolution and growth, partly because of technical or cultural change, and partly as a result of the vicissitudes of the marketplace.

People become attached to the organizations in which they work, to their roles, to their technical proficiency, to the people they work with, and to the symbols that represent all of these. They derive affectional input or support for their self-images from these attachments, which become a significant part of the meaning of their lives. When the attachments are disrupted, people experience psychological loss. Almost all change is loss, and, as reflected in the many social devices we have for dealing with it, all loss must be mourned or the ensuing depression is unrelieved. The emotional burden of unrelieved depression inhibits the successful adaptation of individuals and organizations to their losses. All organizations, therefore, should incorporate methods for coping with the losses brought about by continuous change. Few, however, recognize this issue and do so.

All business organizations are, by definition, accountability hierarchies with levels of power, responsibility, and authority. The definition of these levels constitutes the organization's formal structure, as contrasted with its shape (by product line, by function, by geographical area, by customer, by tasks). Organizations recapitulate the family structure in the cultures in which they operate. Authority patterns and styles of managerial behavior in any organization must be consistent with those of the family structure in that culture or they will create difficulties.

An organization must have a purpose -- overarching aspiration that is never achieved -- and a view of the world framed for that purpose that constitutes its vision. It must evolve a focus within that vision that constitutes its mission. For example, a pharmaceutical corporation may well want to provide means for conquering illness. Obviously, its vision includes the recognition that it can't possibly deal with all of the many kinds of illnesses throughout the world. Therefore, it will concentrate its efforts on two or three, perhaps cancer, heart disease, and tuberculosis. Having limited its thrust or mission, it then establishes goals, long-term steps toward mission, vision, and purpose) and objectives (short-term steps toward those goals). These, taken together, constitute the integrated logic of its mission. Without such an integrated logic, such practices as management by objectives become limited exercises.

All organizations necessarily are attack mechanisms; they are created to attack some kind of problem. The vitality of an organization is reflected in the effective intensity with which it attacks the problems for which it was created. To sustain our biological metaphor, adaptation is aggressive attack on the environment for survival. Fundamentally, all organizations unless deliberately created for short-term goals, must be engaged in perpetuating themselves.

If the practitioner comes from outside the organization as a consultant, the first step is to negotiate the contract. This usually involves defining what one proposes to do, the amount of time one proposes to spend doing it, how one proposes to go about doing it, what other people will be involved in the consultation, how confidentiality is to be assured, how one is to be introduced into the organization, how and to whom the subsequent report is to be fed back, and the projected end point of the consultation. Of course, a critical element is the statement of costs, which should include the cost of questionnaires and other instruments that one might use, if any, and the time necessary for report preparation.

In many cases it is wise to undertake a brief preliminary study by reviewing with the person who is the contracting agent the definition of the problem that precipitates the consultation. This should be followed by interviews with senior executives or administrators, a review of several of the organization's recent annual reports, and a description of the organizational symptoms that reflect its pain. The practitioner might make a proposal for the initial exploratory effort, to be followed then by a more comprehensive proposal for the diagnostic study per se.

In the course of reviewing the statement of the initial problem, the practitioner may well discover that the presenting complaint is not necessarily the basic cause of the organization's pain. Conflict between components of an organization, for example, may reflect conflict between two of its senior officials. A strike may be the product of poor management of change rather than the result of differences about wages, hours, and working conditions. The practitioner will develop initial hypotheses to guide the selection of consultation methods and the formulation of the consultation design.

If the practitioner is a human resources specialist within the organization or has a similar role, probably it will be important to clear what he or she is doing with higher management and to clarify with others in the organization why such a consultation is being undertaken and with what intent, what method, and what feedback. Otherwise, there will be great suspicion when one delves into data that ordinarily are not part of one's professional role. Furthermore, one is likely to be conducting a diagnosis to bring about organizational change, which will require, in turn, the assent and participation of key figures in the organization. In fact, the practitioner may find it helpful to involve some of those key figures in the diagnostic effort as interviewers or compilers of data because they, by sharing in the diagnostic effort, will then have a more direct appreciation of the issues and give more active leadership to the change process.

If the practitioner is a consultant from outside the organization, it will be important to consider the question of why he or she was chosen for this particular consultation, rather than some other person or consulting group. Even if the question cannot be answered initially, the practitioner should develop an answer along the way. That question should give rise to others: Why does this consultation arise at this time rather than some other time? What makes it imperative now? What does the highest-ranking executive with whom one is dealing expect from this diagnostic effort?

Sometimes the expectation is not readily apparent and may become clear only after repeated contact with that person. There is always the risk that the expectations may exceed what is possible. Therefore, the practitioner will have to temper and focus the expectations in keeping with the realities of time, resources, costs, and organizational complexities.

At this time, too, it will be important to assess what boundaries, limitations, and prohibitions the client executive imposes so far as which areas and functions can be observed and which persons or groups can be interviewed, observed, questioned, or even contacted. For example, in one company the chief executive was reluctant to have the consultant contact the union business agent. He said that he had worked so hard to establish an effective relationship with that person that he didn't want to have it disrupted by the consultant. Later it turned out that he was uneasy about a member of the consulting staff whom he regarded as brash and immature and capable of upsetting the relationship. When he had greater confidence in the consultant, he posed no further resistance to that interview.

Internal consultants or external practitioners who undertake a diagnosis to precede addressing an organizational problem should have their own ideas of what questions the diagnosis is expected to answer. Practitioners should also assess whether they can undertake such a diagnosis objectively, whether they should do it alone or mobilize other resources in the organization or other consultants to help, and what the political ramifications might be of undertaking such an effort.

Scanning the Organizational Horizon

As their own most important diagnostic instrument, practitioners should begin the diagnostic process immediately by forming initial impressions of the organization that are tentative hypotheses.

What do you see? What do you sense? What are your feelings about your initial contact? The practitioner should have a notebook at all times and write such impressions down, however vague, illusory, or tentative they may seem. For example, a consultant's initial impression of a new major research laboratory was that it looked like a prison, leading to a preliminary hypothesis that it was autocratically managed; the hypothesis was further validated when the director said proudly that he had chosen every aspect of the design of the building, down to the color of the chair seats in the cafeteria. The practitioner should note what people's attitudes are toward him or her, ranging from the person who authorized the diagnosis to potential recipients of the results. What occurred in those contacts that made you feel good, bad, or indifferent?

Usually the practitioner is taken on an initial tour of the premises. In that tour, one gets a sense of the psychological and physical atmosphere of the organization. How does the tour guide address the employees that you meet? Does he or she introduce you to them? Are they sullen or smiling? Do they treat each other courteously, informally, with a sense of humor, or does the atmosphere seem to be cold, distant, and austere? Is the setting noisy, making communications difficult? Do people have to operate at an almost frenzied pace to keep up with the equipment? Is the lighting adequate and the temperature appropriately controlled? Are the safety practices honored, the food resources and eating facilities adequate and clean, the grounds neatly kept? The feelings you experience about these matters are likely to be experienced similarly by employees, even if they have become inured to the factors that generate those feelings.

During the tour, it is useful to examine bulletin boards not only for their content but also for the manner in which people are addressed. In one company such notices are posted in the ladies' and men's rooms, to be sure that everyone sees them. In another the language simulates military commands. The reception lobby of one company has several large display cases with trophies of the company's employee athletic teams, reflecting a paternalistic orientation. In another company there are no seating arrangements for visitors to await their appointments; people move back and forth through the reception room, both behind and in front of the receptionist's desk. Open doors on both sides of the desk and the easy movement of people indicate informality. That same informality reflects a lack of formal controls and suggests that the organization is operated in a sloppy manner.

In the course of the initial tour and in subsequent contacts, employees will react to the practitioner. Some will be guarded and hostile, others will be open and friendly; some will seek to become the practitioner's ally, others will avoid contact. Inasmuch as these reactions occur without prior contact with the practitioner, obviously they must arise out of people's feelings about themselves, the organization, and the present context. People will then attribute motives and attitudes to the practitioner that will represent their unconscious attitudes toward people in positions of power.

We speak of such attitudes as "transference." That is, there is a transfer of attitudes from earlier experiences to the present situation. People's reactions to the practitioner reflect their own personalities, conflicts, and crises that have occurred in the organization and perhaps an earlier history with consultants. Variations in these attitudes will occur throughout the diagnostic effort, and the practitioner must make note of them and try to understand their significance. In the process, people also will be testing the diagnostician's neutrality. Sometimes this will occur in the form of questions, for example, about whom the practitioner is going to interview, who will get the report and what the practitioner has learned from other interviewees.

The practitioner will bring to the diagnostic relationship attitudes resulting from his or her own personal experiences with authority and with people who are suspicious or hostile or rivalrous and competitive. The practitioner also will have feelings about the way the client organization does its business, manages its people and processes, and shares or disdains the practitioner's values.

Sometimes feelings aroused in the practitioner are subtle, and the practitioner will become aware of them only retrospectively or when he or she blunders. These attitudes we speak of as "countertransference." The practitioner should note them in as much detail as possible. The practitioner should be particularly alert to the degree to which the organization's conflicts and problems touch on his or her own history and feelings. Also, the practitioner should note the degree to which organization conflicts, problems, divisions, and resistances stimulate a sense of helplessness in him or her and should identify those responses that intrude into the diagnostic process.

The practitioner will begin to accumulate factual information. Most immediately available factual information can be found in annual reports and other formal publications of the organization. For a more comprehensive view of the financial condition of a publicly held corporation, one should review the company's IO K report, a public report that such a company submits to the Securities and Exchange Commission. From these reports the practitioner will be able to discern how the company manages its money, how much it depends on stocks, bonds, or loans for financing, and how those financial arrangements facilitate or inhibit its flexibility for cash management and investment.

For publicly held corporations, credit information is available in the directories of Dun & Bradstreet, Inc. Often there is detailed discussion of a company's performance in business publications like *Forbes, Business Week*, and *Fortune*. The IO K report also will list executives' salaries, outstanding obligations, litigation, government actions against the organization, and similar matters.

Whether from these reports or others, one will need to learn the numbers of employees in the various organizational locations, together with demographic information. In large companies, headquarters are often located in metropolitan areas distant from manufacturing plants and operations. These, together with the diversity of the work force, will point to questions about communication, cultural differences, and particular problems the organization may face in dealing with ethnic groups. For example, a corporate headquarters group in Philadelphia employing a largely Hispanic group in South Carolina would have to understand the complexities facing these employees in that particular rural environment, where Spanish is not the local language, where Hispanics are experienced as rivals by local African-Americans, and where the traditions of the community make them feel alien.

The practitioner will also want to get organizational charts early on. These will reflect not only who reports to whom but also the range of roles and functions that ultimately will have to be sampled. Interestingly, when one asks a given interviewee to draw an organization chart, that person's view of the organization may differ significantly from the formal chart. This will be especially true if one asks who the interviewee's boss is. The response will not necessarily be the person to whom the interviewee ostensibly reports but the person who is a conceptual level above the interviewee (Jaques, 1991).

The practitioner will then want to compose a description of the various work settings and tasks. This will provide a sense of who does what, what the nature of the work flow is, what kinds of differences exist in style of work, time frames, criteria for performance, and other dimensions of the work. For example, a research unit will likely have people of a higher conceptual level who operate without the same time demands and efficiency requirements as workers on an assembly line (Lawrence & Lorsch, 1967). Those who are developing products do not have the same time urgency as marketers whose task is to get the product to market as quickly as possible. These sub cultural differences may make for problems among different work groups. Much of the contemporary effort to involve manufacturing people in discussions with customers and to bring marketing staff into early consultation with those in product development are efforts to cope with such differences.

Exploring Organization Direction

All organizations necessarily anticipate the future and are directed toward coping with it. They invest in buildings and equipment, in marketing and advertising, in developing their employees. Many engage in long-term projects like building nuclear power plants or developing oil fields. Most acquire capital either by equity (selling stocks and bonds) or debt (borrowing). It is important, therefore, to understand how an organization perceives its future and focuses its anticipatory efforts. A significant component of that understanding is developing a sense of the organization's trajectory. What is its history? What is its evolutionary pattern? What have been the stages in its development, and how has it managed its transitions (Greiner, 1972)? How would you describe its trajectory, its momentum, its focus? In short, where has it come from and where is it going? With what speed and toward what target?

The most critical aspect of an organization's evolution is the changes in its leadership. How has it managed succession? Entrepreneurs do a notoriously poor job of choosing successors. Political conflicts in an organization may well result in power struggles and the compromise choice of a passive leader who will not favor either faction. In family businesses often the rule of primogeniture is followed, which means that the eldest son takes over, even though another child may be more competent. Some organizations do a very careful job of developing succession with formal executive development programs. Some use psychological testing or assessment centers.

Others, however, leave succession to chance. Some organizations recognize that no leader can do everything well, and succession becomes an effort to compensate for the weaknesses of previous leaders and perhaps to confront new market conditions. For example, when John F. Welch succeeded Reginald Jones as chief executive of General Electric Co., Welch quickly sold off many of GE's businesses and concentrated its efforts on those that were most profitable. The GE of the Welch era is vastly different from what GE was before.

One can get a sense of how seriously an organization is concerned with its perpetuation by the attention it gives to formal management and executive development programs, to assignments for training and development, to the money it invests in such programs, and to the degree of systematic effort it makes to assure its own adaptive perpetuation. Major organizations, like IBM, GE, Motorola, and Procter & Gamble, spend millions of dollars in training and development. They give careful attention to succession planning. Some do so well at this that they are the suppliers of talent to other organizations.

Consumer products businesses frequently turn to Procter & Gamble for managerial candidates. Manufacturing organizations often do the same with GE. In fact, one way to judge how well an organization does in this respect is to learn how frequently other companies seek to attract its managers and executives. Usually, this issue will arise spontaneously as interviewees discuss the organization's history and where superiors or peers have gone. Sometimes it becomes evident in the statistics of managerial turnover. For example, although for many years Digital Equipment, Co. was a highly successful organization, few other corporations tried to win away its executives, as contrasted with the experience of IBM. The reason simply was that Digital was dominated by its founder, Kenneth Olsen, and its structure was deliberately created to diffuse authority. As a result, no one could judge how well any Digital manager would do when he or she became responsible for the total managerial role.

Another important index of how and to what degree an organization anticipates its future is its financial investment in that future. Some wise organizations have systematic plans for capital investment and reinvestment in facilities. Others can't or don't. The latter are therefore likely to lose out in competition that requires increasing efficiency and productivity and lowering costs.

Organizations usually have a core skill that, properly understood, can become their dominant competitive edge. For example, for many years AT&T thought of its core skill as developing telecommunications products. It did not readily recognize that billing millions of customers as it had done for many years was a core skill. Recognizing that fact and taking advantage of it, AT&T quickly became a serious competitor of other credit card companies that didn't have its established mailing lists and collection procedures.

Not only must an organization have a focus, but it also must have an equally widely shared understanding of how it intends to reach its goals. Although there is much talk about vision, mission, goals, and so on in most organizations, in too many those issues are not adequately articulated. Top management may have a sense of where the organization is going, but often, even only a few levels below, not many people understand fully what the thrust is. In some cases processes have not been organized carefully around that thrust. As a result, one of the contemporary buzzwords in the organization literature is "reengineering," meaning aligning the structure and processes of an organization in keeping with what it hopes to be able to accomplish.

All organizations are bombarded with continuous communications from the outside. There is a plethora of information of all kinds. Some inputs, such as newspapers, are broad, while others, such as highly technical reports, are narrow. What kind of information does this organization get, and how does it use that information? Any visitor to a corporation can readily observe on the reception room coffee table and sometimes in the offices of managers and executives a wide array of business magazines -- mostly unread. Typically, managers don't read much. (Even organization development consultants seem not to read very much.) To what extent does the organization make use of the information that comes its way? How does it do that? What information is the basis for common discussion and shared decision making? Who brings what specialized information from which sources into the common pool? What critical information seems to be ignored?

For example, General Motors had to lose 35% of its market share before it took Japanese competition seriously. In sum, how does this organization keep up with the external world? And how rapidly does it respond to threats from various kinds of competitors and from economic conditions and political circumstances? For example, in the face of recession, many companies downsized drastically. Others couldn't seem to face their reality directly and undertook limited downsizing that necessitated their repeating that process again and again, to the demoralization of their people.

Having undertaken the initial exploration and developed a sense of the organization's key figures, directions, financial status, and physical and employee distribution, and of the multiple facets of its work, the practitioner must create a method for organizing the information that he or she will gather. The most convenient way is to create a set of file cards or similar files on a computer, one for each critical topic. Then, as the practitioner gathers data, information can be placed under the appropriate heading immediately, thus avoiding the complex and cumbersome task of later sorting the myriad facts that the diagnostic effort will yield. Overlapping topic categories make it possible for the practitioner to perceive phenomena from several different vantage points and simultaneously to have the confirmation necessary for credible inferences.

There are myriad ways of organizing information. I prefer to do so from the beginning forward, so to speak. The origins of an organization give rise to all else that follows because so much of what ensues grows out of those origins. Few organizations are wiped out, to become only legal shells from which another is later constructed. The evolutionary path of an organization reflects its adaptive methods and patterns. Its communications patterns are an analog to the human nervous system.

The following topics are those under which I gather and organize information (see Levinson, 1972) for a complete outline). The first three topics emphasize gathering facts while the fourth puts heavy emphasis on inferences.

1. Genetic data (identification and description of the organization, its history, and the reasons for the consultation).
2. Structural data (the formal organization, plant and equipment, finances, personnel demographics and policies, general policies and practices, and time cycles).

3. Process data (communications and information transmission).

4. Interpretative data (how the organization perceives itself and its environment; its basic knowledge and how it makes use of that knowledge; the emotional atmosphere of the organization and its capacity to act; attitudes and relationships toward multiple stakeholders, toward the consultant, toward things and ideas, toward power, and toward itself).

The facts and inferences are eventually integrated into an analysis and set of conclusions, followed by a summary and recommendations.

Developing a Sample

Once a method for organizing data has been established, the next step is to develop a sample for individual and group interviews, questionnaires, and observations. Developing a sample is fundamental to diagnosis. The practitioner wants to know that his or her information truly represents the organization. The client system wants to be assured of the validity of the information. Though various members of the organization may differ with the practitioner's interpretations, none will fault his or her fundamental work if they can trust that the data truly are representative and verifiable. (That is, another diagnosis would yield the same data.)

As a rule of thumb, I usually interview all of the members of top management (however that is defined), a representative sample (usually about 10%) of middle management (those below what has been defined as top management and above first-level supervisors), and a sample of line employees (usually about 5%). Depending on the size of the organization, these percentages may vary. In any event, one wants to be certain of sampling the range of organizational activities with sufficient comprehensiveness that when the sample is subsequently described, people in the organization will accept it as truly representative. Sometimes a comprehensive sample is neither necessary nor possible for certain kinds of focal problems. In such instances, it will be important to point out the limits of the sampling.

Interviews

It is particularly helpful for the practitioner to construct an interviewing schedule with the names of people whom he or she has chosen for the sample. The practitioner can then make specific appointments, clearing them with the person to whom the interviewee reports and making it clear to the interviewee that the interview content is confidential and participation is voluntary. In practice, I find it useful to allow two hours for each executive and managerial interview and one hour for those at the line level.

Sometimes interviewees will be dubious about confidentiality and the prospect that anything constructive will come of the consultation. The practitioner can explain that leaks undermine the diagnostic effort and therefore the work of the practitioner and can encourage the interviewee to hold doubts in abeyance until the final results are in.

To provide the basis for a comprehensive grasp of the organization, I ask a series of open ended interview questions (Levinson, 1972). These questions touch on such issues as the history of the organization, feelings about the organization and coworkers, the organization's image, help and training for employees, performance evaluation, benefits, rules, time pressures, communications, sources of information about the work, what the organization stands for and pays attention to in the outside world, and the organization's future. Interviewees seem most intrigued by (and later discuss among themselves) my request that they construct a personified visual image of the organization and describe that "person" to me. Related questions ask how peppy or energetic the organization is and how strong it is.

Questionnaires

In large organizations it is helpful to have a complementary questionnaire. The practitioner may use a commercially available attitude or morale instrument or the Organization and Attitude Inventory (Levinson, 1972) that is intended to complement the open-ended interview questions.

Commercial instruments that provide for computer scoring may be more efficient, even though the resulting information may be less psychologically sophisticated. It is unwise to use questionnaires without personal interviews. The reasons are simple. A questionnaire provides answers to questions one asks but not to those one doesn't ask. Furthermore, the subtleties of response are necessarily missed by the simple responses allowed on questionnaires, which are more expedient for scoring than for understanding complexity.

Diagnosing Leadership

All organizations are the lengthened shadows of their leaders. Sometimes that shadow lasts for generations. Inevitably it is heavily cast by incumbent leaders. Therefore, it is important for the practitioner to assess and describe the behavior of leading figures in the organization and to examine the influence of their behavior on the organization's performance. This assessment is inferred from the responses to questions in the interview about the organizational image and communication of information. It also derives from spontaneous comments of interviewees and from individual interviews with leaders. Sometimes there are business media stories about the leadership. In other instances, such information comes from members of the board or contacts outside the organization.

There may be significant differences among the organization's leaders that offer the disadvantage of conflict or the advantage of complementary effort. In one entrepreneurial organization the chief executive was widely noted for his flood of creative ideas. One of his two lieutenants concentrated his efforts on winnowing those ideas and translating the best into products.

The second, whose emphasis was on the immediate and practical, attended to the day-to-day business of the organization. None of the three could carry on the roles of the others; all were necessary to achieve the organization's goals.

Over controlling leaders will rigidify an organization. Charismatic leaders will tend to overshadow it. Manipulative leaders will be likely to exploit it for their own gain (Kets de Vries, 1989; Kets de Vries & Miller, 1984, 1988). Of course, significant differences in behavioral style, perceptions, and values among organization leaders and managers will make it difficult for the organization to evolve and sustain a coherent competitive thrust.

Observations

From time to time it is useful to observe people at work to see exactly what they do and how it fits into the larger context of the organization. Sometimes, if the work is not too complex or difficult, employees will allow the practitioner to do some of it and experience its requirements firsthand. The greater the immersion one has in the work process itself, the more likely one is to understand some of the issues and problems related to it.

This method also helps to evaluate leadership. By sitting in the office of a chief executive one can observe both the flow of contacts and the content of the issues that arise. Such observations will soon provide a sense of what that particular person thinks is important and how he or she goes about dealing with those issues. There may be a significant difference between what an individual says is important and what he or she actually does in the course of a day's work (Kotter, 1982; Mintzberg, 1973).

Written and Other Information

The practitioner may want to gather all kinds of information: human resources policies and practices; historical data, both formal and from public media sources; references to the organization in trade or professional journals; reports or discussions in industrial or medical histories or similar volumes to understand the place of the organization in its industry, field, or community. Exit interviews are an informative source of information about experiences in the organization. Interviews with competitors, with clients or customers, or with political or other officials with whom the organization has contact add additional perspectives.

Organizations use many different kinds of consultants, and reports by these consultants often yield important data. Sometimes such reports indicate that the same issues have arisen repeatedly and have not been resolved -- or, in some cases, even addressed. In some organizations, consultants' reports sit on shelves. In others they will have resulted in important and sometimes drastic changes, echoes of which may now be reverberating for the practitioner. Change, for example, is poorly managed in most organizations, and its effects may remain as residual problems for years. In any event, the practitioner will want to review such reports, particularly after arriving at his or her own conception of the organization's problems and strengths.

The practitioner should review organization communications in some detail. These include external publications for customers and the public at large, such as the annual report, brochures, advertising, news releases, and similar devices. One might ask of an annual report, for example:

What does the management want the reader to think and believe about the organization? What kind of an image is it trying to present? With what success? How realistically? How large is the gap between how the organization wants to be perceived and how, in fact, it is perceived? Organizational communication also includes internal publications such as bulletins and memoranda. What issues are emphasized in these and other internal communications? What are the repetitive themes? How effective and persuasive are these communications? How much do they contribute to giving employees the information they need and want, as contrasted with superficial pronouncements?

In particular, what is the substance of the communications to customers or clients, to political figures, to regulatory bodies? How does the organization engage its competitors? How does it relate to the communications media and to the respective communities of which it is a part? And, what is its attitude toward itself? For example, "Sensor was a giant hit because of Gillette's willingness to spend heavily on its own brand name and its ability to deliver a product good enough to live up to it." ("The Best a Plan Can Get," 1992.)

The Logic of Diagnosis

Having gathered all the diagnostic information and organized it under the critical topics, the practitioner must now construct inferences from what he or she has learned. That means assessing the strengths and weaknesses of the organization, its resources (financial, intellectual, market position, reputation. and similar facets), its mode of interacting with its environment, its awareness and understanding of the problems it is encountering, and the level of conceptual ability at which it understands those problems. Since the organization's leadership is crucial to its capacity to resolve its problems, the practitioner must assess how far ahead the leadership can conceive of and anticipate issues, how aggressive it is in taking a competitive position, and how well it has developed followership within the organization. The Gillette example cited earlier is a case in point ('The Best a Plan Can Get," 1992):

Gillette undertook a high-risk option to launch Sensor throughout both America and Europe. It added to its risk by planning to back Sensor's simultaneous American and Pan-European launch with an advertising and promotional blitz featuring identical television commercials (apart from language) in every market. Such campaigns often fail; ads that work in one place can flop in others.

Clearly, the Gillette top management conceived of a worldwide strategy to turn the razor blade from a commodity to a product by adding luster to its brand name.

Inferences and Interpretation

The practitioner must be careful in following the path from fact to inference to interpretation. By this time the practitioner will have recorded all of the facts and made the appropriate inferences. The practitioner should be able to cite the facts from which the inferences were made, specify the alternative inferences that were possible, and explain the reason for choosing one over another. This is neither the time nor place to introduce new information. Furthermore, the practitioner must be able to defend his or her conclusions. One can do so only if there is a clear path from the data to the interpretations.

The diagnostic formulation is a comprehensive summary of the practitioner's logic and the conclusion that the practitioner draws from it. The conclusion win also include recommendations about what change efforts are necessary and how they might be accomplished in this organization.

A critically important aspect of the diagnosis is the prognosis. This should be a statement of what kinds of changes are likely to be undertaken by the practitioner and the organization, or by the organization alone, in what period of time and with what resources, limits, and prospective outcome. Unfortunately, this is usually not done. As a result, practitioners frequently are overwhelmed with a sense of the impossible nature of their work. They expect too much of themselves and the organization and therefore frequently are disappointed with the limits of what they and the organization can do. A careful evaluation of a prognosis and a formulation of its boundaries helps to contain the work within realistic limits and to alleviate the sense of overwhelming inadequacy that often follows a diagnosis. Neither the organization nor the practitioner is going to be as good as either would like in its problem-solving efforts. This realistic recognition should not, however, destroy the good that either or both can do.

Feedback Report

The next logical step is the practitioner's feedback report. This should include three basic considerations: (1) a brief history of the organization and its context as a setting for the problem that was posed to the practitioner, (2) what the practitioner did to obtain the information that forms the basis for his or her recommendations, and (3) how the practitioner understands the information and what recommendations he or she makes about what might be done to cope with the perceived problem.

The report then is presented to the chief executive officer or whoever is in an equivalent role. Several cautions must be observed in reporting to that person. First, the practitioner must insist that the chief executive reserve the last two hours of a working day and the first two hours of the next morning for the report feedback and subsequent discussion. If the practitioner does not insist on such a condition, the consultation is likely to be lost. The reason is simple. No matter how much a given executive wants accurate information, he or she is and has been doing the best he or she can. Consequently, a consultant's report, no matter how gently couched, is perceived to be an indictment.

Therefore, I do not give a client a report; rather I read it aloud, asking the client how it might sound to others. I encourage taking notes during my reading, and then after the reading, I clarify any points about which the client has questions. I ask the client to take the report home, read it during the evening, and come back prepared to discuss it the next morning. Inevitably, the sense of indictment will swell into paranoid hostility when the client reads the report. Meeting together the next morning will temper that paranoid reaction, and the subsequent review of the report will bring the reaction back to realistic proportions. I ask the client to review both what has been said in the report and how it has been said. I offer the opportunity for the client to suggest appropriate language changes, if necessary, that will not alter the substance of the report. In one case, I had to review the report word by word, line by line, in three two-hour sessions with the chief executive.

Having clarified the report with the chief executive, the report is then presented to each successive level of the organization. It may be necessary to modify the report for successively lower levels so that it is specific and concrete enough for employees to understand clearly what is reported. Discussion then follows. In some cases, there will be no discussion; the recommendations stand as presented. In other instances, the report may serve as the basis for discussion within the organization about possible options for action. In still others, particularly when there has been no commitment to report throughout the organization, only the person who asked for the consultation will decide on any action to be taken. It is important for the practitioner to understand that the chief executive is the person responsible for the organization and the one who must necessarily determine how to manage the impact of the report on the organization and the subsequent action processes. The practitioner must be extremely careful not to undermine the role of the chief executive.

For example, in a community service organization, the heads of the various departments saw themselves as a collective that made the decisions on behalf of the organization. A major problem in that organization was the failure of the chief executive to demarcate his role and exercise his power appropriately. The department directors protested when I announced that I was to report to the CEO and subsequently to them. They felt, in effect, that they were a collective CEO and that they should all hear the report at the same time. I pointed out that they were not a collective CEO, that the chief executive was indeed the chief executive, and my obligation was to him in that role. I would not collude with them against their leader, however willing he had been to collude with them against his own authority and the interests of the organization that depended on his leadership.

From time to time people will want to quarrel with the practitioner about the validity of the data, the diagnostic method, or the conclusions. It is here that the practitioner's comprehensive sources of information, careful inferences, and logical conclusions will enable him or her to feel comfortable about the solidity of the effort.

Frequently, those who had earlier voiced doubts about the degree to which the practitioner would report what was learned now come forward to applaud the integrity of the work and its results. There can be a highly useful corollary effort. In the case cited earlier, where the chief executive required three review sessions, his conviction about the conclusions was such that he followed each presentation he made to successive parts of his organization with a statement of what he was going to do about the recommendations. His actions subsequently validated his promises.

Having the practitioner then help the organization implement the recommendations usually calls for renegotiating the contract to define what is to be done, within what period of time, with what costs, and what checks on the outcome. If the organization's leadership is left to its own devices to follow up the practitioner's recommendations, the practitioner will have to take leave of the people with whom he or she has worked. It is important to say good-bye to as many of those one has interviewed as is reasonable to those who have demonstrated their work activities, those who have provided special information, and those who have been generally helpful, such as secretaries, administrative assistants, and others who have assisted with accommodations and logistics. All should have a sense of having been personally respected and appreciated for their contributions to the effort. The practitioner, too, will want to close the relationship on a positive note with a gratifying sense of having left something useful behind.

Illustrative Case

Vitech makes measurement and control systems, precision optical products, and glass and medical devices. It comprises four divisions: Graphic Measurement, Precision Measurement, Imprinting Devices, and Government Systems. The first three of these manufacture and sell high-tech instruments, while Government Systems does technical design work for the military services. At the time of the consultation there were 769 employees, of whom 50 were in corporate headquarters and 400 in Government Systems, the largest division. The company was started by its president, Vernon Lambertson, 25 years ago in a garage. Vitech had recently been experiencing difficulties. In 1987 the commercial products divisions accounted for 45% of sales. The latest figures showed that 90% of profits came from the Government Systems division.

The president had ordered both pay and working hours reduced in the commercial divisions, in some cases to a 4-day week. There had been continued indecision about closing the Graphic Measurement division because of low profits, poor management, and inadequate marketing. Layoffs had been announced in the Precision Measurement and Imprinting Devices divisions, but the Government Systems division worked a 50-hour week. Employees in the commercial divisions were disgruntled and worried about their future.

The board of directors had been concerned about these and other matters and felt that Lambertson was spread too thin. He took on a controller and a vice president of human resources, Greg Edwards, as a response to this criticism. The latter felt that outside consultation was needed and turned to The Levinson Institute.

The Course of Consultation

The Levinson Institute had one previous contact with Vitech. Lambertson had agreed to consultation a year previously, but had changed his mind. Now Edwards's urging had pushed him into grudging acceptance. It was felt, however, that Lambertson might abort the consultation at some point and might not support critical activities in the consultation.

The Vitech building was one story of red brick, unpretentious, and approximately 100 feet long. A small sign with a logo stood in front of the building but gave no indication of what the company did. The reception area was small and poorly lighted, and nothing in it described or pictured Vitech. Management offices were small and modestly furnished. Linoleum took the place of carpeting. The cafeteria consisted of a long row of vending machines, a microwave oven, and simple chrome and plastic tables and chairs.

These arrangements proved to reflect Lambertson's philosophy and Spartan way of life. He saw no need for fancy trappings or advertising. In winter, he drove a jeep with a snowplow in case a driveway needed clearing or an employee's car had to be helped out of a drift.

The consulting team reviewed annual reports, 10K reports, previous consultation reports, policy manuals, contracts, government comments, corporate publications, and similar materials. Also available were the results of an annual attitude survey conducted by another consultant. A four-person team interviewed all of the top management, the six members of the board of directors, 16 department heads, and a random sample of five percent of the employees in corporate headquarters and each division. The team devoted 332 hours (the equivalent of 8 weeks) to interviews, analysis, report preparation, and feedback.

Four divisions in one building made for a task-oriented, functional, but cluttered physical layout. Thus, initial questions for the team included the following: How does one define one's place and meaning at Vitech? One's boundaries, autonomy, and support relationships? One's divisional and organizational identity (is there one)? What are the factors that make Vitech a "family," and how do they affect the functioning of the organization, the president, management, and the employees?

Attitudes and Opinions

The need for management development was mentioned by several of the executives who reported to the president. One cited the lack of managers who were aggressive and decisive and could plan. Another pointed to a lack of really skilled and experienced people. The president himself was considered by some to be part of the problem. He was seen as unable to delegate and let go, a trait that hindered Vitech's growth.

At a lower level, engineering managers who were relatively new to Vitech stated that in comparison to their previous companies Vitech had a low level of technological expertise and that their own expertise and creativity were not welcomed. Promotion was seen by this group and others as haphazard and dependent upon seniority and getting along with the president.

Employees had mixed views about Vitech. They were proud of its professionalism. However, relations with customers were tainted by difficulties in responding quickly enough to customers' needs. Although they thought that the Government Systems division and the Graphic Measurement division responded quickly, they viewed Precision Measurement less favorably and the responses of Imprinting Devices as poor. When employees were asked to describe Vitech as though it were a person, responses included the following: an adolescent unsure of where he or she was going; a freight train out of control; an honest, sincere person, competent but not brilliant, who stumbled around hoping things would fall into their proper places.

The culture of the organization was defined as easygoing and informal. There were comparatively few official policies and procedures and a lack of uniformity in the application of policies from division to division. The informality was also reflected in the lack of punctuality about corning to work and a casual attitude about setting objectives and evaluating performance.

Although opinion surveys and market surveys were a regular feature of the operation, Vitech didn't seem eager to accept much advice, particularly from the employee surveys. There was a question about how deeply Lambertson wanted to listen. That attitude was reflected further down the organization by the lack of regular meetings for most work groups. Division managers seemed to have little interest in understanding employees' perceptions. Most supervisors tried to ignore problems until they blew up.

The President

Vernon Lambertson was in his 50s, tall, and stockily built. He was quiet-spoken and seemingly shy. He worked in shirtsleeves. His shoes were scuffed, and he had a number of pens in his pocket. He looked like a hands-on engineer and appeared uncomfortable with social banter.

Lambertson was aware of the poor interpersonal skills of many of his managers. He said they were so good with tangible gear that they thought they were good with people, but he found some of them to be awful managers who produced work situations that were hard to correct. Many middle managers were older employees who had been promoted into their positions and lacked the skills to perform effectively in the present business environment. Lambertson was troubled over this fact and sensitive to his responsibility to these employees who were not able to function as productively and as creatively as newly trained managers might. His loyalty to them, his protectiveness, and his inability to solve the problem resulted in his leaving the situation as it was.

Lambertson, himself, was not very open to change, but he was not intransigent. For example, three years previously he had not thought it important or even appropriate, to share information with employees. However, working with consultants who conducted the regular employee attitude survey led him to change his mind, and communications had improved. On the other hand, Lambertson's tight control meant that nothing got done unless he wanted it done, and managers had to approach him individually and try to get his approval. This tended to stifle creativity and produce frustration.

Lambertson was the first to admit that he was neither a good manager nor a good salesman, but employees had a great deal of respect and affection for him as a person and as an engineering genius. Employees saw him as sincere, honest, and concerned, but also as somewhat incompetent, an opinion they felt guilt in expressing.

Lambertson appeared to hold two ego-ideals. On the one hand, he embodied the traditional image of the compulsive, detail-oriented engineer who was dedicated to results, comfortable with the abstractions of numbers and the specificity of tasks, but uncomfortable with interpersonal relationships and the surfacing of emotions. He was satisfied by task accomplishment and being valued by others who appreciated his solutions to their technical problems. But circumstances from within and without had thrust him into the role of president of a growing and troubled high tech company. He therefore, on the other hand, aspired to be a good president. He saw that his role logically demanded monitoring of the outside world, developing managers and teams of managers, and exercising broad conceptual management skills. However, at 59 years of age and after 10 years of coaching by consultants, he did not think he had changed much, nor was he apt to change, although he had tried and was still trying.

Summary, Inference, and Interpretation

This was an organizational family that had a clear sense of identity, was troubled by and concerned over a member who was very ill (the Graphic Measurement division), and was looking to the future with feelings of apprehension and hope. Whether it would survive the near future in its present form; how it would meet the internal and external challenges it now faced; and how the family heads would ensure its cohesion, health, and growth were questions that weighed heavily on all the members. The company, like its founder, in many ways was hidden from the outside world. Both were unable to explicitly assess and state what they were, what they did, and how well they did it. They were resistant to self-knowledge while making attempts to learn about themselves and hoping to change.

Vitech was described as an organization in the adolescent phase of its life. It had now outgrown its old clothes; the informal management procedures and methods of operation were no longer working. The time for introspection had arrived. Responding to the question of imagining the organization as a person and describing what that person was doing, one employee described Vitech as a teenage boy engaged in his first fistfight: finding himself slugged and stunned, he knew he must fight back, but he was not exactly sure how.

Vitech had not been able to move successfully from its entrepreneurial state to one that was fully professional (Greiner, 1972). It was inhibited by the inability of its chief executive to let go. The chief executive's over control of his own aggression and his need to punish himself were reflected in his severe superego, his over control of others, and the minimal comforts of the work environment. He was able to tolerate neither the expression of his aggression nor the expression of more affectionate feelings, except through a paternalistic sense of noblesse oblige. Furthermore, he was heavily dependent on his professional skill not only for his self-esteem but also as a means of avoiding being dependent on others. This life-long personality pattern was not susceptible to significant change, but inasmuch as the chief executive was responsive to the opinions of the consultants and was face-to-face with economic circumstances that threatened to compel him to contract his company, the consultants believed it might well be possible, with sensitive support, to assist him in taking gradual steps to distance himself from operations. Although Lambertson's paternalism and technical proficiency created conditions for identification that could hold the company together, the changes would have to take place, for Vitech had to differentiate itself more clearly and become more competitive. The prognosis was optimistically guarded.

Recommendations

Numerous recommendations were made for improving Vitech's functioning in many areas. The central recommendation was that Vernon Lambertson be provided with a more permanent form of managerial assistance than had been available to him in the past. That assistance would take the form of an executive vice president or chief operating officer. He or she would provide managerial expertise, complement Lambertson's technical strength, and spare him the extraneous problems he had to deal with under the present structure.

Although Lambertson seemed to understand his own limitations as a manager, it did not follow that he could easily accept the addition of an intervening executive, as his over controlling character and past reactions to such suggestions indicated. It was believed that a psychological consultant would be helpful in supporting Lambertson in his relationship to the new executive and in enabling him to anticipate his inevitable retirement. Careful, sensitive support would be needed to preserve Lambertson's self esteem while helping him recognize his limitations and their cost to the organization.

The central issue for Vitech was the development of a more sophisticated approach to management. Vernon Lambertson could not do it alone. The provision of additional managerial expertise to support the CEO was the foundation upon which the other recommendations rested; implementation of all the other recommendations without addressing the core problem in this manner would mean little for the future of Vitech.

Management, like all disciplines, is subject to fads as executives seek quick and easy solutions to complex problems (Levinson, 1992). But, there are no quick and easy solutions. Various managerial techniques are applied to organizations without addressing the following basic questions: What is the specific problem in the organization? What are its multiple causes in the context of the economy, its own industry, and its unique organizational history? How well is the organization able to cope with its problem?

An ethical consultant must answer such questions, report what he or she has learned in a manner that can be understood, and recommend steps for change. These recommendations can be the basis for discussion within the organization and for evolving a plan of change that is in keeping with the organization's capacities and competence. All this requires a formal, comprehensive diagnostic process, such as outlined in this chapter, and solid psychological skill.

CHAPTER 3

SECTION ONE

IMMERSION AND DIAGNOSIS

IMMERSION 3

A Psychologist Looks at Executive Development

Harvard Business Review, September-October, 1962, pp. 69-75.
... and shows why there are so many failures with present approaches and how management could use psychological principles to strengthen its programs in the future.

Almost every company today is concerned about the development of executive talent to ensure its long-run survival. Many companies have undertaken management development programs to meet this need. These programs frequently are of high caliber – carefully planned and well organized. But often there are psychological barriers within the organization that subtly counteract the development process.

In this article I shall discuss a series of barriers that every manager should know about, recognize, and understand. We shall see that:

• A major factor in a manager's development is the opportunity for him to identify with those who have more experience, skill, and power than he has.

• The coaching and appraisal process, as usually carried out in U.S. business, falls short of the mark because it does not support strong relationships and contacts between a boss and his subordinates.

- Among the most important reasons for this failure are that most line executives do not give enough time and thought to working with their juniors; the climate in business is not tolerant enough of mistakes and individual needs to learn; and rivalry between bosses and subordinates tends to be repressed instead of acknowledged.

These ideas have the most vital implications, as we shall see, for the way executives should work with their assistants, for the scope of coaching and appraisal, for the scheme of executive rewards, and for the role of staff men assigned to training.

Relevant Axioms

To understand the leading barriers to development, let us review several psychological principles and then examine some contemporary management development practices in the light of these principles.

Among most clinical psychologists and psychiatrists, there is general agreement on several axioms:

- *Early influences shape personality.* The early relationships of the child in the family play a critical role in character formation, in the evolution of personality traits, and in the development of attitudes toward others. This axiom is widely recognized in the proverb, "As the twig is bent, so the tree will grow."

- *These early influences are primarily emotional influences.* They have to do with feelings, particularly with the ways in which people come to balance and to express the constantly present twin forces of love and hate. Every human being tends to repeat unconsciously in other situations those modes of seeking and giving love and those patterns of expressing his aggressive impulses which he learned in the family. Thus, people often are reacting emotionally when they and others think they are responding intellectually.

- *As a result of these early influences, organizations of people tend to assume qualities much like those of the family.* This is tacitly recognized in business circles in the frequently heard phrase, "We're just like one big family," and in the many efforts of business organizations to facilitate the identification of the employee with the organization. In the work situation a person unconsciously continues to seek many of the gratifications he once obtained in the family, and to resolve some of the psychological problems which were not resolved in the family during the course of his growth. For example, the pursuit of status and status symbols may be viewed as an effort to obtain indications of esteem from authority figures. Psychologically this pursuit is little different from the effort of the child to obtain love from his parents and to vanquish his sibling rivals.

- *One of the essential avenues for psychological growth is the process of identification.* A boy has difficulty learning to become a man unless he can identify himself with his father and, later, with other parental figures -- teachers, Scout leaders, grandfathers, and so on. All these figures are men who have more power than he has. Given affection and encouragement by such men, and particularly the freedom to express his own feelings of affection and anger toward them, he introjects or incorporates into his own personality the behavior and values of these models. He acquires some of their power, some greater ability to master both his own impulses and his environment. "A chip off the old block," we say.

In such relationships there is always rivalry as well. The boy not only tries to emulate his models, but also to do better than they. Unconsciously he seeks to displace them, to become more powerful than they are. It is out of this rivalry that the spirit of competition is born.

Implicit in such relationships is the opportunity for the boy to depend on the adult for guidance, direction, and support. Gradually, his independence increases, provided the adult encourages his growing independence.

These effects -- the acquisition of adult perspectives and powers, the spirit of competition, and growing independence -- are products of a relationship. If the relationship is impaired, to a certain extent psychological growth is impaired. A boy may be unable to have a good male model for identification; his father may be too weak a person with whom to identify, or too harsh and rejecting, or a highly transient figure -- or he may have died. In such circumstances, without adequate father surrogates, it becomes difficult for the boy to establish the foundations for evolving his own identity as a unique, mature, adult male.

➤ *Identification continues to be a mechanism for growth over a lifetime.* No man is so perfect or so self-satisfied that he gives up seeking to attain some of the qualities of other men; witness the international respect for Albert Schweitzer. All religions hold forth models with whom to identify. In professional training one identifies with those more learned in the field. Where it is made possible in business or other organizations, one identifies himself with his superiors, and thus acquires some of the perspectives, values, attitudes, and behavior required for survival and progress in the organization.

➢ A person carries with him images of identification models, some quite consciously, and strives to meet the expectations these people have (or are thought to have) of him. When executives are asked to discuss their work history, they are likely to mention some older person in business or private life who took a special interest in them. Frequently they will use the phrase, "He was like a father to me." In my experience, rarely is such a person spontaneously mentioned among hourly people and foremen. Although the thesis has not been verified by formal research, in my judgment *one of the significant differences between those who become executives and those who do not lies in the presence or absence of certain kinds of identification models.* Some awareness of this phenomenon lies behind the question that is sometimes asked of aspirants to management positions: "Who were your childhood heroes?"

This is not to say that identification alone leads one to become a good executive. Many skills and talents are required. Having a model, then, would seem to be a necessary condition but not by itself a sufficient one.

Missing Ingredient

These axioms have important implications for business and industry, and for management development in particular.

According to our axioms, a major factor in psychological growth is the opportunity for a person to identify with those who have more experience, skill, and power than he has. This means that the younger, less experienced men must have continuing personal contact with their superiors in relationships whose quality of encouragement and affection (in the very broad sense of that word) facilitates identification.

No matter how good the formal development program -- and many are very good -- it cannot replace the personal relationships which are also required for growth. *But the training responsibility is usually assigned to staff people in the organization who, regardless of their competence in their jobs, have very limited authority and power.* Therefore, they cannot themselves be adequate identification figures for men who are pursuing increasing line responsibilities. When important line executives do not play a significant role in management development, it should not be surprising if the man who is being "developed" comes to feel that the process to which he is being subjected is only an intellectual exercise.

Why Coaching Falls Short

To cope with this problem, top management frequently supplements the formal training programs with coaching or appraisal systems. In these structured relationships, superiors are to help their subordinates grow into more mature and experienced executives. Superior and subordinate are expected to meet at given intervals, to evaluate the subordinate's experiences, to set future goals, and, usually, to prepare a written summary of their discussion.

But the coaching and appraisal process, despite its many real and possible values, has not achieved widespread, enthusiastic acceptance. Apparently, it has not yet become the medium for identification that it might be. Why not? Five reasons stand out.

1. Lack of Time

Though chronological time may be set aside for coaching and appraisal, the coaching and appraisal relationship is often limited to the times marked on the calendar. More important, though the superior may go through the motions, he may not have the "psychological time" to give to the subordinate. That is, he may invest himself only superficially in the coaching process.

Why don't superiors have time? Hasn't the corporate president agreed that the development of executives is important? Hasn't the company demonstrated its conviction by spending large amounts of money on the development program?

The answer in both cases is, "Yes, but. . . ." Though the president may have agreed that executive development is important, though a budget may have been provided for the development program, and though provisions may have been made for executives to coach their subordinates, *rarely is a line executive in a business organization rewarded for developing young executives.* When the president talks with his immediate subordinates, too often his discussion centers around cutting costs, increasing profit margins, developing markets, and so on. Too often he evaluates their performance in these terms. There is nothing wrong with an evaluation which deals with the realities of business life. But when the president appears to be relatively unconcerned, except as an afterthought, about developing his own subordinates and how his subordinates are developing others, his behavior makes it clear that anyone wanting to help develop others undertakes an extracurricular activity of dubious commercial value.

2. No Mistakes Allowed

A vice president of an electronics firm who had "grown up with the business," reflecting on his experience in a seminar I was conducting, observed that he had made many mistakes in the course of his career and that he had learned much from them. He then added, somewhat to his own surprise, that young executives in his company were no longer as free to make mistakes. I think his comment is revealing.

The contemporary climate in American business and industry seems to be one in which mistakes are increasingly less tolerated or permitted. With ever-larger amounts of money at stake, with increasing amounts of data on which to base decisions, and with continuing expansion of rules, policies, and procedures, there is a concomitant demand for levels of performance which more closely approach perfection. This demand is stimulating in an intellectual way, but it forces executives into many kinds of conflict situations, of which these are examples:

(1)   The general results obtained are never good enough in many companies, leading to more pressure from superiors for improvement, rather than help toward growth. This pressure is often viewed as punishment for mistakes, as a result of which the subordinate learns not to make mistakes by not demonstrating initiative. In turn, the superior is required to tell the subordinate what to do, which prevents learning.

(2)   The subordinates amass reams of data on all kinds of obscure questions just in case someone should ask for some isolated bit of information. Endless hours of countless staff people are devoted to compiling reports whose sole purpose is to prove that the executive is

"on top of his job".

(3)   The "just in case" files are never really enough to allay the kind of insecurity which brings them about. All too many executives feel that they must also know their subordinates' work in detail, just in case they are asked about it. As a result, they constantly intrude into the work of their subordinates.

The punishment for mistakes, leading to less initiative and greater direction, makes subordinates feel stupid. The repetitive futility of the "just in case" files angers them. The intrusions into their work make them feel they are not trusted. These feelings alienate the subordinates from the superior, making identification difficult. In addition, the close supervision leaves little time to cultivate personal (but task-centered) relationships with subordinates. Such behavior vitiates the effects of even the ideal formal development program.

3. Dependency Needs Rejected

The child must depend on its parents for biological and psychological survival. In the United States, with its strong emphasis on advanced education, the period of dependency now extends for many people into the early adult years. Each person has the psychological task of weaning himself from this dependent relationship in order to become a mature adult. No matter how successfully a person may resolve this problem, each of us continues to have, to some degree, unconscious wishes to be dependent. Some of us can accept these wishes and lean on other people in acceptable ways and at appropriate times as, for example, when we are ill and someone else must take care of us. Others must reject their own dependency wishes and go to lengths to demonstrate that they do not need to lean on anyone else at any time for anything.

Any person who is responsible for the work performance of subordinates is required to let other people lean on him in the sense that to varying degrees under different circumstances they must turn to him for decisions, direction, and encouragement. This is not an easy psychological position for a superior because most people have enough trouble dealing with their own wishes to be dependent, without having to accept the dependence of subordinates.

As a result, many executives have difficulty with increasing responsibility for other people. Such responsibility can be more easily handled if they in turn have adequate support from their own superiors.

But how often do they get it? Failing to recognize the difference between legitimate needs for support and overdependence, a typically hard-boiled executive may well reject the subordinates' needs out of hand, saying, "Let them stand on their own two feet. I've always had to stand on my own feet. I'm not going to baby them. If they fail, I'll lower the boom." Such a remark is usually made in anger, an indication of the executive's problem with his own unconscious wishes to be dependent.

When the superior sees only those two alternatives of rejection ("stand on your own feet") or direct interference ("lower the boom"), he has no sense of how to help without fostering dependence. His black-or-white extremes seem to exclude a middle ground -- that of seeking out reasons for difficulties and helping subordinates with them.

When the senior executive fails to meet the legitimate dependency needs of his own subordinates, he (1) increases the stresses for the subordinate and (2) makes it more difficult for the man in turn to accept the dependency of his subordinates. Identification does not flower under these circumstances.

In addition, the senior executive himself is necessarily dependent on the subordinate to get the work done. The executive who cannot accept his own dependency needs is likely to be angry with himself and his assistant because he must be dependent on the latter. Such strong feelings of hostility usually are repressed, but they appear indirectly in the superior's attempt to make the subordinate an extension of himself. For example:

One capable but authoritarian engineering executive invariably responds to his subordinate's request for help on a problem with quick solutions "off the top of his head." However, what the subordinate wants, in my observation, is psychological support from the boss in the form of discussion of the problem and exploration of alternatives. The boss does not know how to give such support -- the boss wants the subordinate to implement the "quickie solutions," and this the subordinate cannot do because the "solutions" have been offered before enough questions have been asked. As a result, they do not fit the complexity of the problems.

The boss wants the subordinate to be an extension of himself, to respond as he has responded. "What did you do about what I said?" he asks characteristically. Yet the subordinate, also a mature adult, cannot be simply an extension of the boss. He can, however, be one who helps and assists the boss provided the latter can accept him in that role. When the senior man cannot accept his dependence, the subordinate cannot feel that he has support, that he is recognized as an individual. The boss's hostility is reflected in his inability to "let go" of the subordinate. The subordinate responds with chronic hostility of his own. Their relationship is a "bumpy" one.

A boss like this one is also likely to feel that his subordinate is not good enough to represent him. The subordinate can never, in fact, seem good enough in such situations, for the underlying insecurity which the superior feels will not permit him to view anyone as good enough. The subordinate is inevitably victimized.

4. Rivalry Is Repressed

Although he may not be conscious of such feelings or may not want to admit them, the superior usually fears being dethroned by his subordinates. As I have indicated, all is not love between father and son. There is rivalry and hostility, too. The conflict between the young and the old was recognized in Greek tragedy and Biblical literature thousands of years before Freud. It finds expression in the business situation, too. The rivalry is usually more painful for the senior executive than for the subordinate; for the latter knows he has time on his side. Only rarely in our culture can the senior executive feel free to express his concern about the rivalry. More often he represses his fear. Its overt manifestation is his reluctance to develop others lest they learn to do his job better than he and therefore replace him.

Unless the executive who is doing the coaching and appraising can recognize that such feelings of rivalry, and their accompanying fears, are universal and not reprehensible, the coaching situation will be blocked with the effects of mixed feelings. If the existence of unconscious hostile feelings toward the rival is not brought out into the open with the boss by his own senior, and if the boss is not reassured by his senior that his position is secure, the underlying hostile feelings of the boss will come through in the relationship. In subtle ways, the superior will attack the subordinate and the subordinate naturally will feel that he is being exploited as a target rather than appraised.

It is not unusual for subordinates, recognizing this phenomenon to some degree, to discount the appraisal and forget about it as quickly as possible. Worse still, the subordinate may find his own ways to strike back at the superior, or he may take his anger out on his own subordinates. One of the most effective ways of striking back is for the subordinate to decide that he does not want to be promoted further. No position frustrates higher management more than this one which, by rejecting what top management values very highly, in effect also rejects identification.

Rear-guard action against the subordinate who rejects promotion may continue for a long time, but rarely does higher management realize that it may have had a part in frustrating ambition, impeding the full growth of a junior executive, and depriving the organization of a promising man.

5. Relationship Is Unexamined

As indicated earlier, much of psychological growth is the product of relationships, and particularly relationships with identification figures. In a superior-subordinate relationship both parties influence each other and both have a responsibility for the task. This is what is meant by the phrase "reporting to." In order to discharge his responsibility, each man in the relationship has to affect the other. Each has a different responsibility, but both share a joint task.

If they are to carry out the joint responsibility in the most effective way, they must be able to talk freely with each other. This dialogue cannot be limited to what the subordinate alone is doing. Each party must have a sense of modifying the other. The talks must also include the joint setting of goals and the opportunity to express to each other how each feels about their working relationship. We are speaking here not of the adjustment of one to the other but of the interaction between them. The former leads to passivity and conformity; the latter is a precondition for identification and growth. Specifically, the subordinate must be permitted to express to the superior his feelings about what the superior is doing in the relationship and what the subordinate would like him to do to further the accomplishment of the task.

No relationship is free of hostility. When the anger can be expressed in relatively controlled fashion, directed to furthering the task, ordinarily it can serve constructive purposes. When it is suppressed, it creates more psychological friction in the relationship. More often than not, however, the superior is reluctant to hear such feelings expressed. Sometimes he feels that he is the boss and that any such expression is disrespectful if not an outright personal attack. Often he is afraid that the anger of a subordinate is a reflection on his management, or threatens his position. Some bosses want to preserve the myth of "one big happy family," unable to recognize that there is no continuous state of happiness in any family.

Usually in a coaching situation the relationship itself remains unexamined. The discussion centers around the performance of the subordinate alone. As a result, there can be little change in some of the major underlying forces which affect performance. Furthermore, neither party is very comfortable about the appraisal situation because both, to some degree, are aware of what they are *not* talking about. The superior often has guilt feelings about appraising the subordinate. He is conscious of some of his own angry feelings if the subordinate has not done too well; he is perhaps conscious of some of his rivalry feelings, and certainly of some of his own mistakes.

Little wonder then that the young executive is frequently insecure in his relationship with his superiors. Despite the first impression that may be conveyed, his own position is frequently "sink or swim." One mistake may obliterate a whole series of successes. It should not be surprising that one of the most frequent complaints in business circles is, "I don't know where I stand."

Here is a situation in which management is trying to do its best to develop executives. Frequently it provides the finest possible facilities and outstanding instruction. Certainly no malice is intended. The problem is not that the intentions are bad, or that no one really cares about what happens, but rather that few executives look carefully at the psychological significance of what is being done.

The result is often the opposite of management's intentions. For example, it is not unusual to find idealistic young executives who have become cynics. In management development programs they have been encouraged to think of human needs and human relations, only to be mocked by the practices of their own superiors. Then there is the man who neatly compartmentalizes his paradoxical experiences. At one moment he espouses human relations principles and the next speaks of progress in his company as a dog-eat-dog proposition. Anger and disillusionment with the organization are not uncommon feelings, nor are psychosomatic reactions uncommon when other stresses are added.

Toward Action

We can draw from this discussion a number of possible corrective steps:

(1)   If growth of executive capacity depends in a large measure on identification, and identification in turn depends on the relationships between superior and subordinate, then the psychology of this sequence should be recognized by all executives who ought to be identification figures, from the president down.

(2)   If the strength of the relationship between superior and subordinate is significantly related to the freedom each has to express his feelings to the other about that relationship, then the superior must make it possible for the subordinate to express his feelings without being considered immature or inadequate for doing so. True, not everyone is skilled in eliciting feelings. There are, however, a good many seminars and sensitivity training laboratories where such skills can be learned.

(3)   If both superior and subordinate share responsibility for the task which the subordinate is doing, then coaching and appraisal or development efforts must look at what they are doing *together* to fulfill the responsibility, not only at what the subordinate is doing by himself.

(4)   If executives are to feel responsible for the task of helping their subordinates to grow, two kinds of payment will be required. Each executive (a) will need psychological payment in the form of the same kind of attention from his own superior and recognition of what he is doing, and (b) will also need to be compensated for development. One criterion by which an executive should be evaluated and paid is how well he helps others to grow, as shown by the records of advancement of his subordinates.

(5)   If the development of executives is important for the survival of the organization, then it is the responsibility of each executive to whom others report. It cannot be delegated.

Given the acceptance of this responsibility by line executives, a staff department devoted to management development can make an effective *complementary* contribution. The staff department can help the line executive develop his own coaching and interviewing skills. It can help him learn and apply understanding of individual and group psychology. It can keep him up to date on advances in business knowledge. In short, it can truly serve a development function. In such an arrangement, no longer would the staff be asked to solve huge, complex problems by training, with inadequate access to line executives and top management.

A former chief of staff of the United States Army once said:

"The leader must be everything that he desires his subordinates to become. Men think as their leaders think, and men know unerringly how their leaders think." Field-Marshal Sir William Slim, Commander in Chief of the 14th Army in World War II and, more recently, Governor General of Australia, said that five qualities are necessary in a leader: courage, will power, flexibility of mind, knowledge and "the last quality, on which all the other qualities have to be based, is integrity -- the thing that makes people trust you."

The individual who aims deliberately at convincing others that he possesses integrity is foredoomed to failure, because the very attempt to convey such an impression is an almost certain indication that he is in doubt either as to the validity of his own code of ethics or as to his ability to live up to it. On the other hand, the individual with an understandable and simple standard of personal conduct, who is clearly devoted to the task in hand and puts it in front of personal interests of any kind, almost invariably attracts the adherence and commands the loyalty of other people. If he is in a position of authority, that authority is accepted because it is manifestly directed to the common purpose and does not challenge resistance by raising doubts whether followers are being asked to serve that purpose or merely to minister to the leader's egotism or ambition.

Possibly it is this element of self-forgetfulness, of unconsciousness of role, which is so common an element in successful leaders, which, in addition to the difficulty of isolating and expressing actual activities of leading, renders so many of them inarticulate about the subject. They do influence people, but largely because they do not attempt to do so. Indeed, many of them would appear to share the philosophy expressed in Robert Browning's lines:

'Tis an awkward thing to play with souls, And matter enough to save one's own.

Robert Tannenbaum, Irving R. Weschler, and Fred Massarik, *Leadership and Organization: A Behavioral Science Approach.* New York, McGraw-Hill Book Company, Inc., 1961, pp. 427-428.

CITATIONS:

1. **Bearding the Lion that Roared**: A Case Study in Organizational Consultation,   with Sabbath, J. & Connor, J., *Consulting Psychology Journal, 44:4*,1-16,
       Fall 1992.

2. The Practitioner as Diagnostic Instrument. In:.A. Howard (ed.), *Diagnosis   for   Organizational   Change.* New   York: Guilford Publications, 2, 27-52, 1994

3. A Psychologist Looks at Executive Development. *Harvard Business Review*, Sept.-Oct.,1962, 69-75

CHAPTER 4

SECTION TWO

COURAGE

On Executive Suicide

Harvard Business Review. Jul.-Aug., 1975, 118-122

Corporate executives who commit suicide make headlines. One in New York City leaped to his death from his window. A routine check following his death disclosed that he had authorized a bribe to a foreign official in order to prevent an increase in export taxes that would have harmed his organization. In Texas a top executive shot himself. He left behind a note that alleged he had been involved in political wrongdoing on behalf of his superiors.

In each case it was easy to conclude that the man had taken the only way out to avoid the intolerable consequences of guilt. That conclusion, however, is too glib; behind such incidents lay complex mechanisms that make certain executives particularly vulnerable to suicide, especially in times of economic distress. In self-interest, the special nature of these factors should be widely understood in management ranks.

Suicide always raises the question, "Why?" The question is especially important during a recession, when the suicide rate always rises. Both of the men were very successful, as their top-ranking positions indicate. Both had strong consciences, or their behavior would not have troubled them. What intense pressures for achievement or approval forced these men to comply with actions that violated their consciences? What rigid self-demands made them think that death was the only way out of their dilemmas? Why do some executives attach so much importance to their roles? Why are their aspirations so high and crucial to them that if they face business reverses, their only solution is to punish themselves with long hours of fatiguing work and perhaps eventually with death?

In this chapter, I want to explore some of these questions; to examine the character of the executive likely to be vulnerable to suicide, and to suggest why suicide can appear as a way out to a dynamic individual. Then I shall discuss ways in which people can recognize the symptoms of severe depression in themselves and in others, thereby, perhaps, preventing suicide.

The reader should appreciate the limitations of a brief presentation. All we can do here is try to understand a little about a very complex phenomenon and hope that understanding may cause someone to cry to for help instead of escape to death.

High Aspirations, Low Self-Image

A bright, aggressive, middle-aged corporate controller thought himself to be in line for the position of vice president of finance. He approached the company president and asked whether he would be appointed to that position. The president said that he would not, whereupon the controller left the company and became the financial vice president at another company. On the first day in his new post he jumped from the eighteenth-story offices of the company. His suicide was inexplicable. Many years after the event, his former employer still blamed himself for refusing the controller his promotion.

In this example are some of the common elements surrounding suicidal behavior: intelligence, ambition, disappointment (and, for those who were close to the person, uncomprehending guilt). These elements are particularly germane for executives.

Executives are men and women of high aspiration. As a rule, they are very ambitious, seeking power, prestige, and money, and nearly always they are competing intensely against other executives. In psychological jargon, they have extremely high ego ideals that revolve around power. They have deep-seated, unconscious pressures for attainment; their conscious goals are merely the tip of the iceberg. People who have such high levels of aspiration are frequently nagged by the feeling of being a long way from achieving their goals. No matter what their achievement, it never seems to be enough. As a result, they always view themselves as inadequate.

All of us try constantly to narrow the gap between the ego ideal and the self-image. The failures of people with irrationally high self-demands, lower their self-image and thereby increase their anger at themselves. We experience self-directed anger as depression. While depression is widespread and is usually amenable to treatment, in its extreme form, as we have seen, it often leads to suicide.

Early Traumas

The problems of high aspiration, high ego ideal, and low self-image start very early in life and contain significant components of irrationality. Some infants react to frustration s a product of a hostile world and take a fighting stance toward it. Others interpret pain and frustration as a product of their own inadequacies and therefore are prone to blame themselves. This is a depressive position and becomes a context for self-flagellation when later frustrations or failures confirm already established belief. Regardless of any achievements, such persons always see themselves as deficient and, according to their logic, deserving of self-punishment.

Among those particularly subject to depression are people who early in life lose one parent or both. And if the parents of a person who attempts suicide were separated from him or her when he or she was a child, the separation is more likely to have been intentional (such as through divorce), than natural (such as through death.) The consequent loss of love and support in childhood results in anger at the loss. Through primary-process thinking (explained in a moment,) the child becomes angry with the lost parent for deserting them, which the child thinks is their fault because they are unlovable or inadequate. Irrationally, they become enraged with themselves. Although the rage in time subsides, it leaves a psychological bruise, and new losses such as business losses can stir up the rage again. The person is now more vulnerable to self-punishment.

A second element of irrationality often underlying depression in later life lies in what is called primary-process thinking. In this state, the child equates thinking and feeling with doing. When the child is frustrated, his or her anger mounts and his/her wish to attack the frustrating object frightens them. In his or her anger with parents or others, the child fears that his or her thoughts alone will destroy them. Simultaneously the child feels he or she is bad for having such thoughts.

In an effort to cope with these feelings, the child frequently develops a pattern of behavior in which he controls the expression of feelings so they do not show. They become unconscious; he or she is no longer aware of them. The child tries to be so good and so competent that nobody will ever believe he or she has harbored bad thoughts. This pattern underlies the elevation of ego ideal aspirations to unrealistically high levels; the consequent pressures to achieve perfection follow the person through life, though he and she does not know why.

Dr. Margaret Proudy, former chief of pediatrics at Jackson Clinic in Madison, Wisconsin, has reported cyclical occurrences of depression among a selected group of children from seven to nine years old. Her profile of these youngsters corresponds strikingly to the problems of the ambitious, depressive adult: "The majority are perfectionists, have a poor self-image and find that their classmates, parents and teachers cannot measure up to their expectations. They have much need of affection and approbation, trying hard to please and be good. They have a high incidence of anxiety and dependence and poor ability to express antagonism….One of their chief personality defects is an almost total lack of sense of humor. Life is indeed real and earnest and they have no ability to laugh at themselves or others." The future will find many of these children, and children like them, in managerial roles and other positions of responsibility and power, where their intensity, seriousness, and drive to perform well will make them high achievers and superior workers.

Through adolescence and adulthood, the ego ideal demands are stimulated further by external pressures for achievement, by the expectations of parents and other influential figures, by competition for preferred places on athletic teams, in colleges, for professional training and preferred jobs, and by competition within organizations. In short, those who may be coping with repressed childhood rage this way demand much of themselves and much is demanded of them.

Threat of Failure

When scholastic, professional, or organizational achievement is a cherished dream, the threat of failure, real or imagined, is a constant companion.

One of the major problems with the kind of aspiration that is a product of the tremendously high ego ideal is the fact that no achievement is good enough no matter what one attains. Because the underlying motivation becomes unconscious as the child grows up, conscious achievement simply cannot gratify it. There are two separate worlds of thought and feeling: the conscious and the unconscious. It is the unconscious world, that which is the terrain on which the ego ideal – self-image struggle is so increasingly fought out. It is on this terrain also that one has the repetitive experience of inadequacy and therefore the feeling that one is not good enough. To feel that one is not good enough, in the face of an unrealizable ego idea, is the same as to feel that one is bad. That demands self-punishment.

This makes for the sense of deep vulnerability which all such people have. That vulnerability is increased to the extent to which one feels oneself responsible for whatever "failures" occur both literally and figuratively. It increases to the extent to which the entrepreneur creates an organization as an extension of himself or herself and "marries" it. Therefore in effect he or she does assume full responsibility for it. That vulnerability increases further to the extent to which one has high moral and social standards and has feelings of guilt for not having lived up to them.

If both the organizational responsibilities and the personal, moral and social responsibilities are part of cherished dreams and those dreams seem to be no longer possible of attainment, then one becomes even more angry with oneself for denying one's own fulfillment. Of course, such an experience of failure is more likely to occur in times of economic recession or depression, and when all people in management ranks are increasingly vulnerable.

Thus, one of the major difficulties with this state of affairs is that one's greatest asset is simultaneously one's point of greatest vulnerability. Conscientious people with high ego ideals, high aspirations that they pursue intensely, are necessarily particularly vulnerable to defeats. Then such defeats move their self-images farther away from their ego ideals and which, in short increase their disappointment with themselves. As this gap increases, they get angry at themselves, become highly self-critical, put themselves down, feel low, inadequate, guilty, and depressed.

For the corporate executive, this depressive pattern is reinforced by the career demanding that he or she absorb his or her frustrations and control his or her emotions ("Don't make waves"), carry on with equanimity regardless of what storms may come his or her way or be stirred up within him or her. He or she must not admit to having problems and must not under any circumstances give way or seek help. In fact, to seek help from a friend or the organization physician is considered a sign of weakness or failure to cope. Moreover, if he or she seeks help from a psychiatrist or psychologist, he or she is either weak or crazy or both. When a conscientious executive with tremendous self-demands recognizes that he or she is failing to cope effectively with a situation under circumstances in which he or she must control intense negative feelings, he or she may see limited options. If he or she does not seek professional help, escape from an apparently hopeless situation can seem possible only by developing psychosomatic symptoms, by attacking himself or herself in the form of accidents, or, in the extreme, by committing suicide.

In the effort to avoid the attack on self, some managers may attack and sabotage their organizations quite unconsciously. They make "stupid" mistakes. They provoke and discharge competent people, reorganize without reason, or go off on what prove to be tangents of diversification. Some try to over control their organizations with rigid systems that allow them to "whip people into line" and punish those who don't "shape up." Sometimes these managers plunge their organizations into bitter, unnecessary strikes or provoke community attacks that ultimately result in their defeat. They ascribe the failure, however, not to themselves but to the organization or someone else.

But people can destroy themselves in many ways other than the physical. Some manage repeatedly to jeopardize or set back their careers; some ruin their marriages or damage their children. Some undermine their own best-laid plans; we have witnessed the example of

Richard Nixon who, if he had planned it, could not have engineered his destruction more effectively than did his own unconscious will. Even accidents can be psychological in origin. These self-destructive events cannot be ascribed only to those who are "pathological," mentally ill, or crazy. As every clinician knows, these experiences are commonplace. When people are under heavy stress from self-criticism, they may atone unconsciously for their fantasized sins by punishing themselves.

Prevention of Suicide

How can one recognize and cope with threats to the self-image that may precipitate depression and, eventually, self-destructive behavior? Here are some recommendations:

*Self-directed aggression occurs with greater intensity in the person who is very conscientious and who has over identified with his or her profession, business, occupation, or major life interest. The more the person has circumscribed his or her sources of ego gratification and organized his or her life around one activity the more vulnerable he or she is. Defeat or loss in that area can be cataclysmic. Therefore one should cultivate a range of interests to which he or she can devote himself or herself. He or she cannot be equally competent in all of them, but when things go badly in one area, he or she can always turn to another for gratification.

*Accurate, honest and frequent performance appraisal is important to enable the executive to maintain a perspective on him or herself. Everyone needs confirmation from others of his or her performance; statistics do not satisfy this need. While the person who is not performing well may suffer a temporary decline in his or her self-image, the appraisal opens up alternatives to failure. Information from outside the organization may provide some input; it is useful, for example, for an executive to learn from another company that his or her peers have similar problems.

The chief executive officer is usually exempt from realistic appraisals, though he or she may often be criticized. A committee of outsiders on the board of directors, who have the necessary knowledge and detachment, may serve the purpose. In my judgment, a major function of the board is to help the CEO cope with the stress that comes with the job. Of course, board members who view anxiety over problems as a reflection of weakness are of no help to him or her.

*When a problem seems insurmountable, it should be broken down into components so that they can be tackled one at a time. Frequently, the advice and consultation of others is helpful in this task. Spouses and good friends have served such a function, and sometimes colleagues in trade associations or other outsiders can help with business-related problems.

*In reporting relationships, senior executives should try to relieve irrational pressures of guilt or responsibility that people express, but not by dismissing their expression with words like "Don't let it bother you" or "Forget it." One constructive way to avoid a buildup of pressures is through clarification of what is and is not the subordinate's responsibility. Job descriptions usually include the former but not the latter. It may be helpful if the superior recounted his or her own past problems and failures in order to help his or her subordinate accept the human quality of imperfection in him or herself and others.

*Be alert to signs of depression. These include loss of appetite and substantial weight loss, sleeplessness or excessive fatigue, heavy drinking, excessive use of tranquilizers or energizers, inability to complete work because of mental paralysis or reverie, increasing irritability, slowness and dull quality in speech, physical symptoms that have no physical basis, repeated deep sighing, and talk of suicide.

An executive who suspects that a subordinate is depressed should not urge him or her to take a vacation or take time off to "rest." The subordinate would only have greater freedom to punish himself or herself and heighten the depression. The person whose depression does not require hospitalization needs to have an atmosphere in which he or she can work on his or her problems, with the support of his or her superiors and preferably with the involvement of others. Above all, seriously depressed person must be treated professionally. His or her superiors, peers, and subordinates may think that the problem is not serious, or that the person will "snap out of it." But such optimism is unfounded unless substantiated by a diagnostician.

It is important for those around an executive who is showing signs of depression and stress to recognize that often they may assume that the problem is not of serious proportions or that he or she will "snap out of it." Even if they do not assume that, they may doubt their judgment because they are not clinicians or diagnosticians. If they conclude the problem is serious, they may have difficulty getting the person to professional help. Sometimes a person who has been severely depressed will have a spontaneous remission. Suddenly he or she will get well again. When this happens in a hospital, it is regarded as a highly dangerous time because it usually indicates that the preciously suicidal person has definitely made up his or her mind to do away with himself or herself, and having made that decision, is now relaxed. Sometimes families think that the person who has relaxed is now in good health. They then remove him or her from the hospital only to have him or her commit suicide. When such circumstances arise, when there is great doubt or concern, the best thing to do is get in touch with a professional person and ask his or her guidance or advice. You may not able to implement that guidance or advice as for example, to call the police when somebody is severely depressed and is expressing thoughts of suicide.

It is important to recognize that suicides occur even in the best psychiatric hospitals, despite all of the staff available and certainly, no layman can hold himself or herself responsible for the events which are beyond their experience, knowledge, and control. However, when somebody does commit suicide and others around him or her have been aware of feelings of depression or ineffective functioning, they tend to blame themselves for not having done something sooner or having been unable to head it off. It's important for those people to meet together in a group with a professional person to talk over their feelings and their experiences and to relieve their own guilt. Otherwise, they will carry the burden of such feelings for many, many years. If one castigates oneself with hindsight, one is doing the same thing that a self-destructive person has already done. For example, a group of students had had a great deal of vigorous interaction with a profession whom they did not regard very highly. They also complained to the administration about the inadequacy of the professor. The professor committed suicide after which the students thought themselves to be murderers and blamed themselves for having precipitated the suicide. As a matter of fact, the professor had been in treatment for an extended period of time and the events in the classroom were merely a reflection of the difficulties he was already having. When the students' feelings were not adequately worked out, they continued to be burdened with them with irrational feelings of guilt on their part.

Point of Vulnerability

When a person suffers a loss or defeat and becomes depressed, he or she usually does one of five things:

1) He or she acts positively to narrow the gap between his or her goals and his or her present position. This is the best course to follow, obviously, but also the most difficult, especially in cases of serious depression.

2) He or she becomes more irritable. He or she turns his or her anger against others: spouse, children, subordinates, friends, and even against his or her organization. (Child abuse increases as a consequence of recession.)

3) He or she seeks to escape his or her feelings of futility and find solace in religion, counsel, or good works. If these avenues fail to bring relief, he or she may flee to alcohol and drugs. Some people flee by "copping out" or withdrawing in some fashion, others by engaging in a frenzy of social activity or by plunging into work.

4) He or she tries to control or deny his or her feelings on the assumption that ultimately they will somehow go away or that he or she can overcome his or her problems.

5) He or she atones for his or her supposed failures or sins. He or she can punish himself or herself by having accidents or by making "stupid mistakes" in which he or she sets himself or herself back. If driven to extremes, he or she can kill himself [or himself].

A person's greatest asset, the wish to succeed, can become his or her point of greatest vulnerability if a significant loss or defeat triggers a torrent of self-criticism. As a matter of self-preservation, each of us must try to temper the irrationality of that torment while at the same time capitalizing on its motivational power – the push to reach high goals. Awareness of these factors will help us remain alert to the danger to ourselves and to others. Executives, whose self-images are always at risk, are especially vulnerable.

CHAPTER 5

SECTION TWO

COURAGE

A Psychologist Diagnoses Merger Failures

Harvard Business Review, March-April 1970, pp. 139-147
Unrecognized motives of fear and obsolescence *lead* to *impulsive
actions which magnify the very problems partnerships should resolve*

Foreword

There are many rational economic and personal reasons for merger. But there arc often more subtle psychological reasons, some of which constitute the basis for numerous disappointments and failures. In this article, the author examines the motivations, assumptions, and relationships that arise out of fear or out of obsolescence. He also suggests four ways to avoid such psychological dangers and handle future transactions with greater understanding and success.

Caught up in all the hoopla and glamour which have characterized the great merger spree in recent years, business executives have been preoccupied with the strategies, tactics, and techniques of acquiring, merging, and selling -- yet, frequently the really crucial factor, people, has been superficially dealt with. Nowhere is this shallowness more evident than in those mergers that have been outright mistakes with destructive consequences for both parties. Such failures have usually been attributed to rational, technical problems.

However, I contend that the unrecognized psychological problems, often heavily weighted by fear and obsolescence, are the real culprits and lead to attitudes that are expressed in words like thesc:

"We're smarter and better than they are. After all, we're buying them."

"We've got to control them. They need our managerial know-how."

"They're out to get all they can from us. They want to be free to do things their own way, but they don't want to be responsible for the results."

Such condescending attitudes on the part of the senior organization lead to efforts at manipulation and control that, in turn, produce disillusionment, disappointment, and a feeling of desertion in the junior partner. Loss of morale, personnel, and profits soon follows. This is not to say that all mergers which fail do so for these psychological reasons. Obviously, in some cases sheer incompatibility or the unwillingness of the junior partner to cooperate is more than a rationalization.

In this article, I shall examine some of the psychological shoals and suggest ways of avoiding them. Since the trend toward mergers is not likely to abate in the near future, it will become increasingly important to carefully consider how mergers might be handled with greater mutual satisfaction and success.

First, however, let me acknowledge that many mergers have been mutually advantageous to both parties. Thus my focus here -- from the perspective of the dominant partner -- is on the many others that have been mutually disappointing.[1]

Psychological Shoals

Any discussion of the failures of mergers rightfully begins with the question: Why merge? There are, of course, many important reasons for merging. For example, there are valid economic considerations: to acquire access to more capital, better professional management, or greater product and technical sophistication; to meet competition more effectively; to acquire new products or round out an existing product line; to acquire innovative capacity or tax benefits; to foster growth; and so on.

In addition, there are many personal reasons for merging: to realize capital gains or protect an estate; to assure the continuity of an organization; to demonstrate one's managerial or financial competence,

---

[1] See, for example, Frederick Wright Searby, "Control Postmerger Change," HBR September-October 1969, p. 4.

or both; to become the chief executive officer of a larger organization; and so forth.

Unrecognized Motives

Between the lines of these rational reasons for acquisitions, often there are two more subtle reasons which are rarely discussed in these terms: *fear* and *obsolescence.* These unrecognized feelings constitute psychological traps because they lead to impulsive actions which compound the very problems that a merger is intended to resolve.

Fear: One pressing wish to merge derives from the feeling that unless the company grows, larger companies will destroy it. Following this logic, destruction is to be avoided only by becoming more powerful. And the fastest way to become more powerful is to buy others.

This sets in motion a process of accretion, and I use the word advisedly, for the process is psychologically similar to that of a man who seeks to become bigger by becoming fatter. Such a man eats too much because unconsciously he is afraid of being so little. There is much folk wisdom to the saying that beneath the bulk of the fat man is hidden a tiny one. While the fat man may be physically large to begin with, he perceives himself to be small for many unconscious reasons and acts accordingly.

So it is with organizations. The initial size of the company may make little difference in this feeling on the part of those in the positions of leadership. The important point is that they feel threatened.

But one of the problems with getting bigger by accretion, whether it happens to an individual or an organization, is loss of flexibility and additional burdens on the internal systems. More than one organization has found itself bigger, with more managerial problems, and with few -- if indeed any -- long-term gains to show in, say, earnings per share or innovation.

Obsolescence: As organizations age, they develop bureaucracies and become more rigidly systematic in the way they define jobs, delineate objectives, and narrow task focus and responsibility. The more rigidly the system functions as a system -- that is, the better the way in which matters are measured, counted, and controlled -- the less room there is for individual initiative and spontaneity. In fact, the purpose of bureaucratizing the system is to reduce individual variation and to foster known, standard modes of action.

Inevitably, organizations, like aging people, become more stereotyped in their ways, less adaptable to changing conditions, and less flexible in their efforts to cope with their environments. In a word, they become obsolescent. The executives, too, become obsolescent. One way of obtaining enterprising new blood, they decide, is to buy an enterprising organization.

All well and good, but behind these two -- fear and obsolescence -- there are frequently underlying unconscious attitudes which are the actual destructive forces. When one is fearful, his first unconscious step in fighting fear is to deny his fear and tighten up. The word "uptight" aptly characterizes this feeling. When one becomes obsolescent, he tends to adopt a defensive attitude of superiority and to reintensify his customary efforts. The fact that he is the dominant party, together with his denial of fear and his air of superiority, leads to the kinds of condescending attitudes we noted earlier.

Controlling Behavior

Condescending attitudes lead to behavior which implements them. The attitudes of top management are taken for gospel by staff people, who concretize them in the form of practice. Thus the pivotal issue becomes one of controls. The dominant organization must, they argue, have the same processes and procedures in all of its components. The newly merged junior organization must serve the system. Ergo, no sooner bought than controlled.

As the dominant organization imposes control systems from its established bureaucracy, it stifles in the junior the very quality it sought to obtain and becomes even more obsolete. The very words "control" and "controller" specify the problem. They assume by definition that someone must police, ride herd, and keep people in some kind of box.

Some managements from the very beginning intend to impose controls and to make arbitrary changes in keeping with their own ways of doing business. However, they never convey such thinking to a prospective merger partner because they know the prospect would hardly be likely to merge under those circumstances. Thus they begin by wooing the prospect, promising him they will change nothing. When the merger is sealed, the original intentions are acted on, and the new partner feels he has been" conned." The underlying contempt of the senior partner for the junior one becomes magnified; the junior now feels he has let himself be taken in.

Perpetuation Problem

Fundamentally, the problem to be dealt with in a merger is the same task every organization always has -- namely, to build in perpetuation. This means that from the beginning of the relationship one must create conditions conducive to perpetuation, and develop the capacity in people to assume responsibility.[2] If perpetuation is the basic focus, then control systems and modes of management must foster that intent.

However, if the basic focus is "How do I control the new organization?" then the control devices become the overriding concern. The method is rational; its purpose, fine; and its outcome, efficient control. Therefore, it *should* work. Only when it does not do people begin to ask questions, and then they usually project solutions which fail to fit the problem: higher salaries, profit sharing, competition, and so forth.

I have no brief against controls or controllers per se, but every form of control, like every other managerial process, is based on some implicit conception of motivation. A control system based on policing assumes people must be whipped into shape and kept there by someone else. It conveys to the people who are controlled that they are regarded as inadequate and incompetent, and are therefore not to be trusted.

Contrast this with a conception of accounting data as feedback on performance by which the people can control their own behavior. The person (or department) that furnishes such information might better be called a "facilitator"; and the service stance that goes with it, "facilitating" -- provided that is what he really does.

'Family' Integration

From a psychological point of view, the phenomenon of merger is similar to forming a new family. From the dominant organization's

---

[2] See my book, *The Exceptional Executive* (Cambridge, Harvard University Press, 1968).

point of view, it is much like adopting a foster child. From the other point of view, it is akin to getting a new stepfather.

If the parent is concerned with how to make his child good, he will concentrate on goodness at the expense of the child's development. If he is concerned with rearing the most mature, most capable, most flexible child, then he must be concerned with facilitation of growth, not with control.

This is not to say that controls are bad. To be sure, all children need to be controlled and to learn self-control. Rather, it is to say that when control is the purpose, the whole point is missed. The result is a blob of human clay instead of a living being. Clay may respond to someone else's manipulation; it has no growth potential.

Furthermore, the stepfather who assumes he is going to have to beat the child into shape is in for a running battle. The child will feel deserted and betrayed by the stepfather who promised him affectionate esteem. He will fight if he can, withdraw in anger if he cannot, and leave the family at the first opportunity. So it is with merged managements and even line executives. Suddenly, the dominant management finds itself bereft of the very innovative men it thought it had acquired.

In many mergers, therefore, one finds organizations left with the hollow shells of their name and structure, and with the necessity of bringing in a completely new management group. However, the kinds of managers brought in as replacements will tend to be more bureaucratic or "take charge" types. They are unlikely to be people who have started organizations themselves or who have established records of imaginative innovation.

If those in the merged, junior company were previously in an innovative organization either because they could not work under more bureaucratic controls in the first place or because such controls inhibited their creativity, they will now feel that someone is always looking over their shoulders, or that they have become puppets. Even if they remain, they will no longer trust the organization or its leadership. They will spend the rest of their careers going through the motions. Some, with their backs up, will have to be fired or retired early, while others will have to be placed on some innocuous managerial shelf.

I have observed organizations, even as long as 20 years after a merger, in which there was still residual anger at being taken over. Some employees who had been members of the acquired company were still idealizing the old company and comparing the "new" unfavorably with their former circumstances. In their view, everything had been so much better before.

A Case Illustration

Here is a typical example of an outcome which was not what the dominant management intended. It illustrates that, however rationalized, control focus on the part of the parent organization is essentially self-defeating:

A small scientific organization, which had operated with relative success in its own naive way because its scientists and technicians were free to be innovative, was acquired by a larger company. The major stockholders of the small organization wanted to realize capital gains and long-term appreciation. The purchasing corporation wanted to diversify.

Following the merger, the dominant management discovered that the junior's financial picture was not as good as it had thought. The immediate response to this discovery was quick imposition of controls by a new take-charge president who had demonstrated previous success in salvaging losing situations. He imposed all of the usual textbook methods and standards on his new organization, and he promptly began to lose its key people.

Fortunately in this case, he was quick to call for help. Then, to work the situation through, he shifted from trying to control the new people to facing them with the realities of what the organization was up against.

Knowing what they faced and being responsible people, they dug in and brought the company back into the black. The realities of their financial circumstances were control enough; they did not need a whip.

What about the parent organization's leaders in such a situation? They had the fantasy that *everything* would go up -- sales, rate of return, profits. They fully expected that the people in the smaller organization would love them for being merged into their larger, more protective nest with its greater advancement opportunities. They were disillusioned, angry, and frustrated when the opposite occurred. After all, they were not ogres -- or were they? If not, then why did people desert them when they were only trying to do what was right to save the smaller organization from its own follies?[3]

Manipulation of Personnel

Although there have always been mergers (the usual practice has been simply to incorporate one company within the other) where little thought was given to the consequences, this is no longer advisable. When organizations merged, say, 25 or 30 years ago, people stayed, even if they did not like the new parent company. Furthermore, most jobs were routine and promised to remain that way, even at the middle- and upper-management levels.

Today, the traditional, heavily dependent employee-management relationship based on loyalty and long service is outmoded. Competence alone now counts. If there is competence in the junior organization, no management can afford to squeeze it out by doing what it did years ago. If it does, it denies people's expectations about gaining greater opportunity out of the merger, in terms of their growth and development, their responsibility, and their advancement.

What one needs, in contrast to the stability of a pre-World War II organization, is one characterized by flexibility and adaptability. This requires adaptive, innovative people, and a context in which they can solve problems.

'Identification Crisis'

There is an additional factor to be dealt with, which I shall call the "identification crisis." In earlier years, people were less likely to feel it was their organization. It was clearly the boss's organization, and they were seen by him all too often as chattels. In more recent times, managements have gone to great lengths to integrate people as members of the corporate family, to encourage them to identify themselves with the organization, and to see it as their own.

Even when people felt that the organization belonged to the boss, they had some feeling of obligation to him. Later, that obligation was reinforced by paternalism. Now, with dispersed ownership, there is

---

[3] See Richard E. Davis, "Compatibility in Corporate Marriages," HBR July-August 1968, p. 86.

less likely to be a feeling of obligation and loyalty, and merger undermines that even more. In fact, the stronger the identification, the greater the possibility of the feeling of being deserted when merger takes place.

One response to this is mobility. People begin to look for the best "other pastures" break. Newspaper articles are already beginning to report "floating middle management," and too many good executives are spontaneously retiring early to the dismay of their superiors. There are two problems with this:

With the decreasing age of company presidents, the potential for mobility declines earlier, so organizations tend to retain people who cannot move but who also have no enthusiasm. This means many hit a plateau. It also means much disillusionment in the very people who should be making contributions. When people do move, largely because they feel hemmed in or without challenge, they are saying, at the most elementary level, "The organization doesn't love me. It doesn't use my talents. It uses me as an expendable device."

There is need for continuous reorganization and regrouping to maintain flexibility to cope more easily with new problems. Regrouping is harder when people basically cannot trust the organization. No matter what work groups people find themselves in, the basic identification must be with the organization, or there is no organization.

Vicious Circle

When managements do not see their own tacit con game assumptions -- the product of their trying to "sell" the other party, and their own fears -- they are left to suffer the consequences without beginning to understand why they occurred. Manipulation as a technique suffers from the fact that it always carries the seeds of its own destruction.

For some organizations, this process has now reached frightening proportions. They buy others, impose controls, lose key managers, put in a new leadership group, lose innovative capacity, and then go out to buy more to make up for the new burdens. This vicious circle hinges on an underlying fallacy: controls produce profits. Controls are necessary for guidance. When they become the major method of staying profitable, they eventually become self-defeating.

Profitability and survivability derive in the last analysis from adaptation to the marketplace. The greater the attention management directs inwardly on the organization, the less attention it gives to the outside world. People become preoccupied with contemplating their own navels. They are taught to beat themselves, to go on economic diets.

To be sure, contemplation and control are highly important, but such self-preoccupation is more characteristic of monks than merchants. Self-flagellation is no substitute for innovative imagination and aggressive pursuit of those dreams. By the time all the internal squeezing is done, whatever the temporary contribution to profits, skill in coping with the outside is lost. To make matters worse, people feel driven. Morale declines. People have the feeling no one cares and that they are working only for the dollar. Ultimate financial objectives are seriously threatened.

Some organizations can get away with the manipulation process for a long time -- squeezing cash reserves, manipulating accounting methods, selling off less profitable units, and so on. Large organizations with assured resources -- like banks, insurance companies, and public utilities -- can continue for many years unaware of their losses. But even the largest manufacturing organizations are now having difficulty, as repeated complaints about quality control testify, and the largest financial institutions are having difficulty getting young people; in addition, they have already been outflanked by newer types of financial organizations.

Reality Gap

Fundamentally, the problem is: What does the senior president want? If he wants to evolve a more adaptive organization, he can't get there by the usual means executives have been following. If he merely wants to be a big man and is not concerned about the price, then he is like the man who does not care about his family so long as he gets the income.

How does such a problem come about? Why is there such a gap between the "real" and the psychological? Why is it so difficult to reconcile the two?

The business executive is fundamentally a rationalist. He is heavily trained in business method and economic logic. He is largely unaware of the fact that with every technique or process he uses -- whether or not it is rational in its own right -- he is making an assumption about motivation. The problem is that his assumptions often do not fit people's actual motivations and feelings.

While it is true *theoretically* that the shortest mathematical distance between two points is a straight line, it is equally true *practically* that while the shortest distance, in terms of time, between two points may be a superhighway, one may have to make many circles to get on it. When it comes to matters psychological, all too often the executive is unwilling to make the necessary circles. He thinks he is more practical and direct when he does not; but he is neither, as repetitive efforts to solve the same old problems show.

The self-defined realist equates real with palpable, material, measurable, and visible. That which is more subtle is to him "unreal" and therefore easily disregarded. But that is like trying to treat polio only with warm baths or external medication. The executive, like the physician, must evolve ways of seeing that which is not readily visible to the naked eye and of grasping its reality.

There are other reasons for the gap between the real and the psychological. Executives as a breed tend to run scared. They are continuously trying to "make it." They fear failure. In addition, they feel themselves to be under tremendous pressure for results by forces outside themselves. They feel they must respond fast and on the basis of hard facts. As a result, they have not learned to delay action long enough to think about its psychological meaning. They tend to look on such considerations as a luxury they cannot afford.

Minimizing The Impact

There are, then, two major problems to be dealt with: (a) the executive's anxieties, and (b) the meshing of two organizations into one so that the marriage yields a family and not merely an association of convenience. Obviously, there are problems in all mergers, as in all marriages. The concern is not to eliminate all problems. Rather, it is to make the choices more rational and the modes for coping with the problems more effective. Here are four suggestions that may be helpful in minimizing the negative psychological impact of mergers.

1. Introspective Assessment

Every management which is thinking of buying up another company should ask itself seriously why it is doing so. "Of course," you say, every management does that." It does -- it asks itself about everything except the psychological issues in the situation. While much thinking goes into the financial and marketing analyses and into evaluating the managerial and product potentials of the organization to be acquired, almost never does the same kind of thinking extend to introspection, particularly with respect to such issues as aspirations, fears, and wishes for power.

After determining why it really wants to emerge, every management should then ask itself if it wants to merge for the wrong reason. If it wants simply to get bigger, out of fear, is fear alone a sufficient motivation? Are there no more rational ways to deal with fear? How rational is the fear? How much of a panic psychology is it playing out? If the motivation is fear, then that underlying pressure is likely to continue, resulting in the whipping of the smaller organization and thereby destroying the very goal management wants to attain. If the motivation is to add zest to a sluggish organization, is it not more reasonable to rejuvenate the old one than to fight obsolescence by merger?

2. Projected Assumptions

Having assessed its own motivation, the prospective parent organization should next ask itself what assumptions it is making about the other party. It can infer these from its attitudes toward the other organization and what it is keeping to itself for fear that the other will refuse to merge if all of the intentions are clear. How are these assumptions likely to get management into trouble?

The prospective parent organization must take an honest look at its own control intentions and -- beneath those -- its assumptions about its projected partners (read "subordinates" instead of "partners" to understand the unconscious motivation better). If the parent management follows the strategy that it will persuade or sweet-talk the other president into merging and, then, that it will show him what *real* management is, it is laying the groundwork for its own failure. Such an attitude is often found when the junior company has behavioral flexibility such as dress and time freedoms -- which is unacceptable to the senior organization.

If the assumption could be put into words, it might go something like this: "You crazy scientists who won't come to work on time, we'll show you." Behind such a statement would be the anger of the parent company toward the others for their success in spite of being so crazy, anger about being dependent on such types, and anger over the need to prove itself better than they in order to justify its own existence.

If a management has such. feelings, it would do well to examine them critically. Why have such feelings? How justified are they? What will happen if they are sprung after the merger is made? What resentment and resistance will follow? What will be the cost of the consequences?

3. Organizational Pulse

If management is going to make an assessment of a company which looks attractive, in addition to assessing financial, marketing, and management talent, it should ask itself what the other company is all about psychologically. Why are these people here? Why are they together? What gratifications are they getting? What is their perceived image of themselves? What is their feeling about the organization of which they are a part? Management should not stop with the top executive structure. How do lower level people feel about these issues? Management will have to live with them, too. This does not necessarily mean taking an opinion survey of the whole organization or talking to each individual.

For example, in the small scientific organization I cited earlier in the case illustration, turnover at both managerial and worker levels was very low despite the fact that similar companies were paying higher salaries. This suggests that something was holding those people together; if it had held them together over a long period of time while others nearby were earning more, it constituted a psychological cement.

However, the purchaser failed to examine and take seriously the basis of that solidarity. When he failed to recognize the underlying value system and sense of common purpose, and instead, tried to institute seemingly rational managerial goals and controls, he chipped away some of the psychological cement and the whole organization began to crumble.

One can sense the pulse of an organization very easily by the spirit of its people, the way they talk to each other, what they talk about, and their attitude toward strangers. If the plant abruptly shuts down cold and tight for a coffee break -- regardless of work in process -- and if the people rush madly for the door at quitting time, these are elementary signals of how people feel about their work.

Part of the problem is that organizations try to be too rational about the things they can measure. Most of the critical elements of an organization being acquired have to do with people's feelings, and these are not so easily measured. Most executives will say, "Yes, I know feelings are important," and then promptly go about disregarding them.

4. Harmonious Atmosphere

Having assessed some of the feelings of the junior organization, what are the differences between the way *those* people feel about their organization and the tenor and tempo of the prospective parent organization? This is not to say which one is right, but only to ask, "How do they differ?" A hard-nosed, no-nonsense, high-pressure sales organization will have a difficult time assimilating one that depends heavily on service and customer consideration. This is one of the critical points at which a clash is likely to arise.

At the bargaining table, the prospective partners would do well to indicate to each other what they wish from the merger, how they see each other's organizations, how they feel about apparent differences, and how important those differences are to them. In particular, both organizations should be able to answer with psychological honesty, "What does he want me for, really?" Then the prospective partners can jointly evolve their modes of compromise and integration. Such a process also creates a mechanism for the continuing solution of problems which arise subsequently.

All organizations need devices for solving problems at critical integration points.[4] This is as true for organizations which merge as it is for divisions or units within a company. For example, the personnel department of the smaller organization, which may have had certain

---

[4] See Paul R. Lawrence and Jay W. Lorsch, *Organization and Environment.* (Boston, Division of Research, Harvard Business School, 1967.)

ways of doing things in response to its top management, now has to deal with the personnel department of the larger organization as well.

How are such issues to be resolved with mutual satisfaction? How are future issues to be confronted? The larger organization must be able to hear the anxieties and pains of the smaller. Where does it hurt as a result of this merger, or where is it likely to hurt?

Most organizations woo the other, persuade it, effect the merger, and then go about business as usual -- their way. This is often further compounded when the negotiations are first carried on between presidents, and the president of the smaller organization is assigned to report to a vice president of the larger one. Here is what happens:

The vice president, responding to the demands of his own boss for greater control, profitability, and productivity, in turn makes similar demands on the president of the smaller company. The latter now has to deal with his feelings of being deserted, in addition to whatever feelings he may have about being conned and taken over. These feelings may become more acute when whatever he wants to try innovatively is now squashed flat from someone he did not bargain for and with in the first place. His one channel, short of pounding the table or quitting, is through the man to whom he is reporting.

With these contemporary events, there is a growing general feeling that expectations in mergers are not being fulfilled. This feeling may in turn make it more difficult to consummate mergers as time goes by. Even worse, people may enter mergers as a good many enter marriages these days: "I'll take a chance, and if it doesn't work, I'll leave." That kind of a tentative commitment inevitably undermines a marriage; it will inevitably undermine a merger. It usually means that the relationship is bound by all kinds of secret clauses and reservations, as well as hidden expectations, which then continually burden both parties.

Complicating these forces is an increasing frequency of feelings of guilt on the part of presidents who sell out after having built organizations that are loyal to them. The long-term identification is exploited by the senior organization, control modes are introduced, procedures are changed arbitrarily, and the cohesive organization, with the close relationships people had with each other, now becomes just another place to work.

In such cases, people have learned an important lesson: it does not pay to be loyal, to identify, to invest themselves in an organization or its leadership. They will be sold down the river.

The old presidents are then angry with themselves for what they have done and communicate this anger to others who may be in the same position. The old presidents fight as long as they can, but ultimately quit or are eased out. They are left with residual feelings of anger, guilt, and resentment, and the depression which follows.

Of course, many presidents will disregard such experiences. They are like middle-aged maiden ladies still looking for a husband for security. They are prone to take whatever comes along, later finding the price too high to pay, and, subsequently, seeking ways out.

Thus it is important not to try to con the junior organization's managers. The senior partner may buy them, but it will also lose them. Even if the senior partner acquires the people, the products, and the plants, it will have unwilling, resentful partners who feel they have been taken. They will buck every way they can, and the senior partner will have lost their trust permanently.

The dominant management needs to be as straight and as factual as it can, and not withhold information about what it plans to do. It will only be kidding itself.

In fact, the senior partner would do well to let the junior's managers examine its own organization and talk to a wide range of people. Above all, management should never promise more than it can deliver. That is a business failing. For example, many organizations these days are promising young people creative possibilities, but most are not organized to permit such innovation. They therefore get rapid turnover and mutual disillusionment. Who needs it?

A contemporary example of this fourth suggestion being put into practice, at least according to a published account[5], was the merger of AMK and United Fruit. Eli M. Black, President and Board Chairman of AMK, it is reported, operates with the philosophy that the best way to win such a company is to win its management. After proffering the merger, Black told John M. Fox, Board Chairman of United Fruit, that he would make no further moves toward gaining control without the approval of United Fruit's management. There would be no raids, no end runs, no fights. AMK wanted only a minority position, not control, on the UF board.

The two managements met daily during the negotiating process, and Black invited the UF management to visit AMK in New York.

---

[5] Chris Welles, "The Battle for United Fruit," *Investment Banking and Corporate Financing,* Spring 1969, p. 27.

Black's whole concern was to create an atmosphere of harmony and rapport. In that he succeeded, for, according to Fox, "Black never went back or changed a single thing he had promised us. He never acted without consulting us. He lived up to his word."

Conclusion

There are many reasons for merger, including psychological reasons. Many mergers have been disappointing in their results and painful to their participants. These failures have been attributed largely to rational financial, economic, and managerial problems.

I contend that some psychological reasons for merger not only constitute a major, if unrecognized, force toward merger, but that they also constitute the basis for many, if not most, disappointments and failures. At least those that have turned sour, or have the most dangerous potential for turning sour, are those that arise out of some neurotic wish to become big by voraciously gobbling up others, or out of obsolescence.

Such mergers flounder because of the hidden assumptions the senior partner makes, and the condescending attitudes toward the junior organization which then follow. These result in efforts at manipulation and control which, in turn, produce (a) disillusionment and the feeling of desertion on the part of the junior organization, and (b) disappointment, loss of personnel, and declining profitability for the dominant organization.

To cope with these issues, I have suggested that senior executives of the dominant company should:

Probe their own motivations for merging.

Review the psychological assumptions that they have about the other party in the merger.

Assess the psychological relationships and attitudes of the people in the junior organization, and note how they may differ from those in the senior organization.

Out of open, honest discussion of these motivations, assumptions, and differences, create a harmonious atmosphere in which problem-solving mechanisms are set up so that the anguish of the junior organization can be heard and acted on, and operating modes can be evolved rather than imposed.

These suggestions depend for their validity on the recognition of the reality and power of feelings, and particularly on the fact that both the senior and the junior organization will be equal in psychological power despite vast differences in economic power. Either the senior management understands the psychological power of its partner and acts accordingly, or it stands to lose what it sought in a merger.

The importance of these considerations goes beyond corporations per se. If contemporary modes of merger result in widespread loss of initiative, increased constriction of imagination, and floating populations of executives, this has not only self-defeating implications for organizations, but also has powerful negative effects on society.

Mr. Levinson is the Thomas Henry Carroll Ford Foundation Distinguished Visiting Professor of Business Administration, Harvard Business School, and President of the Levinson Institute. His article, "On Being a Middle-Aged. Manager" [HBR July-August 1969], was a co-winner of the McKinsey Award for the best HBR article published in 1969. His most recent book, Executive Stress, has just been published by Harper & Row.

CHAPTER 6

SECTION TWO

COURAGE

Beyond The Selection Failures

*Consulting Psychology Journal, 46:1,*3-8. Winter 1994

The recent business press has been replete with stories about the failures of top executives. These failures have been attributed largely to problems in organizational cultures (Levinson, 1994). Less conspicuous in the headlines and news stories, but nevertheless equally important, are reports on the turnover of other senior and chief executives. When Christopher J. Steffen resigned as chief financial officer of Eastman Kodak Co., his departure was attributed in the press to conflict between him and Kay R. Whitmore, Kodak's chief executive officer (Cowan, 1993). When Ervin R. Shames left his role as chairman and chief executive officer of Stride Rite Corp., it was said that he wasn't "entrepreneurial enough" and didn't understand the shoe business (Biddle, 1993). Harvey Weiss' departure from Thinking Machines Corp. was attributed to his laidback style (Server, 1993).

The respective failures of individuals in their roles were costly to both the executives and their organizations. The directors of Eastman Kodak had hoped that Steffen would enable the organization to cut its costs and regain its profitability. Stride Rite reported an 11 percent drop in its fiscal third quarter (1993) net income. Similarly, Thinking Machines Corp. was fighting hard to gain profitability. In each instance, the officer who was unable to achieve the desired ends found himself in a situation that was not congenial to the maximum use of his skills and talents, as reflected in the fact that all had been successful in their previous roles. The tragedy for the individuals involved and the pain for the boards of directors who shared responsibility for the failures was predictable. Much of it could have been avoided.

To understand why such failures occur, one has to go beyond the publicly offered proximate causes (Pfeffer, 1993). Proximate "explanations" describe certain aspects of the behavior of the individual in the context of the corporation, but they do not address the question "Why?" in any depth. Several factors in the selection process offer an explanation for these failures.

Inadequacy of Search Firms

The first of these is the inadequacy of the work of search firms. In my limited contact with them, my impression is that they think they do a careful job of fitting prospective candidates to the job requirements and culture of their organizational clients. They interview the senior officials of the firms that retain them and have available various forms of financial reports and other data. Although some headhunters may have long experience and great intuitive skills, they are not psychologists. They are unable to delve deeply into the subtleties of the thinking, feeling, and behavior of a candidate and the significance of that behavior for the candidate's ultimate success or failure in a given organization. Often however, they think they do. In at least three instances when I suggested evaluation of candidates and diagnosis of the fit of the candidates to their prospective roles, the headhunters told me that is what they do. They themselves usually do not recommend psychological evaluation to their clients, nor do they seek a comprehensive diagnosis of the organization.(Levinson, Spohn, & Molinari, 1972).

In one instance, when I was asked by the top management of an international organization to assess four candidates that a search firm was presenting to head the American operations, I reported negatively on all four. One was naively narcissistic. Another, who professed democratic management, was actually an autocrat. A third was too immature to handle the complexity of the role. The fourth was so intimidating that he had no business running anybody's company. Fortunately, management did not rely on the headhunters for screening and judgment of fit.

I do not mean to condemn search firms. As in all other professional activities, some are more proficient than others. But I do mean to point out that they are not psychological diagnosticians and organizations run great risk if they stop in their selection process with the recommendations of headhunters and interviews by their own management.

Limits of Psychological Methods

A second reason why selection processes fail lies in the limits of the psychological methods used. (These are not necessarily used by psychologists.) There are always three elements in a selection process: 1) the psychology of the individual, including the capacity to handle complexity both now and in the future, how much he values the work he will be doing, and the degree to which he is likely to commit himself to the prospective employer; 2) the kind of person who is going to supervise or manage the candidate, and his boss, the manager-once-removed; 3) the nature of the organization in which he or she is going to work. I don't know many psychologists who take all three seriously into account.

Assessment centers, for example, have become widely popular for selecting candidates through middle management levels. In some cases, variants of them have been extended to selecting higher level executives. While assessment centers provide a picture of a person's behavior in the context of the assessment process, that integrated view is necessarily cross-sectional, that person at that point in time in that context. Usually, the assessment is not juxtaposed with an organizational diagnosis that details the multiple aspects of the organizational context in which the candidate is going to work, nor the size and complexity of the prospective role, nor what kinds of changes could occur in a candidate's behavior with appropriate supervision or management under conditions that would maximize the usefulness of what otherwise might seem to be a personality deficit.

I think of one man whom I was ready to reject because of his apparent immaturity, subservience, and annoying repetition of verbal phrases. The glimmer of creativity that sparkled dimly through the negative aspects of his personality, together with his experience, was enough to make him worthy of a try. His prospective manager saw it, too, and was willing to work with him. Now, five years later, he has established himself as a highly valued support of his chief executive.

Similarly, an entry-level candidate was rejected for a prospective managerial role because recruiters didn't recognize the clues to his potential. A late bloomer, he blossomed in an independent entrepreneurial role, as a result of which he was then sought out by the same corporation in which he is doing well.

Still a third candidate, fresh out of college and not yet fully hatched from that academic cocoon with its casual, laid back climate, appeared for an interview with unmatched socks and heavy shoes. Fortunately for him and a manager 'who, supported by psychological findings, was willing to invest in him, he gave a good account of himself as he grew into mature adulthood.

These are examples of late bloomers, a feature I don't see often in psychological test reports. Even some that might seem unlikely candidates because of their pathology might serve highly necessary functions. For example, a somewhat suspicious, hostile person might be exactly the kind of candidate one would want to employ as an auditor for IRS surveillance of its own staff or the manager of food service inspectors in New York City.

The same issues apply to most paper-and-pencil psychological testing. The view is also cross-sectional. There is little or no diagnosis of the organization and much of the time no assessment of the person to whom the candidate is likely to report, unless a psychologist has a long-term relationship with a client organization that enables him or her to know the organization's culture and its managers, let alone the manager-once-removed (Ideally, the manager-once-removed should be the person who determines to what role a person should be promoted or assigned for developmental purposes.)

Many of the test reports are canned printouts of ready-made interpretations. Often managers abdicate their responsibility in selection to the tester rather than use the test results as only one form of data. Much, if not most, of the time in testing for selection there is no adequate counseling process after testing so that the individual knows thoroughly what the test results mean for his or her in this likely role in this particular organization.

And sometimes the interpretations are clearly naive. In one instance, for example, a newspaper reporter was tested by a psychological testing firm. The psychologist's report concluded that she was in the wrong role because she didn't socialize readily, was somewhat distant from others, and even somewhat suspicious of them. Obviously, it seemed, she couldn't do well establishing and maintaining contacts. She pointed out in rebuttal that it was exactly the qualities that were being judged negatively that made her successful. That she didn't socialize readily kept her from becoming overly familiar with the people she was writing about that might impair her objectivity. That she was somewhat distant and suspicious enabled her to dig for information rather than accept press releases and being manipulated in self-serving interviews. The psychologist apparently did not appreciate the nature of newspaper reporting or the subtle nuances of the role.

Of course, one can find many instances of error or bad practice in any professional activity. It is not my intention to pick nits, but only to illustrate problems that psychologists involved in selection should be dealing with.

A difficult problem is the fact that the higher in an organization the prospective role, the less valid are the criteria to which one is predicting. Norms for managers in general do not differentiate performance requirements in IBM from those in Sears Roebuck from those on the Santa Fe Railroad. Sometimes a psychologist with long experience in an organization will develop norms for managers in that organization. The definition of a manager will vary widely from a high-tech company involved in biological research, to one supervising a yarn plant in North Carolina. And when it comes to predicting candidates for top management roles, to my knowledge there are no norms for the top executives of major corporations.

Furthermore, correlations between individual paper-and-pencil psychological tests and the managerial criteria to which they are predicting are notoriously inadequate. A correlation of .40 leaves 84 percent of the variance unaccounted for; batteries of tests, given the criterion problems, usually do not account for much more.

Even where there is a well-established psychological testing program in a given corporation whose criteria and norms have been developed carefully by competent psychologists, there are critical features of a person's career path that usually cannot be predicted from paper-and-pencil tests.

For example, a highly regarded psychologist who had devoted years to a well-respected internal selection program was troubled because of the unpredictable failures that resulted from self-destructive behavior after managers attained certain levels of success. To make judgments about such issues requires careful clinical interviews based on the sophisticated understanding of unconscious motivation. Even then, the accuracy of the prediction would depend significantly on the clinical competence of the psychologist, in addition to understanding the role requirements over a period of time and the degree of observation and supervision to which a given person will be subjected.

Paper-and-pencil tests purport to describe an individual at the time of testing. Although one can argue that with high test-retest reliability, the results likely will be the same at a later date, and there is a certain consistency to characterological behavior, test interpretations usually do not attempt to predict the trajectory of a person's career.

It is not enough to predict cross-sectionally. People who are highly successful in a given role may well become inadequate when promoted or assigned to another. They may not value the work or the role may be too complex or require skills they had not used before. Some who are highly effective will become bored as soon as they have mastered present challenges. Some will continue to progress up the executive ladder, while others will remain on a plateau. Ideally, we should be able to predict when a person will need a new challenge and of what kind. A client, whether an organization or an individual, usually would like to have such information. What is a person's potential and where can he or she go in the organization? Little in the literature, except the work of Elliott Jaques (1976, 1989, 1990, 1991,1994), helps with this task.

Jaques has posited eight levels of conceptual capacity or mental processing, each bounded by the longest time forward an individual can carry out the complexities of a role. These time boundaries are three months, one year, two years, five years, 10 years, 20 years and 50 years, and the unbounded mental capacities of the Einsteins of this world.

He has also delineated a range of career trajectories through which individuals mature conceptually as they age. An individual's trajectory will vary depending on native endowment, education, skill, training, opportunity, and development. The trajectory can be predicted by a method called Career Path Appreciation (Stamp, 1988), together with an extended interview.

Jaques' work (1994) reports four levels of mental processing: declarative, serial, cumulative, and parallel. These occur at two levels of sophistication and are reflected in an individual's responses when he or she is asked to explain his reasoning for his position on a controversial social issue, like abortion, or to discuss something that is personally important to him. With these conceptualizations, psychologists will be able to predict career trajectories.

For some decades there has been significant literature on adult development, particularly for men (Erikson, 1950; Levinson, et al, 1978). It is continuing to grow (Nemeroff & Colarusso, 1990). The literature that describes the stages in adult life reflects shifts in values with age, and shifts in assertiveness, men tending to become more passive and women tending to become more aggressive (Gutman, 1987). Little of this seems to be considered in psychological test reports for selection.

What Else Do We Need?

To turn from the general to the more specific, namely individual potentially pathological behavior, there are other fundamental subtleties about which we should be making predictions. Chief among these is what is likely to happen to certain behaviors with time, in addition to those changes in the management of aggression just described.

For example, although successful managers and executives need a certain amount of narcissism in order to have self-confidence, as they are promoted, some risk becoming increasingly narcissistic as supervision and control decreases. Their subsequent grandiosity then can be costly if not destructive to the organization. Such negative narcissism is often reflected in the extreme in the aggressive pursuit of perquisites, luxury retreats, expansive acquisitions, and fleets of aircraft. Under less extreme circumstances, there is nevertheless a high cost: the greater the attention one lavishes upon oneself, the less one is likely to attend to developing subordinates and the greater the likelihood that performance appraisals will be distorted. Such people exploit the organization and their subordinates to meet their own pathological needs.

A similar problem arises with abrasiveness. Under reasonably tight control, many abrasive people can function effectively, particularly in individual contributor roles. Indeed, some are highly regarded for their expert knowledge and therefore promoted into managerial roles. When they are assigned to managerial roles, and especially if they are less well controlled by their managers in those roles, then, in the extreme, they risk becoming like one of *Fortune's* ten toughest (most over controlling) bosses (Dumaine, 1993). They abuse others, condescend to them, and are unable to develop them, except sometimes in their own image. Ultimately, in many cases, with great pain, managements are forced to terminate talented managers whose behavior undermines their managerial effectiveness. Earlier predictions by psychologists that also defined the likely need for specified kinds of supervision often might help managements save and utilize such people.

I am not referring here to that obvious hostility and abrasiveness that becomes apparent in the answers to many personality questionnaires. Rather, I am calling attention to that specific potential behavior that may well occur under circumstances of increased power and higher position with less managerial control. Intensity of competition in business organizations means that more people will be self-driven. One has only to consider the difference between the relaxed old-school tie nature of financial executives a generation ago, as contrasted with the intensity of such managers and executives in similar positions today. The latter are heavily conscience-driven, or, in psychoanalytic terms, they have powerful highly self-critical superegos. In turn, that harsh self-criticism makes them vulnerable to depression as a consequence of disappointment. In the extreme, people who cannot differentiate disappointment from defeat and are inordinately self-critical, commit suicide.

It was exactly that phenomenon, exacerbated by public criticism that occurred with an outstanding member of the Clinton administration.

In addition to predicting later trajectories and discerning subtleties, we need to understand the adaptive mode of an individual. Under what circumstances will a reasonably relaxed person become "uptight?" What will happen if a given executive loses a spouse through death or divorce upon whom he or she has become dependent (Bird, et al, 1983)? Some highly successful, publicly prominent, extroverted leaders collapse when they no longer have that support. I know of no test batteries without projective tests that get at that level of functioning.

Under some conditions, managers and executives may well regress to more primitive forms of behavior (Kemberg, 1979). What can be predicted about a given candidate?

While there is widespread understanding of the need to ascertain a candidate's values, which and under what conditions become more rigid, reflecting specific environmental and personal pressures? What effect might that rigidity have on managing diversity, handling problems flexibly, or maintaining organizational integrity in the face of threatening competition?

Which candidates have the capacity to create identification with themselves as generative leaders, as contrasted with fostering identification with the aggressor as was the case with Harold Geneen (1984)? *Fortune's* Toughest bosses may make an organization succeed on the basis of their tight driving control, but, like Geneen, they do not build in and strengthen succession.

In the context of contemporary managerial conceptions that become pressures on managers and executives to abnegate their taking charge, many who want to be viewed as modern and competent become uncomfortable to take charge. Yet, good managers must handle aggression flexibly, now to take tight control, now to be more relaxed. When Walter Wriston was chief executive of Citicorp, he allowed his staff a great deal of flexibility. However, when the New York City financial crisis arose, he moved in and took active charge (Levinson & Rosenthal, 1983). That seems to be difficult for some other prominent executives. According to the media, one of the reasons that Kay R. Whitmore was forced out of Eastman Kodak was that he could not cut Kodak's cost drastically enough to meet the financial demands of his board. The same criticism continues to be made of successive CEOs at General Motors (Kerwin, 1993).

Self-Understanding

A fundamental conception that will become increasingly important is the degree to which a candidate understands himself or herself. Now that managers and executives are likely to have a range of roles during a career, to what tasks and at which times in one's career does he or she fit a given role?

John Sculley recently yielded the CEO role at Apple Computer Corp. (Deutschman, 1993) ostensibly because he had exhausted the contribution he could make as a marketing expert and recognized the need for a technical expert now to head Apple. Besides, he wanted the challenge of building an organization of his own (Rebello, 1993). Ideal candidates should understand themselves well enough so as not to exhaust their welcome and thereby do their companies, as well as themselves, an injustice. They must understand their evolving ego ideals (Chasseguet-Smirgel, 1985), the likely shift to more nurturing and passive roles as they age (Gutman, 1987), and the need for them to mentor and to develop others.

In addition, each at some point will have to give up his particular role. When Reginald Jones was CEO of General Electric, he saw as his major task to turn over to his successor a better organization than he himself inherited (Levinson & Rosenthal, 1983). That task is required of many chief executives. However, not all retire as easily as Jones who did so at the age of 62, in part because he knew his organization required a different style of leadership in a more intensely competitive environment, which is exactly what his successor, John F. Welch brought (Tichy & Shennan, 1993). It is important for a person in such a role not only to recognize his own limits and the need for a different kind of successor, but also to be able to foster and support that strikingly different kind of successor behavior. He also must be able to let go as Geneen, for example, could not. Letting go so often hinges on what to go to, what unfolding trajectory does a person evolve for himself in this sense?

Finally, what kind of support does this candidate have and what does he or she require? Beyond the issue of dependence on spouse, what about relationships with mentors, confidants, friends, and significant relatives? Who does the candidate lean on? (And I would worry if there were no one.) How often and with what intensity does he or she sustain that relationship, and what is likely to happen if the he or she loses it?

All of these considerations and the limits of testing point to the importance of a comprehensive psychological interview to complement the testing process. No "objective" data can replace the insights and skills of the psychologist, nor can those data replace the quality of the interaction between client and psychologist, which often reveals critical issues of greater subtleties than can be discerned by mechanical responses to fixed questions.

Conclusion

In sum, effective selection requires a comprehensive diagnosis of the organization, including the size and complexity of the prospective role; a careful assessment of the individual taking into account the subtleties of personality, stage in adult development and capacity for managing complexity now and in the future; and an assessment of the manager to whom that candidate is going to report and the manager-once-removed. Only then can a psychologist adequately evaluate the degree of fit between the candidate and the role for which he or she is being considered. In particular, careful assessment requires judgment about conceptual capacity and its trajectory over time with consideration of when a person will mature into and outgrow a given role, what challenges he or she may then need in the context of his or her stage of adult development, and the degree to which a person can detach himself or herself from his or her role to undertake a new career and the post retirement phase of his or her life.

CHAPTER 7

SECTION TWO

COURAGE

Who is to Blame for Maladaptive Managers?

Harvard Business Review, Nov. – Dec., 1965, 143-158

By the time a person enters management; many executives believe it is too late to change his or her "character." To a great extent this belief is true; the experiences of childhood and adolescence are indeed crucial. Many of the troublesome attitudes and actions of managers that are typically blames on "character," however, can be traced to management itself. In other words, although "character" is relatively enduring, many of management's "people problems" are partly products of its own making. Again and again, in my observation of organization, I find that the undesirable behavior of subordinates is precipitated or aggravated by the unintentional actions of their superiors. Such a statement is not news to subordinates; to them it is by now a cliché, but it is often disdained by their bosses as sheer rationalization.

In one sense, this observation is a discouraging commentary on the practice of management today. In another sense, it is a reason to be encouraged. For, to the extent that "people problems" are created by management, it has the immediate power to solve them by changing its approach. It does not have to defer the solution until long-range training programs and education have had a chance to work.

In this chapter I shall discuss six common management actions that lead to troublesome or problematic behavior among subordinates, and suggest supplemental or alternative actions which might be taken to avoid the difficulty. This analysis is based on my review of hundreds of cases presented by managers and executives in seminars that I have conducted.

Each of these cases was submitted in written form, in advance of a week-long seminar, by an executive or manager participating in the seminar, for purposes of discussion in a small seven-person group. The participant was instructed that his or her case should be about a problem between people, preferably one in which he or she was one of the parties, and one that had been particularly troublesome. He or she was asked to describe in the case the circumstances of the problem and the nature of the discussions between himself or herself and the other person. He or she was free to write the case in any way he or she chose, disguising it sufficiently so that it was not identifiable. In the small group discussions he or she did not have to identify his or her case unless he or she wished to do so, although in such a small group, it was often apparent which case belongs to which participant. I reviewed each of these cases and, on the basis of the most prominent aspect of behavior described, assigned it to one of five categories:

Non-management Problems: Of the total submitted, about 10% did not constitute individual problems; another 10% more were not problems of executives (middle management and above, but not first-level supervisors). These cases have not been used in this chapter.

Mental Illness: This category includes about 5% of the cases in which psychiatric illness had already been diagnosed or in which the symptoms as described by the presenter were so severe that they were clearly indicative of illness. In about 2% of these cases, the subjects were manipulative to the point of dishonesty, exploiting customers as well as subordinates, colleagues, and superiors, and clinically would be called pathological character disorders. These cases too, are excluded.

Hostility: This is the most conspicuous symptom or underlying feeling in about 48% of the cases. Of these cases, about 11% cover a wide range of hostile behavior; the other 89% of this group of cases fall into four subgroups: (a) the authoritarian ones, (b) the angry ones, (c) the self-centered ones, and (d) the wounded ones.

Limited personalities: This group includes 16% of cases classified into four subgroups: (a) the anxious ones, (b) the rigid ones, (c) the dependent ones, and (d) the impulsive ones.

Misplacement: In this group are about 17% who had either been placed in the wrong job (the hapless ones) or who had been outgrown by the job (the helpless ones).

The categories were derived from an inspection of the cases; they had not been previously established. They reflect my interpretation of the behavior of the person described in the case. The categories, therefore, are based on the problem as the presenter saw it on the data as he or she perceived and reported them, though not necessarily as he or she interpreted his or her own data. They are not diagnostic categories in the clinical sense. Nor are they mutually exclusive, for they have been evolved from that aspect of the individual's behavior that I understood from the case description to be the most salient.

These cases, then, are reports by senior executives of problems they have had with subordinate executives. The acute or painful aspect of the problem as presented is the behavior of the subordinate executive. But as the discussion elaborates, it turns out that the senior executive also has apart in each of these problems. His or her part results from lack of self-scrutiny, indifference, inadequate understanding, or some other nonfunctional behavior. This is not to say that the senior executive or the organization "caused" the problem. There are always multiple causes for all behavior. Yet in each one of these groups of cases, senior executives have made certain repetitive managerial errors that related specifically to the kind of behavior that the subordinate displays. This correlation between managerial error and subordinate behavior enables us to focus on the former as a means of pointing toward more proficient managerial practice.

Unable to coach and develop subordinates; they concentrate decision making in their own hands while driving their subordinates unnecessarily hard. In short, they are authoritarian. Their individual achievements have led to promotion, and the aura of their record has obscured for a considerable time the fact that they are now destroying or failing to build some part of the organization.

These are the very sort of managers of whom it is frequently said that they could be outstandingly successful if only they could "work with people." Since they cannot, they will either have to leave their organizations or be doomed to the continued frustration of their ambitions. Whether they cannot work well with others because of the kind of people they are, or because of organizational pressures to produce, is not always clear from the cases. It is clear, however, threat both factors usually are involved.

Top management has several options with such managers in those cases were it is not already too late. If management is primarily concerned with building an organization and with making it possible for managers to grow into larger organizational responsibilities, then, contrary to popular conceptions, it must provide for close supervision of them. Such supervision must be pointed to helping support subordinates and to rewarding team, rather than individual, productivity. True, some of the "jets" may not be able to work in harness no matter what is done, and may therefore have to leave; but they will do so without having developed expectations that they can succeed in the organization by hard driving alone and before management builds up unrealistic expectations about their future development.

If a situation is such that it called for heroic rescue or rebuilding efforts by a single person, both he or she and his or her superiors should recognize together the unique value of his or her talents in a particular situation and the likelihood that he or she may have to find a similar task elsewhere when this one is completed. My own observations suggest that a heroic organizing or rebuilding task takes from three to five years. After that, individual efforts which by then have resulted in an organizational structure, must give way to group effort. Rarely is it possible for people who have ranged far and wide in an organization to accept increasing circumscription of their behavior. Usually, at the end of the initial building period a whole new group of managers must be introduced whose talents lie less in their own vigorous attack and more in coordinating and supporting the problem-solving abilities of groups. This phenomenon is an old story in many different contexts, ranging from offensive and defensive platoons in football, to guerrilla units in the military and reform movements in politics. It is not yet widely recognized in organizations.

Error #2: Failure to Exercise Controls

Senior executives, according to some of our cases, often seem to condone behavior which is beyond the bounds of common courtesy. The result is devastating to those who are subject to such behavior and detrimental to the organization. The cost of tolerating this behavior is reflected particularly in that group of 7% of the cases, I call the angry ones. These are managers who reportedly spew their anger about them at colleagues, subordinates, and superiors. These are the people who are described as being unnecessarily critical, as arguing too long and too much, as being crude and rude to others, and as seeming to flail at their working environment.

Again, it is sometimes difficult to determine how much of this behavior results from what is going on in the organizational and how much from the personalities of the managers themselves. But what is clear is the fact that they have got away with their outburst, that the undesirable behavior seems to increase in intensity, that others are hurt by it, and that the angry ones themselves often feel guilty and contrite after their outbursts.

In another group of 8% of the cases, self-centeredness seems to be the most conspicuous aspect of the problem. The major form this self-centeredness takes is the exploitation of and attack on others as part of the subject's efforts to maintain or increase his or her own status. He or she differs from those who are authoritarian and directive in that he or she is more manipulative. The self-centered manager is more clearly out for his or her own self-aggrandizement and often seems not to care what he or she does to others in the process; the authoritarian executive more frequently is sympathetic to others in a paternalistic way.

The striking aspect of both the angry and the self-centered managers is the manner in which they are able to intimidate others and get away with it. Some of them have been permitted to go on in this way for years, often for the reason that the man or woman in question has some particular skill or talent that the organization needs. Even when the responsible executive knows that such behavior is destructive to the organization, to other subordinates, and to the man or woman himself or herself, he or she often permits it to go on. He or she excuses it with such words as "temperamental," or "the problem you have with creative people."

Such behavior may be a way of demonstrating power or a way of getting attention. For some people, any attention, whether criticism from superiors or loving kindness from oneself, is better than none. Anger or self-centeredness may also be an expression of increased insecurity and anxiety, particularly if job burdens are felt to be too heavy and failure threatens. Whatever the reason, as long as higher management condones the behavior or tolerates it, the problem is swept beneath the managerial rug.

What seems to happen in such cases is that the superior is taken aback by the aggressive outbursts or the chronic hostility of the subordinate. The superior may feel afraid of the subordinate's anger, being cowed by it just as lower-level employees are, and may then back away from confrontation or control for fear of precipitating even more anger. Or the hostility of the subordinate may arouse the superior's anger to the point where the superior feels guilty because of his or her angry thoughts toward the subordinate. If the superior feels inordinately guilty because of his or her own angry feelings and doubts his or her ability to control them once they are unleashed, he or she may be paralyzed into inactivity as a way of coping with his or her own feelings.

In either case, the subordinate is left free to vent his or her spleen on others. Those who are victims resent both him or her and the superiors who permit him or her to behave in this way. Working relationships with colleagues are impaired. The superior feels angry with himself or herself for not stopping the aggressive behavior; and the angry subordinate, whose behavior is really a cry for help, continues to thrash about, to his or her own detriment and that of the organization. Thus when the responsible executive does not exercise adequate control, he or she contributes to the malfunctioning of those subordinates who are unable to maintain their own controls.

The first step in the control process is to define the problem. As long as others put up with an angry one's behavior, he or she has no reason to stop it; there is no problem. He or she can easily feel that he or she must be right in his or her anger or manipulation if everyone else puts up with it, particularly if his or her own superiors tolerate it despite the complaints and turnover of lower-level personnel.

Once the superior has defined which aspects of the subordinate's behavior are unacceptable and has confronted the subordinate with a statement of the problem as he or she sees it, then the two need to look at their own relationship. There may be features of the superior's behavior that provoke and sustain the anger of the subordinate. There may be role conflicts among superiors that tear the subordinate apart psychologically. Work stresses may take their toll. It may well be that the subordinate unconsciously is asking for more support from his or her superior. Whatever the case, the two of them need to examine the situation together for possible causal influences. The superior needs to be alert to possible fears and anxieties that the subordinate cannot express, such as the fear of failure or a sense of inadequacy in the supervision of others.

Regardless of whether there are mitigating circumstances, the superior must draw the line for what is permissible. He or she simply cannot permit destructive behavior to go on. If environmental circumstances that precipitate anger cannot be altered, if indeed there seem to be no problems of such proportion as to induce such anger, then it is a reasonably safe assumption that the problem is primarily within the individual and therefore he or she himself or herself must do something about it. The chances are that he or she will have to seek professional help. If this is the case, bear in mind that the organization does not have to put up with the manager's behavior until he or she solves his or her problem. If he or she still cannot control his or her outbursts after the line is drawn, then he or she should be removed from his or her job.

The executive must not assume that undesirable behavior can be stamped out by forbidding it. Discussion of problems means just that: self-critical examination by both parties of their working relationship. It does not mean that the superior tells the subordinate he or she must stop behaving as he or she does and that the conversation ends there. Follow-up is needed. For instance, the superior strengthens the structure of the organization by seeing to it that the subordinate makes use of those organizational avenues, policies, and procedures which presumably are the agreed-on ways by which problems are to be dealt with in the organization.

When a superior finds himself or herself condoning hostile behavior or procrastinating in doing something about it because the subordinate is "too valuable to lose," the chances are that he or she is taking an expensive, short-run view of the problem. More often than not, when pinned down, the senior executive admits that the subordinate is more trouble than he or she is worth and that his or her failure to act arises from his or her own feelings of anger and guilt.

Error #3: Stimulation of Rivalry

The central problem in a group of about 13% of the cases is rivalry. Sometimes the executive presenting the problem recognizes this, but more often he or she does not. He or she may, for example, concentrate his or her attention on the hostility between two subordinates without recognizing why they became hostile, although the rivalry aspects of the problem often seem clear from his or her own description. For example:

*A manager is promoted to a position in which he or she becomes a rival of a senior person. He or she is instructed to "light a fire" under the senior person or is promised the senior person's job, as for example, when the chairman of the board chooses an executive vice president to prod the president. But the subordinate "freezes" in his or her job, failing to show the previously successful behavior that brought him or her to his or her promotion. His seniors cannot understand why.

Frequently the rivalry is between department heads or different functions. For example, between sales and production; and here again the underlying psychological reasons for the rivalry may not be recognized. Thus:

*A production-minded president sees the need for a strong sales effort and employs a competent sales executive, only to resent his or her success. He or she then rejects or sabotages the sales executive without being aware of what he or she is doing or knowing why.

The destructive effects of rivalry thus stimulated are rarely recognized by the presenting executives, in my experience. Executives are not aware of the deep-seated psychological roots of rivalry ad the guilt feelings which immediate personal competition can arouse in many people. Often they have consciously encouraged rivalry on the assumption that al competition is good. They cannot understand why a hard competitor will suddenly stop competing, let alone see the psychological trap in which the subordinate has been placed.

Although executives usually recognize why two colleagues can no longer be friends after one is promoted, or that older subordinates will rebel against a younger boss, generally they do little to prevent or ameliorate such frictions. Some young executives promoted rapidly over the heads of older people have guilt feelings about taking the opportunities of the older people. Such feelings are not recognized by superiors either. In none of the cases with rivalry problems described in our seminars was the issue of rivalry discussed, either by the rivals themselves or by their superiors, as preparation for dealing with their new jobs.

Rivalry, by definition, is the essence of competitive enterprise. But in such an enterprise, where the desirable end product is the result produced by the organization, all effort should be focused on the collective attainment of that result. When a superior plays subordinates off against each other, over stimulates rivalry in other ways, or acts competitively with his or her subordinates, he or she forces them to divert energies from competition with other organizations into interpersonal rivalry. Less attention is focused on problems that the organization has to solve. In addition, the subordinates become defensive, or destroy cooperative possibilities by attacking each other, or maneuver for the favor of the boss. The more intensely intraorganizational rivalry is stimulated, the more acute the problem of organization politics becomes.

Open discussion of and joint solution of mutual problems make it possible for managers to use much more profitably the energy that might otherwise be dissipated in destructive rivalry. In dealing with this problem, the superior needs to take a critical look at his or her own motivation with possibilities like these in mind:

*He or she may consciously or unconsciously encourage rivalry because he or she likes to see a good fight, rationalizing his or her pleasure by believing that the better ideas or the better managers will survive.

People in executive positions have strong feelings of rivalry that are sufficiently aroused by real problems, if the executives are given enough freedom to attack them; the range of ideas in a problem situation is generally wide enough to produce ample differences and critical examination. Playing managers off against each other is merely psychological goading. Those who are not moved by the problems themselves will not be moved by goading either. Instead, they will be even more rigidly paralyzed. One can only wonder about the motivation of an executive who has to goad his or her subordinates into fighting each other, just as one would wonder about a parent who does the same with his or her children.

*He or she may be angry at one of the rivals and use the other as a weapon to displace his or her own hostility.

This is a subtle phenomenon that happens frequently. The senior executive can ask him or herself to what extent he or she avoids one subordinate, speaks harshly of them behind their back, and disdains their communications. If he or she finds him or herself doing these things without clearly being aware of it, his or her behavior is one clue to what may be influencing the conflict between the two subordinates. He or she would do better to talk directly to the manager with whom he or she is angry than to get at them by using another manager as a weapon.

*He may fear the rivalry of subordinates for his or her own position, and either keep them off balance or permit them to destroy themselves by encouraging their rivalry with each other.

Few managers can grow older without envying and fearing the younger managers who will take their places, no matter how much they like and respect the younger manager. Such fears, though natural, are hard for a manager to accept in himself or herself. According to the folklore of our culture, he or she is not supposed to have them. Why should he or she not retire in due time without regret or recrimination? He or she has it made; what more does he or she want? But our feelings are simply not that logical. Moving up through executive ranks is much like playing the children's game, "King of the Mountain." A manager often feels as if he or she is always pushing the manager ahead of him or her off the top, even if it is only a small hill. Inevitably, it is difficult for him or her to relinquish his or her position without feeling he or she is being pushed, too. If he or she feels that way and is unaware of it, he or she perforce will defend his or her position in many subtle ways. If he or she can accept such feelings as legitimate, he or she is then in a better position to control their expression.

*The two rivals may well represent his or her own inner conflicts about his or her identification with different parts of the organization.

Often executives rise through the ranks on the basis of their identification with a particular capacity, skill, or experience. Then, on reaching a high level, they find that new organization requirements make their old skill relatively obsolete or compel them to evolve multiple skills. For example, many a production specialist has risen to chief executive only to discover that we are now in a marketing economy and that he or she must either shift his or her own focus from production to marketing or at least become more knowledgeable about marketing.

To change one's focus or to broaden one's perception can also mean that a person has to change his or her self-image. A production specialist who looks on marketing as manipulation, for example, may have considerable conflict within his or her own conscience about becoming a manipulator. Even though he or she may well recognize the need for marketing, he or she may still not want to be a salesperson. The conflict within him or herself between the wish to continue being what he or she always was and the wish to have the organization compete successfully by competitive marketing may then reflect itself in his or her inability to make decisions.

It will also reflect itself in conflict between the managers who have to carry on the two responsibilities about which he or she is in conflict. In hardly discernible ways he or she will support one, then the other, or make an ally of one then the other. The two subordinates soon find themselves on opposite sides of a fence whose origin is then attributed to "poor communications" or the supposition that "salespeople are always like that." Perhaps only after the third successive sales vice president has been fired might it dawn on the president that something more than a "personality clash" is afoot. The clash within himself or herself clangs loudly in the behavior of those who report to him or her.

In the promotion or transfer of any executive, careful attention should be given to the rivalry aspects of the situation. These should be talked about frankly as problems to be dealt with in the new job. And for those who must accept a new superior or colleague, it can be helpful to reassure them honestly of their own value, to recognize openly with them the inevitable presence of rivalry feelings, and to indicate that, though such feelings exist, the task is still to be done and the new boss has the superior's full support in managing that group toward the required goals of the organization.

Error #4: Failure to Anticipate the Inevitable

Many experiences in life are painful to people. Some, like aging and its accompanying physical infirmities and incapacities, are the lot of everyone. Others are specific to a person's work life, e.g., failure to obtain an expected promotion or the prospect of retirement. We can speak of such painful experiences as psychological injuries.

Such injuries are inevitable. Yet there is little in our cases to indicate that organizations recognize their inevitability and have established methods for anticipating or relieving them. The result is that those who are hurt in this manner have considerable hostility which is repressed or suppressed. Sometimes the thought of retirement is what hurts. Those people to whom prospective retirement is a psychological injury often refuse to train subordinates and become obstructionists, displacing their repressed or suppressed hostility on both subordinates and organization. Physical changes such as hearing loss and heart attack also leave residues of resentment as people attempt to come to terms with their new limitations which they view as weaknesses or vulnerabilities. Other organizational injuries include:

*Having one's judgment rejected.

*Having some of one's responsibilities given to someone else.

*Lonesomeness - wishing to be gregarious but being unable to act that way, and therefore feelings rejected by others, with a resulting hypersensitivity to further psychological wounds.

Judging from the executive seminars that I have lead over my career, superiors are more aware of psychological injury than any other form of impairment, and they try to do more about it. Yet they typically have great difficulty dealing with such problems, especially because the older employees who are more subject to them are managers of long service. In the many cases where superiors have done a good job of providing support for the "problem people" and have saved their jobs, they have done it by hard work and heroic rescue attempts.

However, such extraordinary measures, and the pain and frustration which usually attend them, can often be made unnecessary by advance preparation in anticipation of possible injury. People not only have a right to know what is likely to happen to them as far ahead as such events can be anticipated, but also they can then prepare themselves for the eventuality or choose alternative courses of action. If they are not informed and then experience a sudden blow from higher management, they have every reason to feel manipulated and exploited.

The organization contributes to executive malfunction when it does not:

*systematically prepare people throughout their work careers for the realities which inevitably will come their way;

*provide shock absorbers, in the form of counseling services, to help people cope with psychological injury.

Every important change should be discussed with each person involved before it occurs. A major part of such discussion should be the opportunity for him or her to express his or her feelings, without embarrassment or fear, about the change. When a person can say to his or her superior how he or she feels about the latter's decision or an organizational decision, the acceptance of his or her feelings conveys to him or her that he or she is accepted and respected as an individual. This in turn supports his or her feelings of self-esteem and makes it possible for him or her to deal with the change and his or her feelings more reasonably. No amount of sugarcoated praise will substitute for being heard.

When a person has help in absorbing the shock of injury and support in recovering from it, he or she is in a much better position to mobilize his or her resources to cope with what has happened to him or her. More often than not, a senior executive who would quickly offer a supporting hand to a person with a sprained ankle, and indeed get him or her medical attention, has difficulty seeing psychological injuries in the same light.

Error #5: Pressuring People of Limited Ability

The characteristic and futile way of trying to deal with people of limited ability is by frontal assault. Repeatedly the senior executives attempt to persuade a rigid person to stop being rigid, exhort a dependent person to become independent, or cajole an impulsive person to gain better self-control. Although the executives may know in their minds that the subordinate is inflexible or unable to accept responsibility or assume initiative, they tend to act as if they could compel or stimulate him or her to change. Thus:

*It is difficult for most successful executives to understand that grown people can be frightened and dependent. Sometimes, in a misguided effort to stimulate the subordinate, they open up the possibilities of greater responsibility and more active participation in decision making.

Such gestures are even more threatening to people who are already immobilized than exhortation is. Sometimes seniors actually promote the problem person in the vain hope that he or she will change when he or she has more responsibility or when he or she is sent off to a management development course. It is not understood that such pressure on a person who is already devoting so much effort to controlling or protecting himself or herself (which is what the aberrant behavior mans) will only increase the intensity of the undesirable behavior. If a person is characteristically rigid, dependent, or impulsive, he or she is likely to become more so under increasing stress, which is what the pressure exerted by the boss becomes.

*Impulsive people present another problem for their superiors. Because so often they are intellectually competent, even gifted, their superiors are reluctant to face the problems of their behavior squarely and thus can only continue to chafe at their episodic failure. About 2% of our cases were people like this who did their jobs well "when they wanted to." However, they are frequently absent, often embroiled in multiple family difficulties, and sometimes irresponsible with respect to getting their work done or doing it thoroughly. Here also are the people who, though not alcoholic, will drink too much in the presence of their superiors, and others whose worst behavior will occur when they are with highest level superiors. The self-defeating aspects of such behavior are obvious.

Poor impulse control and low frustration tolerance usually reflect considerable anxiety and insecurity. More often than not, such behavior reflects the need for professional counsel. Repeated admonitions usually serve little purpose.

*Inflexibility is the most prominent reported behavior of about 5% of our cases. For nearly half of these people, the problem is characterized as an inability to plan for or accept change. Several others seem to resist change not because they are personally inflexible, but because the organization has prepared them poorly and they are angry. In one case, the organization was so rigid that the best person available for a given post was not going to be promoted because he did not believe in God!

Rigid people find their self-protection in well-ordered lives. Often they have high standards for themselves. Those who become more rigid under stress are in effect building a protective shell for themselves.

How should management try to deal with problems of the sort just described?

First, it should so delimit the person's duties that he or she can confine himself or herself to standardized, detailed work, with clear policy guidance. It should be made clear to him or her what his or her responsibilities do not include.

Secondly, higher management should consider what demands have made the person more anxious and defensive. As earlier pointed out, change always requires support from superiors if it is to take place with a minimum amount of stress. Much of the time senior management takes it for granted that people can and will change; few can do so without stress. The most effective kind of support lies in joint problem solving in making changes together, step-by-step so that the person can feel he or she is still master of himself or herself and his or her fate, instead of being arbitrarily buffeted about by anonymous forces over which he or she has no control.

Thirdly, management should take a hard look at the "climate" of the executive organization. In our seminar cases a frequent corollary of inability to perform as expected is the report by the presenting executives that the problem people were previously suppressed in an excessively authoritarian structure for years. Some are able to function reasonably well as long as they have the close support of their superiors. Some cannot make decisions themselves.

Undoing dependent behavior is no easy task, particularly when the organization continues to demand conforming behavior. Where conformity is the first rule of survival, no amount of exhortation will produce initiative. Where mistakes are vigorously hunted out and held against a person thereafter, a few people will take a chance on making a mistake. Therefore, close, minute supervision of a person as he or she assumes greater responsibility is not an unmixed blessing. There are rewards and costs for such supervision. This situation often creates great conflict among senior executives: the wish that subordinates demonstrate initiative versus the wish to be in control.

Despite the plethora of psychological consultants, assessment and rating scales, and a wide-ranging literature on promotion, there is little indication in our cases that careful assessments are regularly made t indicate a person's limitations or predict his or her inability to carry greater responsibility. In cases where people have been outgrown by their jobs, there seems to have been almost no anticipation that such an eventuality would come about. As a result, there has been no continuing discussion of the problem, which might help the person become aware of what he or she will have to do to keep up with his or her job. Nor is there support for him or her in facing his or her feelings about becoming less competent to do the job or having to give it up. Instead, whatever the reason a person has not grown, often he or she is left to flounder in his or her job because superiors recognize it is not his or her fault that he or she is failing, but theirs for having placed him or her in that position. Thus the failure is compounded.

In about 17% of the cases of misplacement, by my interpretation, half of the people placed in the wrong job are unable to function adequately in the face of larger responsibilities. Often these are people who did well in jobs of lesser responsibility and who seemed to have promise of being able to carry on a more responsible job. Some people, however, have been placed in managerial position despite the fact that their limitations are known, particularly their inability to supervise others. Some have moved up through the ranks because of their technical knowledge at the time when it was thought that technical knowledge was the most important qualification that a leader could have. The remaining people in this group could not consistently meet the demands of their present jobs. Often they could do some aspects of their jobs well, but not others.

About one third of the cases in this group involve people who reportedly cannot keep up with the continuing growth of the organization and the particular jobs they hold. In most of these instances the person simply does not have the knowledge or the skill for the expanding job. His or her growing job has gone beyond his or her training and experiences and beyond his or her capacity for organizing and making judgments. This problem is even more painful when the incumbent has had long service in the position or when he or she has made highly significant contributions to organizing and developing an activity, sometimes even the organization itself. In these situations the superior bears considerable pain because he or she feels compelled to take action against a person who has contributed so much to the organization. His or her anger toward the person who "forces" him or her into such a situation arouses his or her guilt feelings, and his or her conscience punishes him or her severely.

How much of the failure to keep up with the growth of the organization was passive aggression, failure to do what a person was capable of doing as a way of defeating the company. I have no way of knowing. Often rigidity and plateaus in performance are products of passive aggression. One way of being aggressive covertly is by not changing, not doing what is expected of one, letting the boss down in one way or another. Passive aggression is an extremely widespread phenomenon.

The single most helpful practice for dealing with misplacement is to have a continuing and consistent relationship with a psychological consultant. Psychological testing and evaluation are no better than the person who does them. His or her judgments and predictions can be no better than his or her knowledge of the person, the position, and the organization. If he or she is to serve all three, then he or she must develop a feel for the company, knowledge of specific jobs and the people who supervise them, and, finally, some understanding of the candidate. Standardized batteries given by psychologists who see neither the organization nor the probably position of the candidate among others in the company have limited value. Mail order testing has even less value (apart from the ethical question involved). Occasional referral to a local psychologist is hardly enough to keep the latter in touch with the climate of the organization.

Growth is the essence of living. All of us like to feel that we are becoming wiser as we grow older. Most people seek opportunities for continued growth. Some, however, cannot or do not. This problem is likely to occur with increasing frequency as executive roles become more complex. To avoid failures, organizations will have to evolve methods for anticipating and coping with misplacements before they become a painful and destructive fact. In a continuing professional relationship the psychologist can be in contact with executives from day to day, know when they are under particular stress, and provide support and counsel as necessary. In growing companies one of his or her continuing tasks should be to keep an eye out for those who are not keeping pace.

Conclusion

The contemporary management scene is characterized by frequent complaints about the inadequacies of subordinates and potential executive successors. The validity of such complaints would seem to be verified by the widespread use of management consultants for every conceivable purpose and by the repetitive reorganizations. These phenomena reflect the chronic pain of management, enormous dissipation of human energy, and the palliative nature of the attempted cures. Dr. Karl Menninger coined the term "polysurgical addiction" to describe people who repeatedly demanded operations to cure their multiple, repetitive complaints. It would not stretch the analogy too far to speak of "poly-consultative addiction" to describe this all too frequent mode of solving managerial problems.

This phrase is not meant to reflect on consultants any more than Menninger's phrase was a criticism of surgeons. Both practitioners serve highly important purposes. Rather, it refers to a characteristic managerial way of looking at problems as caused by someone or something foreign to oneself, and as being resolvable by excision or reconstruction, also by someone else. The tragedy of such a tendency is that the executive, like the patient who wants someone else to cut out the presumably offensive part, often has within himself or herself the power to cope with managerial problems. This is especially true with respect to those problems that are of his or her own (if inadvertent) making.

In this chapter, I have outlined, from cases reported by executives, six common managerial errors in the supervision of subordinates, and I have suggested ways which may help avoid or correct each error. Most management problems seem to call for increased investment, more experts, and long periods of planning and execution before results can be expected. The problems described in this chapter do not. Though few managerial difficulties are more troublesome than those that have to do with people, the solutions to them are often relatively simple, given a modicum of attention and sensitivity. The manager needs only to examine more carefully his or her own actions. Of course, some problems, like those that around feelings of guilt, will remain difficult no matter how simple the solutions seem. Even these, however, will be somewhat easier to cope with if the underlying issue is more visible. Perhaps, then, the greatest self-healing managerial talent, as the psalmist would put is, is to "make wise the simple."

CHAPTER 8

SECTION TWO

COURAGE

Easing the Pain of Personal Loss

Harvard Business Review, September-October 1972, pp. 82-90
"Severe personal and organizational damage can ensue when
individuals are cut loose from their psychological moorings"

Dr. Levinson, the former Thomas Henry Carroll Ford
Foundation Distinguished Visiting Professor of Business
Administration at the Harvard Business School, is President of The
Levinson Institute. This article is adapted from his forthcoming book,
The Great Jackass Fallacy, which will be published in January 1973 by
the Division of Research, Harvard Business School.

Foreword

Management is increasingly aware that in pursuing traditional
organizational goals it can leave a wake of human costs (exacted in
terms of employee alienation and reduced productivity). The
experience of loss is a subtle, often overlooked, phenomenon that robs
people of psychological stability and deprives organizations of
effective human resources. In this article, a noted psychologist
maintains that loss is precipitated whenever people "lose" their
psychological attachments to familiar people, places, and managerial
practices. Any change, even promotion, can have a severe loss
component. After describing the four most critical types of
psychological deprivation in organizations, the author presents some
very humanized measures that management and individuals can take to
facilitate a process of adaptation and restitution.

Imagine a tree rooted in the ground. The roots not only transmit nourishment but also give the tree stability against the elements. When any one of these roots is destroyed, the leaves that depend on it begin to wither -- part of the tree dies. If the tree is to be moved, a wise tree mover will cut away some of the more extended roots on one side of the tree and allow the tree time to adapt to that loss by developing new roots; then he will cut away some roots on the other side of the tree, leaving a large ball of dirt in which the remaining roots, including the newly proliferated ones, are contained.

The human experience is much like that of the tree. We attach ourselves to people, places, things, goals, wishes, aspirations, skills, knowledge, and even life styles. Like the tree, we experience loss when our attachments are destroyed. Our loss experience, however, is a deeply psychological one. It includes mixed feelings of deprivation, helplessness, sorrow and anger. The experience underlies alienation, rootlessness, and severe stresses in the family. Yet, while loss is a universal problem and probably the most psychologically costly one, we can, like the wise tree mover, learn how to counteract it.

The loss experience is pervasive in industrial societies, and its effects are conspicuous in organizations. Many managers who are viewed as remaining on an organizational plateau, becoming organizational deadwood or losing interest in the job, even those referred to laughingly as having risen to a level of incompetence[6] carry the burden of depression due to the sense of loss. But the importance of the loss phenomenon for management goes beyond such common experiences, for these reasons:

All change -- promotion, transfer, demotion, reorganization, merger, retirement, and most other managerial actions -- produces loss. Despite the fact that change is necessary and often for the better, the new always displaces the old; and, at some level of consciousness, individuals experience the stress of this displacement as loss.

The destruction of psychological attachments, particularly if it is chronic and is accompanied by a sense of hopelessness, precipitates major illness and even life-threatening maladies.[7] All loss has important psychological and physiological significance. An extreme

---

[6] Laurence J. Peter & Raymond Hull, *The Peter Principle: Why Things Always Go Wrong.* (New York, Morrow, 1969.)
[7] See Thomas Holmes & Minoru Masada, Symposium on *Separation* and Depression, American Association for the Advancement of Science, December 1970.

example related to work is the debilitating effect of long-term unemployment. A less striking example is the psychological effect on employees when there are significant changes in the way work is done, as in automating work processes.

When people are not inhibited from doing so, they automatically begin a restitution process to recoup their losses and compensate for them. Moreover, both the manager and the organization, with little more effort than it takes to ignore the effects of loss, can become facilitators of the restitution process. Thus they are in a position to be both agents of prevention and healers, and, at the same time, they increase organizational effectiveness.

In this article, I shall discuss the implications of the loss experience from both an individual and an organizational perspective. Then I shall suggest some steps that individuals and organizations can take to facilitate the restitution process. Once management is aware of the loss phenomenon, it can readily set in motion processes that will not only help people avoid many of the negative consequences of the loss experience but also simultaneously foster a closer, more effective working relationship between the organization and its members.

Corporate Implications

Everyone carries in varying degrees the psychological burdens of loss from a lifetime of experiences. As a corollary, everyone is vulnerable in varying degrees to the threat of additional loss.

Deprivation of several different kinds of psychological nourishment constitutes the essence of the loss experience. Among the most critical losses are (1) loss of love, (2) loss of support, (3) loss of sensory input, and (4) loss of capacity to act on oneself or the outside world. With respect to people who work in organizations, loss experiences range clearly along these four dimensions.

1. Loss of Love

The death of a relative or a close friend is a general example of this experience. In the business world, the separation from a highly valued business partner or colleague may be equally as painful as separation or divorce from a spouse.

Movement within or out of an organization that involves leaving behind important sources of regard and approval is another example. People are likely to experience loss of love when the organization changes its way of treating them and their attachments to sources of self-esteem are severed as a result. There are numerous examples of corporate' actions that precipitate such experiences:

Closing a plant can cause people to become suddenly rootless.

Restructuring the organization can cause familiar work relationships to be broken up.

Changing the product mix can cause those who made previously highly valued products to lose their favored position.

Embarking on industrial engineering speedup activities can cause work to become dehumanized.

In short, any action or event that decreases the feeling of being valued as a person can be a powerful precipitant of the feeling of loss of love. Moreover, such actions and events usually produce harmful behavioral consequences (e.g., anger and resistance) as well as more subtle psychological and physiological reactions (e.g., anxiety and illness).

2. Loss of Support

When an individual has to establish new organizational ties and relationships, find new subordinates on whom to depend, or generally adopt new ways of operating in the company, he is likely to experience loss of support. This type of loss can be particularly damaging when he is no longer able to depend on once-valued skills, practices, or theories that have supported his personal competence. (Incidentally, it is fear of the latter development that impels people to resist new advances and techniques in business.)

The loss of support is what causes many individuals to become confused in new or changed situations, even when the change results from a long-sought promotion. A person who knows his way around a company, is intimately familiar with its politics, and operates comfortably behind the scenes will find himself at a considerable disadvantage in another part of the organization where he does not know his way around politically and must operate more in the public eye. The characteristically active person will find himself at a "loss" in a situation where he must remain passive. And less competitive people will find themselves to have "lost" their favored ways of behaving when they are required to be more competitive. (The latter phenomenon occurs often in contemporary business as historically staid companies seek to become more aggressive.)

<u>Organizational identification</u>: A more subtle form of loss of support is usually glossed over by managers. When an organization's purposes, goals, and/or leadership practices are changed, people who have identified with them can experience a profound sense of loss. An example is a respected retail establishment that merged into a large retail chain.

The employees took pride in the original store's reputation for service, high-quality merchandise, and leadership in its field and community. But after the merger, the store was enlarged, service ties to the parent organization caused mounting delivery problems, and they no longer had time to serve customers well. Morale deteriorated and the store eventually lost its dominant local leadership. As a result of these developments, the best people began to leave, others marked time as best they could, and the store went continually downhill. Had management recognized the need to maintain organizational support, it might have been able to work with employees and help them replace their loss with new goals such as the challenge of revitalizing the organization, competing with other stores in the parent chain, and so on.

Implicit in such destruction of organizational identification is the lost opportunity to work toward a personal ego-ideal (i.e., the image of oneself at his future best, which constitutes the individual's internalized criterion of personal success). When people can no longer feel that they are working successfully at being good and becoming better, they will become frustrated, depressed, and feel concomitantly worthless, no matter what they have achieved up to that point.

Loss of the ego ideal occurs in a different way when people achieve long-held aspirations -- that is, they have "made it," whatever this phrase means to them. They begin to ask, "What next?" or "What do I do now that I have it made?" or "Where do I go from here?" Such individuals show how powerful and threatening the loss experience can be when they refuse to train successors or yield control of their organizations to others.

A similar phenomenon takes place when a manager, who has moved up and taken with him those with whom he has learned to work well, retires or leaves the organization. Those who have risen with him are suddenly devoid of what gave them organizational interest and purpose. They then experience severe loss, particularly if they themselves had never expected to rise as far as they did. Usually, they are left to regret and mourn-despite their high positions in the company.

3. Loss of Sensory Input

This type of loss occurs when a manager no longer gets the kind of information that helps him to orient himself in time and place. It may not be the absence of information per se, but rather his inability to sense it. For example, it is of no help to a person to read a computer printout if he has not had the training which helps him to understand it.

Similarly, a man promoted from the ranks to a supervisory role frequently loses the ability to learn what is going on among his subordinates because he is not practiced in conducting meetings and in dealing with people who have less power. And when a man who is accustomed to understanding what goes on in the plant merely by listening to the typical plant noises is moved into another role, he will no longer be able to sense those cues and will feel very uneasy about what may be going wrong.

The same is true when people must use new equipment. I still remember vividly the introduction of smokeless welders in an assembly shop. The men who used that equipment became very suspicious when they could no longer see the smoke. They thought they were being poisoned by invisible smoke and that the new equipment was part of a plot to take advantage of their ignorance. No one had thought about anticipating their anxiety. After all, the new machines were easier to work with than the old. And people should feel good about having better equipment.

4. Loss of Capacity to Act

The sense of having lost the capacity to act on oneself or the outside world is probably the single most threatening experience of the contemporary industrial world. Its most common manifestation comes with aging.

The loss of youth threatens the capacity for adaptation and mastery and increases the feeling of having to depend on others. This phenomenon is especially vivid for people in managerial ranks who, with age, frequently encounter the obsolescence of knowledge, devaluation of previous experience, and diminution of the competitive spirit. Simultaneously, they feel threatened by younger competitors and new demands from the marketplace as well as the requirement that they must continually update their professional knowledge. As a result, they feel they are no longer good enough, no matter how hard they have worked or how adequately they may have performed in the past.

The loss of capacity to act produces the feeling of being perennially victimized, of being powerless, and has led to a wide range of hostile social reactions (e.g., race riots) as well as to more structured responses (e.g., consumerism). This loss experience has been given added impetus in managerial circles by the displacement of many middle-management and professional people during the recent recession. Managers who thought they had stable positions in their organizations and communities suddenly discovered that they had neither and that they were powerless to do anything about it.

In manufacturing organizations, I have frequently seen the same type of frustration resulting from ill-conceived, mechanistic change processes that took years to unscramble. For example, in organizations that rotate managers, employees inevitably feel that they cannot readily be heard and cannot act in their own interest, because no manager is around long enough to understand them. They therefore react by organizing themselves in a way that makes it impossible for a manager to penetrate their organizational armor. Visiting such plants and offices is like being in enemy territory.

Managers experience this same sense of loss (a) when they lose some control of their operations to more centralized processes, to higher level managements, or to technical specialists; or (b) when they are threatened with being displaced, say, through job-enrichment programs.

The experience of loss, as is evident from the foregoing illustrations, is costly to organizations as well as to individuals. Whatever psychological reactions it induces, one way or another they become manifest in increased personal problems and decreased organizational effectiveness. Therefore, it becomes important to consider how to cope with these phenomena. Let us turn to some steps that managers and organizations can take to protect themselves from the undue consequences of loss.

What Managers Can Do

How can managers cope with the loss experience? In this section, I shall outline some steps that may be helpful, but it is also important to keep in mind that constructive efforts already have an advantage from the momentum of the reflexive, compensatory process of restitution. That is, just as a spider immediately goes about repairing a broken web, so people go about repairing their social webs. The natural impulse to begin repairing his psychological injury provides the individual with a ready handle for coping with loss. A manager who understands this process can, like the wise tree mover mentioned at the beginning of this article, help both himself and others to restore their psychological roots.

Become Aware of It

The first and most important step a manager should take, whether in the family or in the corporation, is to become aware of the loss experience in himself and others. This statement may sound trite, but unless a manager becomes attuned to loss in its various manifestations, he will not have the sensitivity to deal with it when it occurs.

One way that a manager can increase his awareness is to think about the various kinds of losses he has experienced and the different feelings they engendered. Next, he can observe his own behavior to see how he responds to even small losses. He should review the feelings he had when he left one location for another, one position for another, one boss for another. Despite whatever positive feelings were produced by such changes, he will probably recall an underlying sense of regret. In this way, he can begin to understand the depth and power of the loss experience.

Once managers become attuned to their own loss experiences, it becomes easier to detect signs of psychological pain in the words and behavior of others. Loss manifests itself in various observable ways; here are some typical examples:

When a group of managers has worked together intensely on an organizational problem and the members have then returned to concentration on their usual activities, they will likely feel some sadness at separating from each other, despite their strong desire to get back to what they normally do. This sadness may reflect itself in the heavy emotional quality of the last day, in the jokes of the previous day that deny the sadness, and even in the early departure of some individuals because they cannot take good-byes.

Employees' depressed moods are easy to spot if one knows what to look for. They are usually accompanied by the feeling that impending problems cannot be solved, that no one in power really cares, or that management is inept. Increases in trivial complaints, medical office visits, and even accidents are overt reflections of these feelings. Self-depreciation is another sign of the depression that accompanies loss.

The stress that follows a loss experience usually becomes more intense, and hence easier to detect, when people have to cope with unfamiliar situations. In fact, the experience of loss, coupled with the pressure of new demands, produces the major stress accompanying change. Stress is reflected in increased restlessness, irritability, physical symptoms, withdrawal from others, the appearance of sadness, and a greater sense of fatigue. Often stress is also reflected in more intense busyness or artificial cheerfulness.

Effects of denial: In addition to paying close attention to outward signs of loss, the manager must be aware that people will experience psychological pain without necessarily giving any noticeable signs of doing so. Just as a small child pulls a blanket over his head to cope with a fantasized threat in the darkness, so the adult calls into play the primitive defense of denial. Some people think they should not express such feelings because they are supposed to maintain a "stiff upper lip." Others cannot accept pity and compassion and simply steel themselves against admitting any such feelings.

In short, the ordinary person denies many feelings of loss, particularly feelings of depression associated with loss, and therefore is little aware of how it affects him and his work. Managers, in turn, tend to be relatively insensitive to the significance of this phenomenon; they fail to take it into account when changing people's circumstances, or they simply assume that people will compensate for whatever damage has occurred.

Talk About It

Once a manager becomes sufficiently aware of feelings of loss so that he knows when they are arising or are likely to arise, the most immediately fruitful prophylactic step is to talk about them. People can sometimes bear seemingly impossible emotional burdens if only they can talk about their problems. When feelings are put into words, they can be dissipated or acted on with conscious intent. If they cannot be verbalized, there is no release from anguish and people are compelled to act on impulses which they only dimly perceive.

When a person dies, those who mourn him talk about him frequently and, in the process, gradually relieve their burden. This is the purpose of having friends call. In a less dramatic way, the same process is helpful in all loss experiences. Thus, if a manager loses his job or has to give up the location he likes, associates he prefers, or a department he has built, he should find a way of talking to someone else about his problem.

In the organization: In his role as a superior to whom others report, a manager should create opportunities for subordinates to talk about loss experiences. When a subordinate has accepted a transfer or a prospective move, for example, the boss might well say, "I know you're going to miss people," or he might even ask, "Who and what are you going to miss most when you leave the job?" Such questions legitimize the opportunity for a subordinate to recall and recount the prospect of loss. Then the boss might ask, "In your new assignment, how are you going to replace those things and people?" This makes it possible for the subordinate to begin thinking out loud not only about what and whom he will miss but also about the importance of doing something to foster the restitution process.

Similar questions might be asked about the subordinate's family. The manager might even inquire how he or the organization can be helpful in restoring needed supports. This legitimizes the right and responsibility of the subordinate to ask for appropriate help in the restitution process. After all, if the organization has created the psychological problem for the individual and his family, the boss (the organization's representative certainly has the responsibility to help them cope with it. (I shall discuss the organization's role in more detail later.)

If a number of subordinates are involved in situations like the foregoing, a manager should initiate a series of group discussions. In this way, people can share their feelings together, publicly legitimize their right to have them, and permit them to rise to the surface without embarrassment. In effect, such open expressions of feeling constitute a psychological wake, a group-mourning process, and they are the best way to begin to counteract the negative effects of loss.

Ideally, these discussions should be held well in advance of prospective changes so that the feelings of loss do not interfere with effective adaptation. Too often managers try to reassure people that organizational change will not hurt them or that everything "will be all right." Such reassurances have little effect. (In mergers, for example, they have become the signal that painful change is indeed coming.)

Imperative for action: Some people would argue that in a competitive enterprise there is no room for dealing with feelings and most certainly no room for dealing with them in the interpersonal manner I have projected here. In addition, they would say that managers do not have the competence to use even these simple psychological techniques. I contend, however, that if the competitiveness within a company is of such intensity that it destroys the company's important human resources, or even makes them less effective, then the company is deceiving itself and will pay an inordinate price for this deception.

Furthermore, these simple ways of attuning oneself to people's pain and making it possible for people to talk about feelings and to evolve methods of coping with them do not require advanced, sophisticated psychological thinking. They are well within the capacity of practically all managers. (It should, in fact, be mandatory in all training programs to teach managers how. to recognize and deal with such problems.)

What Organizations Can Do

According to a study by Dr. David Rosenthal of the National Institute of Mental Health, 90,000 Americans were hospitalized in 1967 for depression (many as a result of some type of loss experience) and "many times more never found their way to a hospital."[8] This is merely

---

[8] *Boston Globe*, April 24, 1972.

one indication of the pervasiveness of the loss phenomenon, and it has profound implications for organizations that supposedly depend on their human resources.

By and large, managements are unaware that all organizational change necessarily involves loss. The consequence, as I have tried to show, is that companies often take actions which maximize the loss experience and result in both individual symptoms as well as even more massive resistance to organizational change. In short, wherever there are likely to be continuing and repetitive loss experiences, managements would do well to set up institutional programs for dealing with them.

One such approach is a joint counseling program involving the Los Angeles County Occupational Health Service and the Department of Psychiatry of the University of Southern California School of Medicine.[9] Based on studies showing that both the illness rate and the death rate are higher among those who have lost their spouses than in others of the same age and sex, this program serves employees who have recently experienced the loss of an immediate member of the family. Employees use the service on self-referral or when the health service identifies those who are in mourning by reviewing bereavement leaves. The counseling is carried out primarily by nurses and psychologists.

Another more common example of organizational coping mechanisms is the preretirement program. Some companies hold retirement counseling sessions that commence several years before an employee is due to leave. The employee is encouraged to articulate his retirement plans, and the company clarifies what resources and services will be available when he retires. Thus he is better able to prepare for the coming change and to adapt to it as well as to begin the restitution process.

Provide Relocation Guidance

The organization can do much to help families adjust to relocation. It can, for example, encourage an employee to talk with his family well in advance of a move and, perhaps, suggest that he and his

---

[9] Jean S. Felton, "Occupational Health: Government Program for County Employees," *Journal of the American Medical Association,* July S, 1971, pp. 56-60.

family read a book like Edith Ruina's Moving.[10] This type of approach fosters a joint experience that leads to practical planning and the discussion of feelings. It allows the family to experience the detachment process slowly and to begin the adaptation process.

The company can also prepare the way with information about new communities and introductions to local people who will help the families get settled. In one situation, where six management people were to be moved, the company sent the wives to the new community to examine housing, schools, medical facilities, and other resources. The wives brought back snapshots of homes, schools, and parks and discussed them with their families. By the time the move occurred, there were already familiar images of what was to come as well as mutually supportive group solidarity among the wives.

A similar organizational approach was taken by a hospital in which many of the staff members had worked for a long time. When a new hospital was to be built, the architectural plans were posted on the bulletin boards of the old hospital. The staff was encouraged to discuss the plans and the renderings among themselves and others. When the basic framework of the new building was up, there was an open house for visitors. The staff members acted as hosts, showing the visitors around and pointing out among other features what were to be their own private spaces. They also participated in further planning for the new hospital; and, when the hospital was finally completed, they helped move their own belongings. Then they served as guides for another open house. Gradually, they gave up the old while accepting the new; both processes went on simultaneously.

In a contrasting situation, the staff was moved from a decrepit hospital to an excellent new one, but received no such orientation. Consequently, the new hospital seemed alien to them, and they could find nothing right about it for many months.

Relating to the community: An organization often has to cope with loss in the community of which it is a part. For instance, if it closes a plant that is the mainstay of a community, this action could leave the whole community with a loss experience. The confrontation-adaptation-restitution process in such circumstances is illustrated by the

---

[10] *Moving: A Common-Sense Guide to Relocating Your Family* (New York, Funk & Wagnals, 1970).

American Oil Company's approach to closing its refinery in Neodesha, Kansas.

A year prior to the closing, a full-time coordinator was appointed. After the company publicly announced the closing, it held discussions with employees, union leadership, community officials, and news media representatives. It then implemented a comprehensive plan to find employees new jobs, to keep employees apprised of their benefits and opportunities, to find new industry for the area, and to turn over its property to the community for an industrial park.

By the time the plant was closed, only 28 of 200 employees had not yet been placed in new jobs, and the company engaged a private employment agency to help them. Subsequently, all former refinery workers who wanted new jobs were employed. Moreover, as a result of new industry attracted to the industrial park, the 200 lost refinery jobs were replaced by 300 new ones.

Match Jobs And People

In all organizations, it should be routine for employees being promoted or reassigned to weigh the psychological cost to themselves and their families. Many companies move people around under the guise of broadening the person; yet I frequently find that such moves are merely for movement's sake and contribute little to the broadening process.

Few companies make it a policy to convey to their managers the importance of group and family decisions as supports for prospective job changes. In fact, most take it for granted that the manager wants a promotion; therefore, they offer it and then assume everything will be all right. Managers, for their part, often feel that if they do not accept the promotion, they will lose favor.

These are the attitudes that create the "mobile manager" who lives by temporary expedient arrangements to ensure fast promotion. Such a life style makes the whole process of relating to an organization a self-centered, exploitative one because, consciously or unconsciously, the manager experiences himself as being exploited.

This makes many organizations merely large-scale, manipulative, game-playing devices; and, as a result, they cannot render adequate service, produce dependable products, stand behind trustworthy guarantees, evolve integrated performance, or foster those other qualities which give a business character. It is not without reason that all of these problems are in the forefront of contemporary consumer concern and managerial frustration.

Toward behavioral consistency: In thinking about promotion and reassignment of people, organizational representatives should look more closely not only at the characteristics of behavior that the prospective job requires but also at the degree to which those characteristics are ingrained in the individual who will fill the job.

I refer here specifically to preferred behavioral characteristics. Too many organizations assume that managers will be able to change their behavior in keeping with whatever the job requirements may be. In fact, people cannot change their behavior that readily. A move into a new position can mean leaving behind familiar ways of getting a job accomplished, as well as separation from key people who provided support, and it can precipitate any of the four types of loss experiences discussed earlier.

For example, it is an old cliché in management that when a good salesman is promoted to sales manager, the organization loses a good salesman and acquires a poor sales manager. The preferred ways of behaving for a good salesman often have to do with meeting people, pleasing them, persuading them, and serving them. As a sales manager, however, he no longer has these behavioral supports; he may experience loss in the face of new demands and fail to adjust to the behavioral requirements of his new managerial role.

The same is true of most other managerial jobs and requires that organizations think carefully about matching characteristic individual behavior with situational demands. In training programs and in discussions with superiors and personnel executives, managers should be encouraged, even required, to spell out in detail their preferred ways of handling aggression, affection, and dependency. They should also be asked to define their images of themselves as they would ideally like to become. The managers should then be invited to compare these self-descriptions, verified and corroborated in regular appraisal interviews, with the behavior requirements of the new job which they are being asked to consider.

When managers understand that such self-and-organizational-evaluations can maximize their success and that they will not be passed over for subsequent promotions if they do not behaviorally "fit" prospective jobs, then more of them will make more reasonable choices to the mutual advantage of the organization and its people.

Maintain the Organizational Ideal

As I mentioned earlier in this article, an often overlooked manifestation of the loss experience is the loss of the organizational ideal. Businesses these days are so preoccupied with goals they forget that goals are subsidiary to purposes. When there is no defined purpose, people cannot be "for" anything. They feel exploited in the interest of attaining another dollar for the stockholders or the boss. This feeling of being exploited alienates many people from organizations and has led to much of the contemporary criticism of business.

Top-management groups should hold annual retreats during which they sit down together and discuss what they are in business for and what they would like to leave behind when they retire. Such a formulation of purpose in keeping with the ego ideals of individual executives gives rise to a collective common effort. Subsequently, a set of purposes can be arrived at that form the charter for the organization, and goals can be set to attain these purposes.

For some top-management groups, such discussions may seem maudlin and inappropriate. Others may prefer exhortation, persuasion, flag waving, and similar temporary expedient devices. My experience is that working toward a mutual understanding of common purpose makes sacrifice worthwhile and unites people for the common good. Contrast the purpose-oriented approach to the usual method of playing people off against each other (to their mutual destruction and that of the organization). Compare it with those exhortative and sometimes utterly useless meetings at which colleagues, well-lubricated by alcohol, arrive at temporary liaisons to assure themselves of each other's friendship for survival purposes.

Once a sense of purpose is established in the annual retreat or in more frequent discussions; the organization has an important psychological device for keeping people together and developing organizational momentum in a clearly defined direction. Such an effort on an annual basis is a preventive device. It becomes particularly important when drastic organizational changes have had to take place, when diverse groups of people have had to be brought together, when merger has occurred, or when a significant shift in leadership has taken place.

Conclusion

In an era of increasingly rapid organizational change -- when people feel mote and more alienated and alone and managements strive with increasing frustration to sustain identification with the organization, loyalty, and interest in the task -- it becomes imperative to look ever more closely at how these two separate needs of the individual and the organization can be welded into a common purpose from which individual, organization, and society all profit.

Already we know the cost of organizational disruption in terms of alienation, increase in psychosomatic illness, and decrease in productivity. Now we are learning more about the chronic depression that many people experience when the way they are managed maximizes their loss experience and disrupts their sources of gratification and support. All organizations increasingly will have to evaluate the human cost of loss and change. They are already called upon to think of the cost of their effects on the environment. The next step in the process of social evolution will be to weigh the costs of organizational influences on people.

It is predictable that, ultimately, psychological pollution precipitated by arbitrary and unthinking leadership action will become unacceptable and subject to compensation just as physical pollution and contamination are now subject to compensation. Weighing the impact of one's decisions on people's psychological attachments therefore becomes not merely a do-gooder interest. it is also an important matter of self-interest.

Loss and Possession, death and life are one,
There falls no shadow where there shines no sun.
Hilaire Belloc, 1870-1953
For a Sundial

CHAPTER 9

SECTION THREE

LEADERSHIP

FATE, FADS, AND FICKLE FINGERS THEREOF

Consulting Psychology Bulletin*, 37, 3, 3-11, Fall 1985
*New journal title: *Consulting Psychology Journal: Practice and Research*

Psychology, like other disciplines, gets caught up in fads. This is especially true in consultation, whether to individuals or organizations. All of us, too keenly aware of the limits of our knowledge and skill, and needing to be open to new ideas, want to try innovations. Yet, too often, we fail to test new ideas as hypotheses. We often adopt them naively, with great fervor and partisan zeal. When there are no longer customers for those interventions, we go on to something else. Too rarely do we look back carefully to the reasons why the techniques are no longer in demand or what casualties we have left in our wake. It is one purpose of this paper to review some of those passing techniques in management consultation and to call attention to our need to recognize them and to keep ourselves from becoming victims of professional gimmicks and mechanical assumptions.

Management Fads

The Omnicompetent Manager. Psychological fads occur in a context of management fads. In management practice, fads have been reflected in management styles. The later abandoned General Electric thesis that a good manager can manage anything was picked up by the American Management Association and became the rallying cry of a whole generation of management educators. Along with it" came the Vince Lombardi slogan, "Winning is the only thing," and the model of the dominating charismatic chief executive officer.

The Portfolio Manager. The concept of the omnicompetent manager was elaborated by the model CEO as a financial manager. In this conception the organization was viewed as a series of subsidiaries to be managed as a financial portfolio. Everything that could be so labeled became a profit center, sometimes even those that had no profit responsibility. The paragon of this style of management was Harold Geneen, who built ITT from a quietly ineffectual international telephone company into a $15 billion conglomerate. The move was on to conglomeration. Bigger was better; a good manager can manage anything.

But, as it turned out, bigger wasn't necessarily better and a good manager couldn't necessarily manage everything. Clifton C. Garvin, Jr., chief executive officer of Exxon, was quoted in *Time* as saying ruefully that he didn't think executives of petroleum companies could manage other kinds of companies, as he contemplated the wreckage of Exxon's efforts with office automation subsidiaries, Mobil's failure with Montgomery Ward and Container Corporation, and the abortive movement of Socal into AMAX and that of ARCO into Anaconda.

Management by Objectives. The executive as financial manager concept was coupled with Peter Drucker's (1954) advocacy of management by objectives. A good many consultants picked up that thesis to considerable profitability as they hammered again and again at the need for organizations to define their objectives. Concern with objectives turned into concern with strategy. For two decades there was a heavy emphasis on strategic planning, long-range implications, computer modeling, discounted cash flow, and issues of that kind as organizations tried to become more rational in their competitive efforts.

Marketing. If a corporation couldn't be managed as a portfolio, what then should its thrust be? Marketing, naturally. That was it. A company must sell its product. Look at P&G, at IBM-they were the marketing companies. For the imitators, the emphasis was then on the hype. Between the concept of discounted cash flow, that was said to prove that manufacturing didn't pay, and the marketing hype that seemed to make quality of product irrelevant, we lost the manufacturing edge of a whole range of products to Japan.

Matrix Management. But still, making a product or rendering a service had to be combined with selling it. Ergo, matrix management. That style of management is a highly complex mode of operating which usually creates more problems than it solves. It requires continuous and careful consultation between those superiors to whom any manager reports and a carefully established policy that will govern the behavior of both of those superiors. Fortunately, that one didn't get too far before it fell of its own weight. In fact, that one went fast, no longer than it took for several authors to write books and hang out their consultation shingles.

Culture. No sooner was that dismissed than "culture" became the buzz Word. Culture has been around for a long time. The fact that one can differentiate the characteristic behavior of people in one corporation from that in another corporation in the same industry is an old story. It was even an old story thirteen years ago when I detailed ways of examining organization culture without ever using that word (Levinson, 1972).

With the new wave there was much glib talk about changing organization culture. Many consultants are still talking glibly about it. Any experienced consultant knows that it takes at least ten years to change a large organization significantly. None of the discussions of culture change I have seen indicates that consultants, with the exceptions of Elliott Jaques (1976), appreciate that or that they have had consulting relations with the same companies on culture change over such a period of time.

There are only three ways to change organization cultures radically: a) discharge the current management and bring in completely new managerial cadre; b) employ significant numbers of new people with values and skills different from those already established in the organization; c) change the orientation of the people who are already there. Anyone of these actions requires time for developing effective working relationships, a common language, the management of change, and the creation of identification with leadership. Furthermore, to change a culture one would have to also change the performance appraisal system, the compensation system, promotion criteria, managerial styles, and the organizational structure.

Decentralization. The rush to decentralization, which antedated **In Search of Excellence** (Peters and Waterman, 1982), resulted in creating small empires instead of one large one. Smaller units can be ruled as autocratically as the larger ones and the bureaucracy can become a divisional bureaucracy rather than a corporate bureaucracy. Division heads can stamp their personalities on divisions just as rigidly as can corporate CEOs. When it becomes necessary to reorganize decentralized units to produce systems rather than single products, the previously created feudal lords then usually leave their organizations, as happened at Hewlett-Packard and other companies. When corporations were radically decentralized and managers were pressed to delegate, higher level managers often fled from new responsibilities by offloading them on their subordinates. Frequently they delegated responsibility to subordinates who had neither the perspective, nor the experience, nor the capacity to carry on the level of function required. Often overwhelmed, they floundered. They complained about lack of direction from above. Their recommendations often did little to cope with the complexity of the problems they were asked to address. "Skunk works," advocated by Peters and Waterman may help to develop a single product, but they don't do much for the basic research that is necessary to carry on the theoretical and conceptual underpinnings from which single products may be developed. Nor can they handle the complexities of marketing, distribution, and integration with the larger organization as IBM discovered (Sanger, 1985).

Excellence. And now we have the rush to "excellence." Of course, every body wants to be excellent. Given the history of shoddy products that has led us to lose markets to overseas manufacturers, we did indeed need to become more excellent. However, much of what has followed has been fervid exhortation. All consultants have seen many public statements in company philosophies, annual reports, and messages to the troops that urge excellence. Decentralization, "skunk works," staying close to the customer, all have been urged and, in some cases, practiced.

We can be pleased with the attention to people that the crusade for excellence presumably has fostered. All of us in the behavioral sciences have been advocating more sophisticated managerial attention to subordinates for years. However, we must be dismayed with the glibness with which that word "excellence" is bandied about and with the many misguided efforts in the name of excellence.

It is important, of course, to turn some people loose to be more creative. But which people? Should all people be turned loose? Should only some people be turned loose? Or only some under certain circumstances? And does the pursuit of excellence justify turning out one group of managers for another, as happened in one company with no further logic for the change?

And, what is the role of leadership with respect to those people who are turned loose? In the crusade for excellence, little has been said about the importance of performance appraisal, organizational structure, and styles of leadership and how these three crucial aspects of organization enhance or inhibit excellence.

Psychological Fads. Turning to psychology, from the days of the Hawthorne studies (Roethlisberger and Dickson, 1939) there has been a heavy emphasis on small groups, their norms, their supervision, and their place in the organizational structure. The recognition that people were the important components of an organization and that formal structure and processes were secondary led to a continuing concern over the past fifty years for understanding small group functioning and the relationship of foremen and supervisors to people at work. There was a movement away from mechanical assumptions and measurement efforts for daily work tasks (although never in the old AT&T and Western Electric where the studies took place). This interest carried over in other countries to Trist and Bamforth's (1951) studies in British coal mines and A. K. Rice's (1958) work in the Ahmedabad silk mills.

Ultimately, the structure of the Kalmar Volvo plant was reorganized so that people could learn all the jobs to be done on a given major automobile assembly task. That enabled them to rotate among the jobs, to have the stimulation of a range of kinds of work. These and other innovations led to concepts of leaderless groups.

These efforts in part were derivatives of the historic concern with job enrichment, job enlargement, and the heavy emphasis that Frederick Herzberg (1959) gave to the work itself and the need for autonomy. In the same tradition we were encouraged by Maslow's (1954) self-actualization conceptions, Douglas McGregor's (1960) discussion of Theory X and Theory Y, with the Blake and Mouton Managerial Grid (1964), and with Likert's System Four conceptions (1967) to open up interaction in the organization so that people could voluntarily and collectively do spontaneously what otherwise they had to be "motivated" to do.

These thrusts then carried over into the Topeka dog food plant (Walton, 1982) and into similar experiments in other situations that enabled people to be significantly self-governing in their daily work activity. However, in the process of establishing such efforts, a number of issues were not recognized. For example, in the British coal mines the social structure above the ground. Because the miners lived together in the same mining villages, there necessarily had to be tacit leadership.

Volvo officials themselves said that it was unlikely that they could duplicate in another plant what they did in Kalmar. I have seen no mention of that in the American literature. Simultaneously, nobody recognized that autoworkers in Sweden were more often not Swedes but Finns. When any group of people is imported labor in another country, naturally they will cling together, they will be more spontaneously related to each other, and it will be easier to do with them what one could not do so easily with such a diverse group as automobile workers in Detroit. But even at Volvo, I am told, it became necessary to reinstitute foremen because somebody had to be accountable.

Most of the efforts to use leaderless groups and abolish first-level supervision took place in small plants where a plant manager could himself or herself supervise 50 to 75 people without intermediaries when the work itself was stable and repetitive. I do not know of successful efforts to use leaderless groups in larger plants where the work is varied and there is a need both to give direction and resolve differences.

There is a good deal of research and lay information on the tyranny of groups, on their inability to innovate, on the inability of members of groups to deviate from group norms lest they be extruded from those groups, on the difficulties of employees in employee-owned plants accepting layoffs, and on the difficulties such plants have in maintaining managers. Few of these phenomena seem to have raised questions among those social psychologists who were, and indeed still are, advocating greater group control of the manufacturing process. There are many unresolved problems with socio-technical leaderless group efforts (Hirschhorn, 1984).

I label much of this work fallacious, not because the original work was not praiseworthy, but because derivatives seem to be advocated glibly without adequate thought about the complexities of organization structure, demographics, manufacturing technique, and differences among industries.

Group Decision Making. These activities are part of a strong movement toward industrial democracy, stimulated by successive waves of social psychologists and carried into application by many people in organizational development. The social psychological orientation is that of a fraternal psychology. Its underlying theme, as I interpret it, is that we are all equal and therefore, to oversimplify, signs or symptoms of power are bad. In fact, power is bad by definition, as autocratic forms of political and organizational management demonstrate. It is especially bad if it doesn't arise from the bottom, but rather occurs by delegation. Ideally, the leader is the first among equals. This is what Little ("1984") speaks of as the social aggregate he defines as "group," concerned with individual care, locating meaning in others, and valuing subjective experience. The leader in such a context is expected to give effect to his followers' sense of selfhood and relationship. Followers of the group leader want to be brothers rather than rivals.

In its post-World War II incarnation, this orientation led to a heavy emphasis on group decision making. An organization, it was held, was merely a series of overlapping groups and therefore, obviously, groups should make their own decisions and the leader of the group was to transmit those decisions to the next higher-level group of which he or she was also a part. Such theorizing was short on accountability and responsibility. It had little to say about what happened if the leader, who was presumably accountable, disagreed with the decision of the group. If he or she overturned the group decision, then that finished group decision making. If the manager did not disagree with what he or she thought was a bad decision, his or her neck was in a managerial noose. There followed the idea that first level supervisors, particularly, were unnecessary and therefore there needed to be only lead persons whose task it was to lead group discussions. Ergo, leaderless groups as discussed above. There would be no boss.

That didn't answer questions about what a group would do if its members were in conflict and no one had the authority to resolve that conflict. This is an endemic problem in accounting firms, law firms, other partnerships, and in certain technical operations where people feel they should not be, and indeed need not be, either supervised or accountable to anyone else. It occurs often in self-governing work groups, as Hirschhorn ("1984") summarizes.

Quality Circles. The reincarnation of group decision making took the form of quality circles. Whatever the merits of some quality circles, this was a frequently misguided application from what was assumed to be a Japanese model. High-level management wanted to compete with the Japanese by being more Japanese than the Japanese were. They pointed to first-level supervision and plant managers as needing to establish quality circles. No matter that the Japanese culture was vastly different from our own, including a Confucian tradition with rules for relationships between those of higher and lower status, or that the Japanese companies that were being imitated employed people for life, and that everybody knew what the boss wanted anyway. No matter either that one could not do at the bottom levels of an organization what was not managerially consistent at higher levels of the organization. Little account was taken of the organization value system, its culture, its structure, its operational processes, or its leadership style. Little wonder that it was reported that 80% of quality circle efforts failed in five years, and that for others enthusiasm died in the second year where attention turned from cost cutting and mechanical efficiency to styles of management and management practices. Higher management typically was not interested in those topics.

MBO. Antedating these activities, as I noted earlier, there was preoccupation with Management by Objectives (MBO). While all employees of any organization should clearly understand what it is they are supposed to do and when it should be done according to specified criteria, MBO, in most cases, turned out to be a highly simplified, by-the-numbers mechanistic device. People learned not to set objectives unless they had already accomplished two-thirds to three quarters of them, to set them in steps that were as short-term and as vague as they could manipulate, and to devise means for maneuvering around them. Furthermore, although the "how" of a person's role performance is as important, and sometimes even more important, than the objectives attained, no attention was given to the' 'how". When people are promoted, they take with them not their accomplishments in earlier roles, but their consistent methods of problem solving and the flexibility to evolve new ones that are essentially, their stock-in-trade. It is those methods or managerial "style" that determines whether a person is able to assume various responsibilities.

Performance Appraisal. There has been a renewed emphasis on performance appraisal in the organizational behavior literature. This emphasis has included exhortation, behavior modeling, coaching, and other mechanisms for getting people to do performance appraisal. New rating forms proliferate. All forms and methods have failed so far, witness the repetitively futile effort to devise a successful method. The vice president of human resources of Exxon recently told *Fortune* that even the largest corporation in the world has failed to devise a satisfactory performance appraisal system over the last 30 years.

The reason such efforts fail is that so few psychologists, and even fewer people in other disciplines, have an understanding of unconscious guilt. It is unconscious guilt that undermines all performance appraisal and that must be understood and dealt with or people will: a) not do performance appraisal; b) pile up the ratings at the high end of the scale; c) resort to forced choice methods, based on a curve of normal distribution, that has no validity when applied to small numbers of people (Levinson, 1976).

The performance appraisal system is the fundamental means of transmitting the culture of an organization. If employees can't trust the performance appraisal system, they can't trust the compensation system or the promotion system. The recent rash of suits by fired middle managers against top management for age discrimination, which top management can't defend because few performance appraisal systems have recorded behavioral data, is testimony to the futility of contemporary performance appraisal efforts. Pressure for equal pay for comparable work, for evaluation of professionals like nurses and teachers, for evaluating older people who must be allowed to work until they are seventy, point to the need for greater specificity. Present inadequate appraisal methods can only be regarded as fads when their proponents persist in selling them because others are doing so.

Compensation. Almost all compensation plans are based on reward-punishment conceptions. By and large these are intended to establish fair pay and in many cases also to serve as incentives. However, nobody has ever been able to demonstrate that any mode of incentive compensation, short of commission for first-level salesmen, has done much to incent anybody. In fact, the continuous manipulation of bonus plans, profit sharing stock options, and mechanisms of that sort, serves to tell us how futile most such efforts are. If you ask corporate executives why they continue to use bonuses despite all the problems with them, they usually will answer, "Because other companies are doing it." One might almost speak of most compensation efforts as motivation by manipulation. In another context I have called them The Great Jackass Fallacy (Levinson, 1973). Ultimately, compensation issues will best be dealt with using Elliott Jaques' conception of structure, time-span and time frame. In that conception people's capacity to handle complexity will be the significant determinant of their level of compensation. Meanwhile, as Frederick Herzberg has noted (1959), for most people compensation is a dissatisifier rather than a satisfier. In managerial ranks, incentive compensation is arbitrarily determined because there are so few instances in which it can be tied directly to individual productivity or personal achievement. In fact, some people are highly compensated because of the achievement of their predecessors, who set things up in such a way that their successors can now be highly successful.

Let It All Hang Out. Beginning in the 1950's and continuing through the 1970's, parallel with the emphasis on group decision making and arising from some of the same traditions, we had the "let it all hang out" thesis. This began with T-groups, followed by encounter groups, followed by marathons, followed by EST and its variations. These activities were characterized by almost total absence of understanding of human personality and the defensive structures of human beings. Their advocates and practitioners denied the casualties they precipitated, the damage they did to careers, and the utter futility of it as reflected in the abandonment of the T-group method by its erstwhile leading practitioners. Research results indicated that such groups were (and sought after as) another form of therapy (Lieberman, Yalom and Miles, 1973), despite the denials of their practitioners.

Participation declined when it became apparent that it was a lot easier to take people apart than to put them back together again. In many cases it also became apparent that the practitioners of such activities were indulging in displaced hostility by scapegoating participants or allowing the more skilled manipulators to scapegoat the more easily manipulated. Indeed, in many cases trainers actively encouraged scapegoating. Furthermore, people from companies and other institutions were sent to such activities irresponsibly: untrained people, like personnel directors, were making diagnoses of what kinds of treatment people needed for ostensible behavioral problems.

All behavior, whether individual or organizational, is a resultant of many simultaneously operating forces. Therefore, before getting involved in the application of these and other practices, consultants must be careful to look at the underlying assumptions each technique is making about human motivation, as reflected in what managers are expected to do and what behavior is expected to follow. All actions are based on some assumption, usually tacit, about why people behave as they do. There are few theories in organizational psychology that have a sophisticated understanding of personality. Apart from psychoanalytic theory, there are only part-theories. Different techniques make different assumptions about motivation and these are frequently in conflict with each other.

The consultant needs to look carefully at the organization structure. Does it facilitate getting work done, or is it an effort to "provide incentive?" To the extent to which the structure is to provide incentive, it is likely to fail. There is no underlying psychological logic for it. The only psychological logic for organizational structure so far advanced is that of Elliott Jaques (1976).

The consultant has to carefully examine organizational processes. I have enumerated MBO, performance appraisal, and compensation among others. To what extent are they honored in the breach? To what extent are they merely glib formulae that become mutually contradictory? To what extent are they based on a descriptive psychology rather than an explanatory psychology that takes into account unconscious processes? If they are based on a descriptive psychology, then they are necessarily subject to frequent change because none is satisfactory. No organizational psychology based on manipulation of the environment or rewards and punishments will work for very long. We don't hear much any more about behavior modification as a supervisory mechanism-another fad of a decade ago.

Finally, how does the consultant understand the leadership style of the chief executive officer and its impact on the organization? Some say they are consultants to the whole organization and not to any single person in the organization, however authoritative that person may be.

That, to me, is utter nonsense. As long 'as one or more key people can decide whether the consultant is to remain in the organization and what the consultant is free to do in the organization, then the consultant must necessarily take them into account and deal directly with them.

Furthermore, the consultant who is introducing change into an organization should formulate a prognosis, namely, what kind of effort is going to be invested over what period of time with what potential results? Failing that, the consultation may go on indefinitely or the consultant may try to cover al\ bases. But even more important is the question of how long the change will last. One may recall the changes that occurred in the Harwood Manufacturing Company as detailed by Marrow, Bowers and Seashore (1967). To visit Harwood now is to discover that those processes that Marrow wrote about so proudly are no longer in vogue. The same is true with respect to Harmon International. I suspect if we looked at a number of companies that have been held up in the past as models of participative management or some other style, we would discover that those styles are no longer in practice there and hardly even remembered. This is not to say that there was anything wrong with those efforts, but only that when the chief executive officer wants something to happen in a company, it will, happen. Whether it can become institutionalized in such a way that it cannot be torn apart or disrupted by successive managements is another question. Even the results of the famous Hawthorne studies were never integrated into Western Electric. Successive managements neither understood nor appreciated the contributions those studies had made.

There is even a more painful side to some current consulting efforts, particularly those based on survey methods. One can get all kinds of answers to survey questions and point to all kinds of problems, but rarely can one discern from the replies the underlying "why?" of the problems at hand. To understand such problems requires a more sophisticated understanding of both individual and group processes. It is not enough to leave the consultee with a summary of the raw data and with the problem of what to do after the feedback.

Consultants have frequently worked with levels of management with little enduring effect. Often they couldn't get to top management and more often top management was skeptical about the clichés being offered. Good top executives understand that they are always dealing with complexity. They know that single techniques that do not take complexity into account won't go very far. They believe, and often rightly so, that their leadership style has made them successful. The task of the consultant is to help them understand, without lowering their self-image, that all styles have certain positive and negative elements. Some of the negative aspects of style are amenable to change. Most, however, are not. That often means the compensatory devices and mechanisms may have to be developed. To do that one has to understand personality functioning, and now we are back to square one. That's where most consultants in organizational behavior fall short and why so many are caught up in consultation fads and fallacies. And why we will continue to deal with lower levels of management and employees unless we ourselves become more sophisticated. The fads indeed will be the fickle fingers that determine our professional fate.

REFERENCES

Blake, R.R., and Mouton, J.S. (1964) The Managerial Grid. Houston: Gulf.

Drucker, P.F. (1954) The Practice of Management. New York: Harper and Row.

Herzberg, F., Mausner, B., and Snyderman, B. (1959) The Motivation to Work. New   York: Wiley.

Hirschhorn, L. (1984) Beyond Mechanization. Cambridge, MA: MIT Press.

Jaques, E. (1976) A General Theory of Bureaucracy. New York: Halsted.

Levinson, H. (1972) Organizational Diagnosis. Cambridge, MA: Harvard University Press. Levinson, H. (1973) The Great Jackass Fallacy. Cambridge, MA: Harvard   University Press.

Levinson, H. (1976) "Appraisal of What Performance?" Harvard Business Review, July

August, 1976, 30-46.

Lieberman, M.A., Yalom, I.D., and Miles, M.B. (1973) Encounter Groups: First Facts. New York: Basic.

Likert, R. (1967) The Human Organization. New York: McGraw-Hill.

Little, G. (1984) "Ambivalence, Dilemma, and Paradox: The Nature and Significance of   Leader Follower Ties, with Comments on the Leadership of Margaret Thatcher." Political Psychology, 1984, 5,553-571.

Marrow, A.J., Bowers, D.G., and Seashore, S.E. (1967) Management by Partcipation.   New York: Harper and Row.

Maslow, A. (1954) Motivation and Personality. New York: Harper and Brothers.

McGregor, D.M. (1960) The Human Side of Enterprise. New York: McGraw.Hill

Peters, T.J., and Waterman, R.H., Jr. (1982) In Search of Excellence. New York: Harper and Row.

Rice, A.K. (1958) Productivity and Social Organization. London: Tavistock.

Roethlisberger, F.J., and Dickson, W.J. (1939) Management and the Worker.   Cambridge, MA: Harvard University Press.

Sanger, D.E. (1985) "The Changing Image of IBM," New York Times Magazine, July   7, 1985,   12ff.

Trist, E.L., and Bamforth, K.W. (1951) "Some Social and Psychological Consequences of the Long-Wall Method of Coal Getting," Human Relations, 1951, 4, 1-38.

Walton, R. (1982) "The Topeka Work System: Optimistic Visions, Pessimistic   Hypotheses, and Reality." In R. Zager and M.P. Rosow (Eds.) The Innovative Organization: Productivity Programs In Action. New York: Pergamon.

CHAPTER 10

SECTION THREE

LEADERSHIP

FREUD AS AN ENTREPRENEUR: IMPLICATIONS FOR CONTEMPORARY PSYCHOANALYTIC INSTITUTES

In L. Lapierre (ed.), *Clinical Approaches to the Study of Managerial and Organizational Dynamics.* Montreal: Ecole des Hautes Etudes Commerciales, May 1990

Charismatic authority, Weber (1947) postulated, arises because of faith in a leader believed to be endowed with exceptional qualities. In order to sustain charisma, charismatic leadership must be routinized -- that is, firmly established -- within a framework of rational-legal authority, a belief in the inviolability of formal norms.

That is what had begun to happen when, in. the autumn of 1901, at the suggestion of Wilhelm Steckel, Freud addressed postcards to Steckel, Alfred Adler, Max Kahane, and Rudolf Reitter, inviting them to meet with him at 19 Bergasse to discuss his work (Jones, 1953a). The weekly meetings that followed became the Wednesday Psychological Society and, on April 15, 1908, the Vienna Psychoanalytic Society.

According to Weber, charisma includes five components: 1) an extraordinary "gifted" person; 2) a social crisis or situation of desperation; 3) a set of ideas providing a radical solution to the crisis; 4) a set of followers who are attracted to the exceptional person and come to believe that he or she is directly linked to transcendent powers;

5) the validation of that person's extraordinary gifts and transcendence by repeated successes (Weber, 1947).

All of these conditions were present for Freud. Furthermore, he met other criteria for the charismatic leader (House, 1977): "extreme high levels of self-confidence, dominance, and a strong conviction of moral righteousness of his beliefs" and "a high need to have influence over others." His behavior was consistent with that of other leaders described as charismatic: he offered himself as an effective role model, he created the impression of competence and success, he articulated ideological goals, he communicated high expectations plus confidence in his key followers, and he stimulated them to want to be as capable and insightful as he was.

That Freud was charismatic is beyond question. But why did he seek to sustain charismatic leadership? Was it not enough to become famous for discovering a revolutionary method of learning about and understanding feelings, thoughts, and behavior? Couldn't one, like Einstein, be contented with a place in history for conceptualizing those insights? Obviously, for Freud the answer was, "No." The reasons lead us to the psychological logic behind founding a psychoanalytic organization, and, in turn, to its structure and ultimately the influence of that structure on the theory and practice of psychoanalysis as mediated by psychoanalytic institutes.

Psychodynamics of Entrepreneurial Behavior

According to the various biographies, Freud was the preferred eldest child of a loving mother who required his brother and sisters to defer to him and his need to study. He would also be their somewhat authoritarian teacher. She encouraged his scholarship and professional aspiration. Her doting affection and his family position supported that degree of narcissism that led to a high level of self-confidence. "This self-confidence, which was one of Freud's prominent characteristics, was only rarely impaired and he was doubtless right in tracing it to the security of his mother's love" (Jones, 1953a).

His father apparently was rather weak and ineffectual. Classically, such a family constellation encourages the son to think that his mother prefers him over his father and that he should out-do him. When he is unable to resolve his Oedipal rivalry by solidifying his identification with his father, the rivalry persists. That sets the stage for entrepreneurial behavior. (Schumpeter, 1961). Entrepreneurial personalities, still protesting behaviorally against the father, have great difficulty with supervision and control (Levinson, 1971). Jones (1953a) reports that Freud disliked being hampered and fettered. Entrepreneurial behavior also is characterized by rebellion. As Gay (1988) puts it, Freud came to see himself as a destroyer of illusions and found this stance most congenial, and further, "Psychoanalysis aimed at nothing less than the overthrow of the reigning schools of psychiatry and psychology (p. 499)." McIntosh (1970) argues that charisma can be an "...acting out the universal Oedipal fantasy of the sons rising to overthrow the father through the rebellious qualities of both the leader and the followers." On his 50th birthday, his followers presented him with a medallion with his likeness on one side and Oedipus solving the riddle of the Sphinx on the other, thereby acknowledging his Oedipal role as well as the central position of that role in his theory.

The Freuds were immigrants to Austria from Moravia (now Czechoslovakia) where his father had experienced the hostility of woolen manufacturers. Vienna was not cordial to provincial Moravians. It was even less cordial to Jews. Sociologists generally recognize both circumstances as fertile ground for the development of entrepreneurs.

Inasmuch as his father was hardly a strong model for his masculinity, let alone his professional path, he leaned heavily on his professors and was as devoted to meeting their exacting demands and expectations, as he was to those of his mother. The perfectionistic striving, however, could not have been a product solely of external factors. Necessarily, the unresolved Oedipal rivalry must have left its residue of unconscious rage. That is a major source of the intense aggressive energy that drives entrepreneurs and makes it difficult for them to manage rivalry. The unconscious guilt, the product of primary process thinking that accompanies such rage exacerbates self-critical superego functioning and the resulting press for perfection. Jones reports that in a letter to Emil Fluss, Freud bemoaned his dread of mediocrity and was not easily satisfied with himself. Harshly self-critical, he was also necessarily hypersensitive to criticism by others. That configuration of forces, coupled with the narcissism and rebellious posture referred to earlier, is conducive to condescension. It also is conducive to ready dependency, for self-doubt is never far from a severe superego, despite the manifest self-confidence. "A profound self-confidence had been marked by strange feelings of inferiority, even in the intellectual sphere, and he had tried to cope with these by projecting his innate sense of capacity and superiority onto a series of mentors, on some of whom he then became curiously dependent for reassurance. Thus he idealized six figures who played an important part in his early life: Brucke. Meinert, Fleischl, Charcot, Breuer, and Fliess, all of whom were good friends to him" (Jones, 1953b). They, his later adherents and the public at large, became the sources of applause and recognition he needed to counteract the superego demands that threatened his self-image as reflected in his deprecation of his various papers.

Most entrepreneurs are too rivalrous to sustain close friendships. Freud was an exception. "An intimate friend and a hated enemy have always been indispensable to my emotional life. I have always been able to create them anew, and not infrequently my childish ideal has been so closely approached that friend and enemy have coincided in the same person, but not simultaneously, of course, as was the case in my early childhood" (Jones, 1953a). Breuer, Fliess (on whom he was most dependent when he worked in painful isolation for ten years after separating from Breuer), and Jung were his only close friends. All became enemies. He would also split with Adler, Steckel, Ferenczi, and Rank.

The Leader and the Follower

Weber contended that if the leader does not repeatedly validate his charisma, he loses his authority and the solidity of the movement he started is jeopardized. Trice and Beyer (1986) point out, "Charismatics apparently understand very well the pivotal role of success in maintaining their authority for they go to unusual lengths to claim and redefine success."

That meant he needed followers. A rebel seeking adherents naturally attracts other rebels. The rebel followers are likely to be of three kinds: 1) those who identify fully with the leader and can become his acolytes; 2) those who are tentative, either distantly interested or who become involved and then lose interest; 3) those whose identification with the leader is only a mechanism for grafting their own ideological propensities onto his. The last, after having matured in their own eyes, usually separate to go their own ways. Freud had many of all three kinds. One could argue that the third kind were the Oedipal rebels who had to overthrow Freud's dominance as he had to undermine significant psychological verities of his time. One could argue alternatively that they brought varied experiences to their construction of meaning, and offer even more speculative psychoanalytic reasons.

Freud's organizational troubles seemed to begin when, in its fifth year, Rank became the first paid staff person, the secretary of the Wednesday Psychological Society. Rank's job was to take notes at each meeting, collect dues, and record attendance. He was the first psychoanalytic bureaucrat. The appointment of a secretary was the beginning of structure. Structure implies status, degrees of power and politics. All began to appear. After Rank's appointment, "The meetings grew testy, even acrimonious as members sparred for position, vaunted their originality, or voiced dislike of their fellows with a brutal hostility masked as analytic frankness" (Gay, 1988). Besides, as the organization grew the members became a varied lot, few of whom could approach Freud's level of conceptual thinking. Freud tried to cope with their conflicts by reorganizing the group into the Vienna Psychoanalytic Society, allowing some to drop out or to change their relationship to the group.

In this experience lies a fundamental problem that has troubled psychoanalytic societies since that time. Following scientific tradition, Freud wanted to stimulate the greatest exchange possible among those interested in his work. He encouraged originality. Unlike the classical entrepreneur or other charismatic leaders, he was unwilling to impose inviolable doctrine on his followers. He wanted the respect and acceptance of the scientific community (Gay, 1988). He did not want mere echoes.

Preserving the Creation

But, like all entrepreneurs, he also wanted to preserve his creation, his "baby." The Swiss psychiatrist, Eugen Bleuler, told Freud that he was an artist who wanted to preserve his creation intact and was passionately eager to secure its acceptance (Hale, 1971).

In the business world, entrepreneurs, men who have failed to win their mothers, build organizations and then usually "marry them" (Levinson, 1971). (Few female entrepreneurs have built large organizations.) In effect, they create their own psychological families and become one with them. It is difficult to separate the person from the organization; he is it and it is he. The "baby," and the family of unconscious fantasy, often is more important than their literal families. Indeed, spouses of such men frequently complain that they desert their families for the business. To preserve his "baby," Freud had to start an organization.

Charisma is routinized by: 1) the development of an administrative apparatus that stands apart from the charismatic, to cope with the ongoing operating needs generated by putting the charismatic's program into practice; 2) the transformation and transference of charisma to others in the organization by means of rites, ceremonials, and symbols; 3) the incorporation of the charismatic's message and mission into the written and oral traditions of the organization; and 4) the selection of a successor who resembles the charismatic sufficiently to be like a reincarnation (Eisenstadt, 1968); and *5)* the degree to which the organization (or other collectivity) continues to express, to work toward, and to cohere around the charismatic message and mission of the founder (or reformer) (Trice & Beyer, 1986). To these I would add identification with the *behavior* and underlying psychodynamics of the charismatic leader: narcissism (reflected in pursuit, conviction, promulgation, wish to perpetuate), together with rebelliousness and projective identification.

Weber (1947) suggests that routinization is hampered by the direct involvement of the charismatic in the mundane features of administration. Anything that tends to dilute the exceptionality dilutes the charisma. Grete Bibring (1978) reported that among the members of the Vienna Psychoanalytic Society, there was much dream interpretation and socializing. Freud was much too involved with his followers and their organization and did not maintain sufficient psychological distance from them for idealization to be sustained.

Trice and Beyer (1986) add that when an organization fails to develop a strong reinforcing culture -- including ritual and ceremonies to transfer and diffuse charisma, together with written testament and oral tradition to guide behavior -- the organizing force behind the charisma tends to fade away over time. None of that was sufficiently present in the early days of the Wednesday Psychological Society or the Vienna Psychoanalytic Society. Although most of the followers at the time wanted to be able to think like Freud, they seemed to be more concerned with becoming practicing psychoanalysts.

In short, the ego ideal of the entrepreneurial Freud was in conflict with the ego ideal of the scientific Freud. That made it impossible for the Vienna Psychoanalytic Society of Freud's time to become the model society and to meet Freud's hoped-for support and perpetuation of his work. Yet, the imperative need for such support of prominent men is well established (Bird, et al, 1983).

Karl Abraham and Max Eitingon in Berlin, Ernest Jones in London, and Sandor Ferenczi in Budapest became the rescuers of Freud's hopes and ambitions. Their ego ideal task was primarily to protect the "baby." At one time or another, they all had been guests at the Wednesday Psychological Society. Abraham founded the Berlin Psychoanalytic Society in 1908. Subsequently, that Society developed its own clinic and training program that became the model for the rest. Societies took root in other countries. Their big advantage was that they were distant geographically from Freud and therefore could idealize him. At Freud's instance, Ferenczi proposed the formation of the International Psychoanalytic Association at the International Congress of Psychoanalysts in Nurnberg in 1910. This proposal reflected the fact that Freud had now turned from Vienna to a worldwide network. He had intended all along that his work be recognized worldwide and to have a worldwide effect (Gay, 1988).

Two persistent nagging problems drove the protective effort. One was the threat to the reputation of the nascent movement by "wild" analysts and others, now in various parts of the world, who would not only vitiate or trivialize its findings, but also undermine its scientific reputation. Freud was uneasy about what the "human rabble" might make of his work.

The second was the need to "hold on to the homogeneity of the core" of psychoanalytic knowledge and practice as more people became psychoanalysts by the mere expedient of declaring themselves to be. He wrote to Bleuler that he feared the extravagances of some of his followers and needed a central headquarters to control their polemics (Hale, 1971).

Beneath both problems was Freud's need to preserve and perpetuate his "baby" and to immortalize himself. In addition, Freud had to cope with the hostility of the Vienna medical and neurological communities and those outside of Vienna, the growing criticism of his ideas, and the defections from the Vienna Psychoanalytic Society. Sandor Ferenczi, Otto Rank, Hans Sachs, Karl Abraham, and Ernest Joncs, at Jones' suggestion, (Jones, 1953a) in 1912 formed a protective coterie around Freud. "I daresay it would make living and dying easier for me if I knew of such an association existing to watch over my creation," he had said about the formation of that group of six. Obviously, the broader, more comprehensive worldwide group would be even more important to him.

Developing Institutes

To foster that group he recognized, required not only developing the International, but also training institutes "to guarantee the authenticity of his teaching and the competence of the taught." "Freud took the initiative not only in organizing the movement in Europe and America, but also in defining a psychoanalyst as one who accepted his theories" (Hale, 1971). In these efforts, Freud turned out to be what Gay (1988) describes as a true politician, " more devious than in the rest of his conduct, and his struggles with Adler brought out all his latent gifts for navigating among contending forces in pursuing his program." These efforts took much of his time and energy.

Clark (1972) has identified five "carrying missions" essential to fulfill organizational sagas: 1) a key group of believers who routinize the charisma of the leader in collegial authority; 2) program embodiment, which involves the visible practice with which claims of distinctiveness can be supported (that is, unusual courses, noteworthy requirements, or specific methods of teaching); 3) a supporting social base among outside believers devoted to the organization; 4) an allied student subculture, which "steadily and dependably transferred this ideology from one generation to another;" 5) imagery of the saga "widely expressed as a generalized tradition in statues and ceremonies, written histories, and current catalogs even in the 'air about the place' felt by participants and some outsiders."

Under such circumstances all members gain charisma just by being members (Kanter, 1972). The routinization is most likely when "secondary leaders have taken the initiative in advancing their interest" (Madsen & Snow, 1983).

The Berlin Psychoanalytic Institute worked out a detailed training program with courses on theory and technique. Some, like Grete Bibring (1978), felt it to be rigid. "That was different from Vienna where we were not rigid. We were what we would call *schlumpig; schlumpig* is sloppy". But under Abraham and Eitingon, it was solid because both were unswerving admirers of Freud. Candidacy at that time, as Hans Sachs put it, corresponded to a novitiate in a church because the guidelines mandated a training analysis (Gay, 1988). In 1925, at the Ninth International Psychoanalytic Congress at Bad Homburg, Eitingon reported that in five years there had been sixteen didactic analyses. At the same meeting the concept of endorsement by local societies of the applications for training by the many from overseas who sought to get that training in Berlin and Vienna was approved. By 1929 admissions and training standards were in place, including the concept of being analyzed oneself before analyzing others. The primary emphasis was on becoming a good practicing analyst.

That emphasis carried over into the United States. The American psychoanalytic movement began with two streams, one primarily in Boston and the other in New York. The Boston stream started with Freud's journey to Worcester and his Clark University presentations, followed by his visit to the summer home of James Jackson Putnam. With Putnam's endorsement and leadership, given his prestigious academic position, and that of others of like repute, psychoanalysis took root. But it was not until Ives Hendrick, John Murray, M. Ralph Kaufman, and Helen Tartakoff returned from Berlin and Vienna that a more formal structure evolved. Gifford (1978) reports that Hendrick exaggerated the standards of the Berlin Psychoanalytic Institute where he trained and applied them to the newly formed Boston Psychoanalytic Institute: "He seemed to create a model of efficiency more German than the German analysts themselves, and this personal model of strictly impersonal regulations, and a concrete complex structure was imposed on the Boston analytic community. Hendrick's unswerving pursuit of this ideal may also have influenced the procedural apparatus of the American Psychoanalytic Association through his indefatigable work on its committees."

In New York, A. A. Brill was the dominant figure. The early New York analysts, under Brill's leadership, insisted on psychoanalysis as a medical discipline, an issue never fully resolved with Freud. The New York group tended to be the most orthodox and over identified with Freud. Its training program became a yardstick for others (Levine, 1962).

There seemed not to be much theoretical debate of the kind that characterized Freud's original followers, except among the American pioneers themselves. However, there were vigorous debates in both the Boston and New York Institutes about how standards were to be maintained and who should do so. These debates threatened the older analysts who had pioneered those societies and who wished that authority remain with them as training analysts rather than be taken over by the education committees as the International required. The younger analysts, fresh from their European training, advocated meeting the standards of the International. They won. Sicherman (1978) contends that the new orthodoxy transformed the American psychoanalytic movement from an optimistic and reformist creed to a professional specialty.

A crucial question was who becomes a training analyst and how. Discussions on that topic had been going on for years. Early on, after the era of simply declaring oneself to be an analyst, those who wished to become proficient psychoanalysts attached themselves to an established analyst. Then came the Institutes and their rules. But one still had to be analyzed and that analysis had to be accepted as valid by the education committee of a psychoanalytic institute. Earlier the International had delegated that task to the oldest member of a society it favored in each city (Hendrick, 1961). The Boston Society imported Franz Alexander to be its training analyst, the New York Society invited Sandor Rado. Hans Sachs, said by some to be the gadfly of the Boston Society, took the traditional position.

Hitler precipitated the influx of European analysts, representing the first generation of Freud's students' analysands. They readily became training analysts and influential figures in the American institutes. In addition to their culture and learning, they brought another perspective: some of the Europeans' condescension toward Americans (shared by Freud himself because he was fearful of the Americans as potential charlatans) and a sense of being elite, but they invigorated what before had seemed to be a small club. It subsequently became a larger, more rigid club.

Insider Games

"Most human systems," says John W. Gardner, (Gamarekian, 1989) "...move toward being what I call insider games. They set up barriers against outsiders knowing what's going on, perhaps even unintentionally. And successive regimes strengthen those barriers so that they can carry on their businesses without a lot of interruption. Unless there is someone out there who insists that is not the way it is going to run, you get yourself into a terrible mess. Pretty soon the system doesn't even work for the insiders."

That is what seemed to happen to many psychoanalytic institutes. The organizations were stymied significantly because these now old disciples maintained their elite manner as guardians of the truth and the method for getting it. First there was the general problem: who was a training analyst? The Education Committee of the International said one who was a practicing analyst in an affiliated society for five years and who had made at least two contributions to the psychoanalytic literature. But in some institutes, the Boston Psychoanalytic being one, no one knew how to go about becoming a training analyst. People were tapped on the shoulder by one of those who was established in that role. Others were left in the dark. The social structure of the Institute, it is said, became more rigid with hapless candidates at the bottom of the ladder who had to be examined and write papers. Gone was the tradition of open discussion as the second generation disciples guarded the treasure.

According to Jacobs (1983), "Through Freud they (the devoted teachers) had been given the gift of psychoanalysis to preserve, to nourish and to develop and by exercising that responsibility with care and wisdom and with creativity, they sought to make that dream come true." The ego ideal still was to be a guardian, to protect the "baby."

As a result, there soon began to be defections. In New York, Rado, Karen Horney, and Clara Thompson were read out of the party. Elsewhere there were splits. Open discussion of theoretical ideas was not tolerable. Whatever the specific manifest issues, behind them lay the issues of power and status on the one hand and intellectual examination on the other, together with the possession of the charisma.

The internal pressures against the over control were exacerbated in the 1950s and the 1960s with the growth of numbers of candidates and analysts, and the liberating spirit of the increased openness that characterized the rest of society. To the older analysts it sounded as if the younger ones had no confidence in them. For the younger ones to be able to interact with their seniors in the psychoanalytic institute was as expectable as their customary interaction with their parents, teachers, bosses and public officials. And, after all, was the psychoanalytic society not a family, a metaphor used widely? To be a family member was to share the charisma.

The conflict between these issues -- preserving the "baby" and sustaining the tradition of open discussion -- was reflected in the conflict between the membership and Board of Professional Standards of the American Psychoanalytic Association (Kris, 1976). On the one hand, the task of the American is to establish psychoanalysis as a profession through high standards of training. On the other, its purpose is also to advance psychoanalysis as a science and to become a partner in the quest for scientific knowledge and the welfare of man. Although nominally the Board of Professional Standards has a responsibility for setting and reinforcing the standards for Institute training, as a matter of fact it is a toothless tiger, Kris reported, and, he said, the Institutes wanted it that way. As a consequence many Institute graduates did not apply for membership in the American which in effect required them to be certified again.

That the Institutes want to retain their power seems to be consistent with Kemberg's (1986) criticism. Kemberg argues that all too often the atmosphere of the psychoanalytic institute is one of indoctrination rather than exploration in which "certain teachers ignore others and discuss Freud uncritically." He contends that candidates are sheltered from sharp disagreements, that they don't hear about their supervisors' cases and do not learn about the theory of technique from snippets in the literature. Furthermore, he feels the idealized literature doesn't present a realistic conception of the true nature of psychoanalytic work, that training analysts don't share with candidates what they do in a continuing way. This results in candidates' idealizing psychoanalytic technique and senior members of the faculty. It also results in the ultimate authority lying with the training analysts and not the rest of the faculty that then deprecates the authority of the faculty and the education committee. That, he argues, makes the training analysts the real bosses, the supervisors secondary and the courses tertiary. Those who are not training analysts and the junior faculty become demeaned. They do not get involved in evaluating the candidates, withdrawing from those who are privileged or are non-performing. All this then creates a paranoid atmosphere as a senior faculty reactivates the fantasy of the secretive Oedipal couple. He feels that the apparent arbitrariness of the appointment of training analysts is often political and further exacerbates these negative conditions. Furthermore, this mode of functioning results in diminished creative thinking and scientific productivity as well as narrow intellectual view. He argues that there is a need for explicit public policies for appointment and there needs to be explicit criteria of faculty functioning so that incompetents are not protected as their work is then exposed to their colleagues and students.

Kernberg argues that the candidates should be exposed to all theories and techniques so that they can evaluate them for themselves. He argues further that the faculty should be willing and able to engage in scientific debate, to expose their theories and clinical work. Otherwise the self-perpetuating elite will tend to exacerbate the idealization to retain maximum power to compensate for their waning creativity, productivity and sexuality, and financial security. That then paves the way for ambivalence leading to idealization, leading to splitting and to other schools of thought. The training analyst doesn't lead as he or she should and can be corrupted, a point made by John Gardner quoted earlier. In effect then, the analysand identifies with the aggressor. Balint (1954) had earlier discussed the training analyst's unconscious wish to mold his analysand into a clone, rather than offer the kind of treatment he would to a non-candidate patient.

Cultural Changes

Through the extended period from the early 1900s when Freud's work first began to get attention in the United States, his influence expanded as anthropologists, sociologists, social workers, psychologists, historians, and others applied its insights to their work. Many sought psychoanalytic training to enrich their efforts. Early on, also, work began with adolescents, child guidance clinics, and in psychosomatic medicine. These were offshoots of European efforts but gained new momentum in this country. Franz Alexander became the first professor of psychoanalysis at the University of Chicago in 1930 and Hans Sachs was appointed to a similar professorial post at the Harvard Medical School in 1932.

Research on psychosomatic medicine, on infants and children, in child development, and adult life stages expanded the purview of psychoanalysis. In 1932, Clifford Beers, assisted by mental health professionals, organized the first international conference on mental hygiene. That signaled the beginnings of the development of a citizen action organization to reform mental health facilities and foster public education in mental health. Because of the constriction of psychoanalysis as a medical discipline, non-medical psychoanalytic centers developed and trained psychologists and social workers. All of these diverse activities broadened the conceptions of psychoanalytic institutes to include the application of psychoanalytic thinking to the wide range of social issues and problems that Freud had envisioned.

During World War II, the military psychiatric leadership had been psychoanalytic and significant advances in the psychiatric treatment of military traumatic casualties demonstrated both to physicians and the military that psychoanalytic understanding had much to offer. Following that war, large numbers of physicians sought psychoanalytic training. In addition, as a product of that military experience, many psychiatric departments were headed by psychoanalysts and psychoanalysis became a necessary credential in many such settings for both admission to the faculty and advancement. Training facilities developed over the country, facilitated by the Veterans Administration.

Many who were in psychoanalytic training were also heads of clinical facilities as part of their training and professional growth. Their function in these new roles also brought them face-to-face with the complexities of organization structure, authority relationships, and group processes, which they saw first hand, had an effect on their staffs as well as their patients. Already they were involved with the families of their patients. That direction, in turn, led to family therapy. The need to help people who were not appropriate candidates for psychoanalysis, or who could not afford it, or for whom there simply were not enough resources to help them that way, led to group therapies and a range of brief therapies that were intended to help people with specific problems. The pragmatic view simply had to prevail in the face of the ego ideal therapeutic intention.

Psychoanalytic centers moved westward but the political strictures remained rigid, still guarding the "baby." There was severe conflict within the American Psychoanalytic Association even while psychoanalytic leaders were moving to unshackle the American Psychiatric Association from its rigidity by the formation of the Group for the Advancement of Psychiatry that they headed.

Although there was considerable effort to maintain the American Psychoanalytic Association as a federation of psychoanalytic societies, it became increasingly centralized and authoritarian, producing more splits (Millet, 1966). The American ethos of openness, questioning of authority, and pragmatism collided with psychoanalytic propositions. These were insufficient to deal with the complexity of the phenomena to which some wanted to apply psychoanalytic theory as the complexity extended beyond what the theory could handle. In the words of Kuklek (1989), in another context, "The Americans were not content that an aristocracy of the talented should lead them and they questioned the scientific ideal embraced in the nineteenth century." Some spoke of the inadequacies of a hydraulic model in an age whose paradigms were based on information processing and electronic telecommunications.

Then came psychopharmacology. The various pharmacological agents, it turned out, were lifesavers. Although they didn't cure mental illness, nevertheless they made it possible for many people to leave institutions and others to operate more comfortably in their daily lives. Although the slower psychotherapeutic processes often were more effective over the longer term, pragmatic therapists of all disciplines were soon prescribing drugs and various therapies, including behavior modification, social learning, and other conceptions that frequently were helpful for specific kinds of problems. Genetic research that demonstrated that certain kinds of illnesses ran in families under girded some of the application of pharmacological agents. All this, in turn, moved psychiatrists more in the direction of medicine as they sought to differentiate themselves from social workers and psychologists on the one hand, and to identify themselves with neurobiological advances on the other. Fewer psychiatrists were willing to undertake the extended psychoanalytic training. More psychologists and social workers did. Following the anti-trust suit filed by psychologists, the barriers of medical training collapsed and a new era began in which the psychoanalytic and psychotherapeutic proficiency became the new version of the professional ego ideal for those mental health professionals as well.

Unwilling to accept the theories about women, which even Freud himself felt he would be criticized for, female psychoanalysts moved to study more carefully their own psychological dynamics. They began to offer a more accurate understanding of the psychology of women. That contradicted the passivity with which male psychology used to characterize them. They called attention to their particular sensitivities to the feelings of others as well as their capacity for greater empathy than men. The theory began to yield, as it had already started to do to accommodate object relations theorists, as well as concepts of Klein, Kohut, and Kernberg.

Diminution of Central Controls

Peter Drucker (1989), whom the *Wall Street Journal* labels one of America's wisest essayists, points out that we live in an age of pluralism. Governments don't try to evolve comprehensive policies much anymore, but they tackle each issue separately. Central cities are losing their importance as work sites because so many work centers are now in the suburbs and so many people work at home. Given the need for using "knowledge workers," and for making decisions closer to the point of action, much of the power of executives has been delegated downward. In what may be an important parallel to understand with respect to psychoanalysis, he notes that economists must make do with special theorems that apply to one problem. They don't any longer presume to fit those concepts into an overarching economic theory such as Keynesianism. Cool pragmatism drives policy, he says, and moral crusades no longer have any power. Charisma is a remnant of a past era; most of the achievements in this country are the work of people who are not charismatic.

Contemporary chaos theory from physics now applied to social phenomena suggests that we are affected by things we can't even measure. According to the so-called butterfly effect, butterflies flapping their wings in the Amazon affect the weather in Chicago.

In management, delegation of authority to the point of action and the disappearance of status boundaries when the action becomes necessary, is reflected in a wide range of businesses and industries and in many different studies (Pfeiffer, 1989). "The chain of command is much in evidence but when tension is running high, all work together as specialists among specialists on an equal footing in a more collegial atmosphere...the system works."

With increased telecommunications, more people have greater knowledge. It becomes impossible for the Soviets, for example, to exercise control over their people once telecommunications develop. They have had great difficulty ever since Sputnik, when they had to begin to get scientific knowledge from outside their sphere. That together with the growing pressure everywhere for young people to be involved in the decisions that affect them means that all over the world there is more interaction as hierarchy is narrowed and those at the bottom become more empowered and unencumbered by managers. There is a parallel of greater equality in clinical practice as those who seek help who once were invariably called patients are these days more frequently referred to as clients.

Lodge and Walton (1989) describe how many large corporations work much more closely with their suppliers and their customers to the point that they have their staff people in their customers' suppliers' establishments. They seek to increase the quality of their product or service, to lower the costs for the user and at the same time meet the user's particular needs. Lodge and Walton note that such a drastic change in the way of managing was disruptive to many industries, particularly the financial industry. That industry was fragmented in the early 1980s as a result of the breakdown of the older more traditional relationships. There was a period of unusual innovation and experimentation, however, through the instability. Both suppliers and users of capital have been searching for more stable and secure relationships in the future. A new form of integration based on long-term relationships will arise. They note that in the future there will be teams of managers, each one of whom will be skilled at a different function. This mode of operation is already old hat in mental hospitals, where the teams of health care professionals have for years been concentrating their specialties on the needs of patients. However, one implication of greater quality is that those same people want to take part in the governance of their institutions. No doubt that participation will increase. The psychoanalytic society may well become an alliance of specialists who preserve an evolving core of basic theory when it becomes clearer that specific variants of practice may well fit specific patients or problems.

Implications for Psychoanalytic Institutes

Psychoanalysis is gaining considerable support from recent research on brain functioning. It has become clear from recently reported studies (Goleman. 1989) that feelings come before thoughts and actions. The thesis upon which psychoanalysis has long stood now is verified experimentally. No doubt there will be many other studies that give a systematic scientific footing to the theory. That, together with research on psychoanalytic therapy and the greater emphasis on the need for psychoanalytic diagnostic criteria before undertaking various therapies, will serve to facilitate clinical interaction and at the same time foster that research, that exchange of ideas, that Freud so devoutly wished and encouraged.

Going beyond Kemberg's suggestion of the psychoanalytic institute as a combination art school and university college, and to take advantage of the now wide ranging fields with which psychoanalysis should be related, Holzman (1990) argues that the best way for psychoanalytic institutes to get in touch with new knowledge that might enrich psychoanalysis is for psychoanalytic institutes to give up their night school practice and to become components of universities. There their faculties could interact with members of other disciplines, participate more actively in research, and be abreast of evolving trends in many other fields. Simons (1990) feels that psychoanalytic institutes are increasingly ready to move in that direction.

Holzman proposes, and I agree, that psychoanalysis, whether in contemporary psychoanalytic institutes or in university settings, be taught as a classical technique. Although the clientele base has been narrowed, there still is no more effective way to grasp what goes on in people's minds and to have a criterion against which to judge the merits of technical and theoretical variations and departures. Once a trainee has developed basic skill and understanding, then he or she would have a frame of reference for the debates that Kemberg argues for. Then, with rotating mentors who are not involved in the trainee's analysis, the trainee's technical skill might well be broadened. In addition, trainees might minor in other disciplines, as is currently the university practice. In some cases for instance, among non-psychoanalytic professionals, psychoanalysis in effect would be a minor if another discipline is major.

Professional schools that are not integrated into university settings run the risk of becoming merely independent trade schools. Of course, not all university departments are creatively productive, nor is psychoanalysis necessarily research-based. The mere movement into universities by itself would not guarantee renewed innovation and intellectual excitement. But, stimulation and cross-fertilization is much more likely than isolation to stimulate debate, foster conceptual advances, and counteract dogma. Freud never got the professorship he so ardently sought. As a result, he formed his own supporters outside the university. Since so many prominent in psychoanalytic ranks also hold professorial appointments, perhaps now is an ideal time to explore the possibilities of integration with the academic community.

The fact of the activation of many competing factions in the contemporary psychoanalytic movement seems to bear out the thesis I have advanced and which the experiences of Kris and Kemberg seem to verify. Rangell (1988) expresses a sense of gravity and concern for the science. He feels that the separation between competing schools has become all but overt. He has little faith that gathering the competing schools under one administrative umbrella will do much for integration, "...group formations to preserve and further psychoanalytic theory have never been satisfactorily achieved," he contends, because individuals within those subgroups are not independent of group pressure.

Meissner (Kirschner, 1988) is more sanguine. He sees the fragmentation as a necessary dialectic, "less a series of conclusions than a method." "The human experience is always of some kind of fragmentation." he observes. "Whatever integration that occurs is always partial."

In his discussion of what is not adequately taught in business schools -- namely about human behavior, Leavitt (1989) observes that business schools teach students how to analyze problems, but not much about how to act on them in a worldwide context, "about the critical, visionary, entrepreneurial, path finding part of the managing process." The coalition between large mass-production factories and the academic commitment to measurement, observation and scientific authority drove the individual pathfinder away from large organizations and drove out path finding and pathfinders.

There was parallel within psychoanalysis. The ego ideal of preserving the "baby" drove away innovators. Now the innovators stay within the family normally, but if Kemberg and Rangell are to be believed, the alliance is tenuous.

Healing those divisions perhaps calls for another metaphor. Wray (1989), drawing on the work of Robert Terry, offers the metaphor of improvisational jazz in which no one is totally in charge, people playoff each others' strengths, in which anyone picks it up, and in which there are different voices that are respectful of differences. People are individually competent but contribute to a whole that is greater than the sum of its parts, although there is room for solos. This implies individual and group competence, together with sensitivity, and flexibility of roles changing over time. That, it seems, was what Freud was trying to encourage from the beginning.

CHAPTER 11

SECTION THREE

LEADERSHIP

THE AGE OF LEADERSHIP

Mobil Services Company Limited, Internal Publication. 1974

There are four issues with which all leaders have to work: the problem of organizational change, the problem of leadership, the need to understand motivation, and the need to understand and cope with dependency.

Confronting people with prospect of organizational change is a bit like telling them they should use another typewriter keyboard. They know very well that another keyboard would be more efficient. But everybody's operating this one. So it will take a long time before they consent to learn another one.

Regardless of how ineffective the present structure is at least people know what to do with it. They know to whom they are responsible, and there are a set of enticements, or rewards, to go with that structure –such as salary scales and the opportunity for promotion. However, when employees have been with the organization for a few years, if they become dissatisfied, or if they feel that if they or the organization has become less effective than either might be, it is then difficult for them to leave. The more dependent they are on the organization, the more vulnerable they become to manipulation.

Of course changing an organization is a slow process. It's much more complex than most of the behavioral approaches to management would believe.

As a short cut, many organizations have tried to get at their problems through attitude surveys and morale studies. Though useful, these have severe limitations. For example, you get only answers to the questions you ask. If you ask the employees of most companies, "Are you satisfied with your work?", up to 80 percent of them will say "Yes." But that's like asking people when you meet them on the street, "How are you?" Eighty percent of them will say, "Fine," though their heads may be throbbing and their intestines churning.

Furthermore, people may say, "Yes, the work is monotonous," and "No, I don't get paid enough." They might really be trying to express their anger because they don't have any control over what happens to them. Unfortunately nobody's asked them the question that elicits that response.

Essentially, most companies still tend to operate on carrot and stick – or, reward and punishment – assumptions. This is akin to enticing the jackass with a carrot while brandishing a stick at him. Depending on how he responds, he gets either the carrot or the stick.

In part, this represents a social lag problem. Organizations are using methods that worked in an autocratic age. But they don't work as well in today's climate of egalitarianism. And they will work less well in the future.

Today, organizations are hiring increasing numbers of young people who have been taught to be independent. Of course nobody can be truly independent, but we can accept dependency to the extent to which we are *interdependent*. You will accept favors from me to the extent to which I will accept them from you. But if I don't accept them from you, then you are not going to become psychologically obliged to me.

We live in an age of nuclear social problems. And business, like all institutions, must contend with pressing issues of alienation, helplessness, and demoralization.

In this age, a psychology of leadership is crucial, and it transcends business management. It is crucial in politics, in business, in public institutions – hospitals, churches, schools, governments – even in the family. As parents, we must be identification models for our children. In the same way, we must be, and provide, such models for employees, citizens, and students.

Even institutional forms such as communes, in which people denied the need for structure and leadership, often weren't able to hold together unless they had either an ideology or a dominant leader.

In terms of organizations, we're going to have to spend a lot of time developing leadership. We can continue training people in management, but they will tend to be insufficient: not that there shouldn't be management, but given the next step where more people will have a personal orientation, it's going to take much more active leadership to hold things together. This leadership will have to have transcendent purpose and high goals related to that purpose; what's more, it will have to bring people face to face with their realities and to support them in the process of overcoming their problems.

Having a transcendent purpose is analogous to the question of what does one do with his or her child and how does the parent help the child to become an autonomous, functioning adult. One way or another the parent says, "This how you is what I stand for." Sometimes the parent can't say it in so many words, but it becomes very clear that some things are acceptable and others are not. However, for employees, followers and others, that purpose must be clearly defined.

Several years ago, social psychologist Roger Harrison developed a conception of four types of organizational character: the power-oriented, role-oriented, task-oriented, and person-oriented. I've been elaborating that conception as a way of understanding the course of organizational development and the implications for leadership and motivation. For example, historically most corporations were established by entrepreneurs who controlled the organization. As a result, these organizations were essentially power-oriented. Characteristically, the entrepreneur, as a child, was a person who had experienced intense rivalries with his father; having struggled with rivalry, he was unable to tolerate it within his organization. Therefore, he built in followers who wouldn't compete with him.

The Shift to Role-Orientation

When these dominant figures left the scene, they tended to be replaced by leaders who took fewer risks and had less initiative. They were administrators or bureaucrats rather than entrepreneurs. There was a resulting shift from power-orientation to role – orientation. That is, the organizations more often performed a service than competed for power. Public utilities are a case in point. The contemporary university president and hospital administrator represent this type of orientation.

The third generation tended to be technically competent people with a task-orientation. For them, the important thing was to get a given job done. Often they had to surmount crisis problems in order to remain viable. They didn't necessarily run the whole business, but they had to rescue the business. They had to refocus the organization's efforts on the tasks it had to do to survive. Management systems are attempts to obtain clearer focus. One also sees task-orientation in project-type matrix organizations, for example, if a company is going to build a refinery, it must bring together people with certain kinds of skills. When the task is completed, they disperse, and the manager goes back and assembles another team for the next task.

But in the fourth stage the head of an organization becomes faced with the super ordinate task of defining where the organization is going, and how it is going to get there. In this stage, we are dealing with a personal-orientation; that is, where people come together because they want "to do their own thing," which in turn relates to the ideal of the organization. The more an organization moves in that direction, the more the task of the leader becomes not management but leadership.

When that happens, the only glue that holds the organization together is identification with the leader that requires knowledge of what he stands for and where he is going. The leader must hold himself out and say, in essence, " Here's what I stand for, here's what I am trying to do. These are my values, this is what I want to get done in this role." So he becomes a sort of beanpole. People can then wrap themselves around the aspiration he has created.

They in turn can say: "Yes, that is where I want to go." Or: "I'd like to modify your statement with a little bit of my own so we can share a common purpose."

President Kennedy and Pope John Paul offered this kind of psychological image for cohesion. Now we are crying for it in terms of leadership that will stand for something. If a leader doesn't stand for anything, then he's either a manager or an administrator. If he is merely a manager, the organization runs serious risk of manipulation.

Of course some organizations remain essentially power-oriented, tightly controlled at the top; some remain role-oriented and become heavily bureaucratic; some remain task-oriented and can last as long as there are tasks that they can accomplish. The telephone companies are a case in point. The more innovative an organization has to be, the more likely it is to be person-oriented. The general cultural trend would seem to push us toward organization structures that are less rigid and provide more personal gratification.

Leadership by Sanction

The relationship between leader and follower is based on a kind of unconscious psychological contract. I had an aunt in Brooklyn once who had a contract with two entities – God and Franklin D. Roosevelt. Her contract with God assured her of enduring heavenly survival. Her contract with Roosevelt implied that he was going to do good things for her and people like her.

When a leader wants to do something, he has to get sanction. And he gets this sanction by defining the problems – that is, touching people where they hurt, putting a name on it, and opening up avenues for them to do something about it. But if he merely labels the problem and makes lots of noises about it, people may deny him this sanction.

For example, a new president comes into a formerly autocratically run company where people are dependent, and he advocates decentralization and greater risk and initiative. Before he can proceed, he has to gain the permission of the people. Otherwise they will continue to be passive. Of course he can fire some of them. But he can't fire them all. Only if they identify with him can he gain the necessary sanction.

Preventive Leadership

My old boss, Dr. William C. Menninger, was chief of psychiatry in the U.S. Army during World War II. He often said that the mental health of the men in a unit was more dependent on their leadership than on any other factor. This observation was reinforced years later when I began studying business organizations. I was primarily interested in prevention: that is, keeping healthy people functioning well. At that time, the literature told us what to do about psychiatric casualties, but we didn't know much about how to keep well people well.

Since then, I've worked extensively with organizations and I have changed my focus from such problems as accidents, absenteeism, and alcoholism. I've realized that they are symptoms, and that the key problems had to do with the organizations themselves.

When an organization is operated for short-term, expedient reasons, then manipulation becomes the rule, and this has a destructive and demoralizing effect on the employees. But when an organization is managed for its own perpetuation, rather than on a short-term basis, that tends to be good for its people. The members face reality and cope with it effectively, and there is a minimum of manipulation.

After studying organizations in this context, one can develop a diagnostic method. This then becomes helpful in understanding complexity, particularly motivational complexity. It encompasses the dynamics of individual people, the dynamics of the group, the history and personality of the organization, and the implications all of these factors have for action. With this kind of approach, one can choose a course of action that's going to get people where they would like to go.

Many corporations bring people together for courses in management development. In these, there is a great deal of talk about human relations and the need for self-actualization. Such sessions often provide new insights. However, there is a great tendency to substitute buzzwords for knowledge and slogans for psychological understanding. Because such training experiences don't have a theory of personality embedded in them, they can't focus on critical issues such as personal values and unconscious motivation.

Managing Dependency Needs

Self-actualization doesn't mean much to me, because we don't really know what anyone's potential is, or how to find out. Even if one were to fulfill his or her potential, there is no indication that you would be very happy. As a result, what basically we are dealing with is not the fulfillment of potential, but people's ego ideals. All of us strive to meet the high expectations we hold of ourselves. That means executives – or, leaders – have to understand that the most powerful of all motivations is the desire to like oneself. People are always trying to do that in their behavior, no matter what they're involved in.

A major problem in all organizations – and one that is widely disregarded – has to do with dependency. We all start out as helpless infants, dependent on our parents. And in our older years we become increasingly dependent again. In between, we still have to manage our dependency needs.

Most of us manage those needs by seeking employment organizations that provide us with money, power, skills, and various kinds of support. Sometimes organizations deny those needs. Take, for instance, the case of the person being sent overseas and having to make a major cultural adjustment. When problems arise, they're often attributed to culture shock. But, more accurately, they tend to be problems of dependency.

While the husband may get along well in another country because of the stability he derives from his organization and his work, his wife may not. At home, she got along quite well because she owned a car that enabled her to draw from the environment the resources she needed. She usually lived close to a church and a shopping center, and was able to call her mother. Suddenly she is relocated to Tokyo. There she is unfamiliar with the language, local customs, socializing patterns that separate men and women and she is not the kind of person who historically has taken adaptive initiative. Under the stress of adaptation, both she and her husband become more rigid, making adjustment increasingly difficult.

All change involves undermining ones preferred ways of handling dependency needs. One way one can help people with cultural shock and change is anticipatory guidance. People can be drilled in the kinds of problems they're likely to face. Also, if a leader can decompress people under stress by taking about their problems and can explore them in finding ways of dealing with their problems, a leader can make life considerably easier for them

But leaders have to know these things about the people who are working for them. They have to be able to comprehend what it takes for a person to be able to have self-esteem. What, in short, is the person's ego ideal? And how do both relate to the personality of the organization – and the leader him or her self?

With a better understanding of these phenomena, then the leader can more effectively cope with the organization's task and the nuclear issues of alienation, helplessness, and demoralization. In short, he or she can truly lead.

LaVergne, TN USA
16 September 2010
197285LV00004B/2/P